Call to Faith

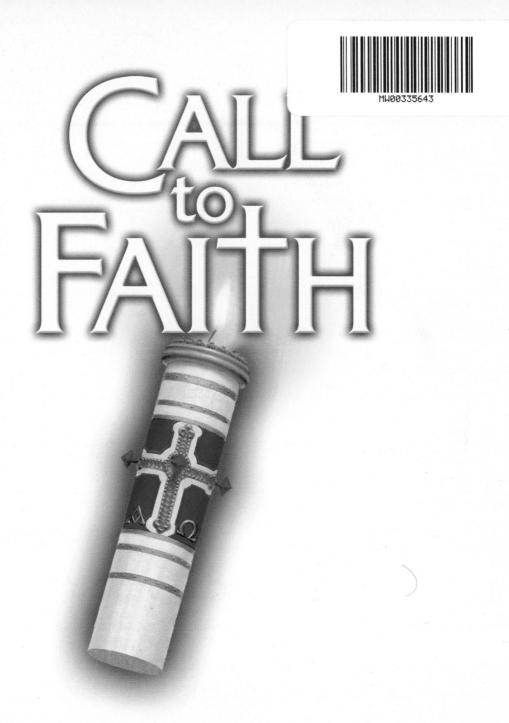

GRADE 8

Harcourt Religion Publishers

www.harcourtreligion.com

Nihil Obstat
Rev. Dr. Steven Olds, S.T.D.
Censor Librorum

Imprimatur
✝ Most Rev. Thomas Wenski
Bishop of Orlando
February 1, 2006

The Ad Hoc Committee to Oversee the Use of the Catechism, United States Conference of Catholic Bishops, has found this catechetical series, copyright 2007, to be in conformity with the *Catechism of the Catholic Church.*

The imprimatur is an official declaration that a book or pamphlet is free of doctrinal or moral error. No implication is contained therein that the person who granted the imprimatur agrees with the contents, opinions, or statements expressed.

For permission to reprint copyrighted material, grateful acknowledgment is made to the following sources:

Division of Christian Education of the National Council of the Churches of Christ in the U.S.A.: From the *New Revised Standard Version Bible: Catholic Edition.* Text copyright © 1993 and 1989 by the Division of Christian Education of the National Council of the Churches of Christ in the U.S.A.

International Commission on English in the Liturgy: From the English translation of *Ordination of a Deacon, Priest, or Bishop.* Translation © 1975 by International Committee on English in the Liturgy, Inc. From the English translation of *The Roman Missal.* Translation © 1973 by International Committee on English in the Liturgy, Inc. From the English translation of "The Angelus" and "Come, Holy Spirit" in *A Book of Prayers.* Translation © 1982 by International Committee on English in the Liturgy, Inc.

International Consultation on English Texts: English translation of the Apostles' Creed, the Lord's Prayer, Gloria Patri, and the Nicene Creed by the International Consultation on English Texts.

United States Conference of Catholic Bishops, Washington, D.C.: From the English translation of the *Catechism of the Catholic Church* for the United States of America. Translation copyright © 1994 by United States Catholic Conference, Inc.—Libreria Editrice Vaticana. From the English translation of the *Catechism of the Catholic Church: Modifications from the Editio Typica.* Translation copyright © 1997 by United States Catholic Conference, Inc.—Libreria Editrice Vaticana.

Printed in the United States of America

ISBN 0-15-902281-9

1 2 3 4 5 6 7 8 9 10 073 11 10 09 08

GRADE 8 CONTENTS

ABOUT YOU

Finally, one year more before high school . . .
This year will be the best ever . . .
I'm anxious about my classes . . .

You may have thought you'd never get to eighth grade. Sure, lots of things are changing at home, with your friends, and inside of you. You might surprise yourself, and others, with some of the things you say and do. Sometimes you probably feel like you are stuck between two worlds with high school right around the corner. The good news is that this year can get you ready for the responsibilities and exciting new times you'll have. But this year is really important for the here and now, too. You'll get to know yourself a lot better, and begin to understand what choices you want to make and why. You'll have fun with friends and family, and push yourself in ways that you might not have imagined. Think of this as the beginning of a great adventure.

ACTIVITY

LET'S BEGIN Name three things that are important to you right now and tell why. Do you think these things will be more or less important to you at the end of the year? Why?

ABOUT YOUR FAITH

When everything is changing around you, there is one thing you can count on to remain the same: God never changes. His wisdom, his Church, and his love will always be there to help you make it through. We live in a world where everything changes all the time—and not always for the better. There are few things we can depend on to help us no matter what. That's why faith is so important. Things are different when you let God the Father, his Son, Jesus, and the Holy Spirit into your life.

This year you'll get to know what it means to be Church. You'll find out what it means to be part of our Church and how the Church continues Jesus' work in the world. You'll look at the things happening in your life through Jesus' eyes, and you'll discover that the faith community can help you make good choices about lots of different things.

SHARE YOUR FAITH List three things you want to find out about what the Church does and what it means to take an active role in the Church.

1. _____

2. _____

3. _____

▶ **Now, partner with someone you don't know well. Share your questions with each other and then find out what others in the group are wondering about.**

ABOUT YOUR BOOK

When people say you shouldn't judge a book by its cover, that's about not judging people by the way they look. You've got to get to know them. You may think you know what's in this book after looking at the cover—and you might be right. But take another look.

In addition to the stories of today, the Scripture stories, the Catholic teachings, and the activities, here are some of the extra features you'll find.

GO TO THE SOURCE sends you directly to the Bible to find out more about the scripture passage or story explained in your book.

WHERE IT HAPPENED is just that—a mini-tour of where biblical or Church events took place and where the saints lived their extraordinary lives.

GLOBAL DATA gives you interesting facts and statistics about various countries and regions of the world as well as about the Church in different locations.

CATHOLICS TODAY offers a view into the way people live out their faith by the ways they pray, the stands they take, and the choices they make. This is about how Catholics from all over put their faith into action, and how you do, too.

CHECK THIS OUT! points out different faith facts and bits of information that connect to the main topics you are learning.

Words of Faith define core Catholic teachings and help you to understand the "what" and "why" of your faith.

PEOPLE OF FAITH puts the whole message of the Good News into real-life circumstances by presenting biographical sketches of ordinary and extraordinary people who responded to Christ's call to follow him.

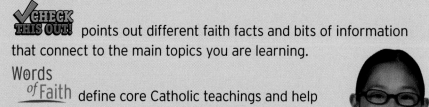

CONNECT YOUR FAITH Choose one of the features above and find out how it's used in the first unit of your book. What new bit of information or insight did you gain from the feature?

A CALL TO FAITH

PRAYER

Leader: Let us take time, here and now, to gather for prayer,
in the name of the one who calls us to follow his call.
Jesus calls us together and forms us as his Body
moving and acting in the world today.

Reader 1: Where there is inequity,
where people don't have the things they need,
where children go hungry,
and people are hurting,
let us be your justice, Lord.

All: **We are called to act with justice.**

Reader 2: Where there is hatred,
where bullies rule the hallways,
and accusations fly,
where eyes are lowered, fingers pointed, and tempers rise,
let us be your love, Lord.

All: **We are called to love tenderly.**

Reader 3: Where there is a job to be done,
where others can benefit from our gifts and abilities,
where people long to have hope,
and to hear the Good News,
let us be your servants, Lord.

All: **We are called to serve one another.**

Leader: We are your Body, your hands and heart and voice in the world.
You call us to act with love and justice,
to serve you in those around us.
Give us the guidance and strength to follow your call.
We ask this in your name.

All: **Amen.**

 "We Are Called"
David Haas, © 1988, 2004 GIA Publications

1 IN GOD'S Image

PRAYER God, help me to see what matters in life.

How do I know what's really important?
What's my purpose in life?
How do I know the right way to live?

Darryl was cutting through the park on his way home from school when he saw Aunt Peggy sitting by the pond, feeding the ducks. He sure was glad to see her today. As always, she gave him a big smile and then asked if he wanted to sit for awhile. As always, she asked, "So what's new in Darryl's world?"

Today, he just blurted out his frustration. "I am so mixed up—you won't believe all the stuff people want me to do. Hannah and Bobbie begged me to come to their house tomorrow because they are having a party. But Gerry had already asked me to help him study for our chemistry project because he knows I aced the last test. Then Mom and Dad said that we have to go visit Grandmom Hoyle because she is feeling lonely. And that is only tomorrow! It seems like every time I turn around, someone wants me to do something or help out. I don't want to let any of them down. What am I going to do?"

Aunt Peggy looked at him with her calm, dark eyes for a moment and then asked quietly, "Do you really think you can meet everyone's expectations at the same time?"

Darryl didn't say anything, but he suddenly felt like a ton of weight had been taken off his shoulders. He shook his head and smiled a little. Then she asked him, "What are the things that are important to you?"

Wow. Darryl thought a minute. Maybe he should just relax, enjoy his aunt's company, and take time to think that question out with her. That's when he turned to her and said, "Can we go down the corner to get some ice cream?"

ACTIVITY

LET'S BEGIN What effect did Aunt Peggy have on Darryl? What would have happened if Aunt Peggy had told Darryl she didn't have any time for him?

▶ **What do you do when you are torn in different directions? Where do you go to simply talk or get advice? What helps you put things in perspective and figure out what really matters?**

JOINED WITH GOD

We all have expectations put on us and our time. Our family needs us, our friends want to hang out, and our schoolwork takes time, too. With all of these expectations and demands, you might wonder what's really important. How can you know what matters or make decisions when everything seems to have the same value?

Well, everything in life isn't equally important. You've already experienced that firsthand. The challenge is to find out what really matters, and to build your life around that. You can have lots of things going on, and still live a life of purpose and direction.

Purpose and Direction As humans, we all share the same purpose. By our very nature, we are made to have a relationship with God: to be his friend, to know him, to love him, and to help others do the same. This is our purpose and our calling in life. How we respond to the expectations placed on us, and how we create expectations for ourselves, should be based on which ones lead us toward friendship with God.

Because God wanted to have a relationship with humans, he made us different from the rest of his creation. You were made in God's image and likeness, with a body and a **soul**—the spiritual principle in you that reflects God. With only a body, human beings would be like all the other animals. Because God has breathed his own divine spirit into every human person, you are both a physical and spiritual being. You have an intellect that makes it possible for you to think, reason, and judge, and a **free will**—the ability to choose and make decisions on your own without being forced by instinct to choose or act in a certain way.

▲ *Hands of God and Adam,* detail from *The Creation of Adam* in the Sistine Chapel, by Michelangelo Buonarroti (1475–1564)

This unique combination makes you an image of God. You are related to God. The journey of life involves the ways that you live out that relationship with God.

 How would you describe your journey of faith so far?

8

Jesus' Example Jesus taught us what friendship with God is all about. He showed us how to love God by the choices he made, the ways he prayed, and the priorities he had in life. He showed us how to love God by loving others. He recognized the dignity of all people, even when society did not. He welcomed people others ignored, he forgave people who were truly sorry for their wrongs, and he cared for people in need. He showed compassion. Jesus was also responsible to Mary and Joseph, and followed the rituals and feasts of his Jewish faith.

Having a relationship with God the Father was not something Jesus did separately from the rest of his life. It was part of who he was with his family, friends, and followers. It was part of the choices he made and the things he did, simply eating a meal with his disciples or performing a miracle like feeding 5,000 people.

✝ **SCRIPTURE** Jesus once told his disciples not to worry about what they were going to wear or eat. He told them, "Look at the birds of the air; they neither sow nor reap nor gather into barns, and yet your heavenly Father feeds them. Are you not of more value than they?" He was not telling them that material concerns were not important, but he didn't want them to be constantly worried about them. He wanted them to depend upon God and to be focused first on God's kingdom. (See *Matthew 6:25–33*.)

❓ **What is really important to you? What is really worth worrying about?**

❓ **How would things change for you if you followed Jesus' advice about worrying?**

soul

free will

covenant

Decalogue

Ten Commandments

CATHOLICS TODAY

Jesus shows us that our happiness comes from trusting in God and being one with him. This is what God created us for, and when our lives are lived with this purpose, everything else leads toward it. Jesus was able to model this relationship with God because he is fully human and fully divine. As Paul said in his Letter to the Colossians (*1:15*), Jesus was the "image of the invisible God." Through Baptism, we are as brothers and sisters of Christ. We are in some ways an image of the invisible God. Though not perfect like Christ, each of us shares in the image of Christ.

ACTIVITY

SHARE YOUR FAITH In what ways can you be called an image of the invisible God? How is your family an image of God? Your school?

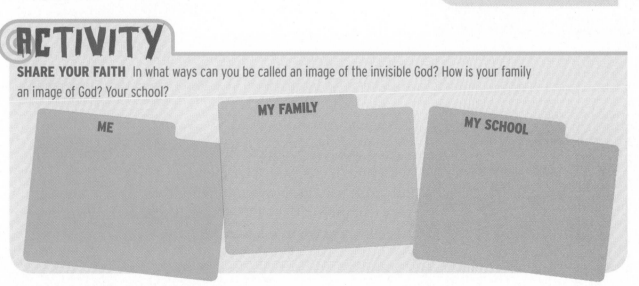

ME

MY FAMILY

MY SCHOOL

CALLED TO COVENANT

Focus What is a covenant with God?

Even though we are free to make choices, we do not always choose what is right. Sometimes we show God's goodness, and at other times we fail. Whether people are good or bad, God never stops offering his love. But people might still wonder, "If God is so good and loving, why is there sin and evil in the world?"

God created our first parents in his very own image and likeness. They shared fully in his holiness and goodness. They also shared in God's gift of freedom and, sadly, chose to disobey him. Because of their choices and actions, they lost the holiness and justice first received from God.

Yet, God remained perfect in his love for Adam and Eve. Instead of abandoning them, he promised that all humans would once again share fully in his life. He made a covenant with them. A **covenant** is like a contract between two persons, but it is more serious and heartfelt than a legal contract. It is a sacred promise or agreement between God and humans involving mutual commitments. In the stories of the Old Testament, God showed over and over that he will remain faithful to the covenant, even when humans fail in keeping the covenant.

 What covenant or sacred promise do you and God have?

Called by Name God seemed to surprise people in the Old Testament with the way he called them to serve him.

▶ Jacob was chosen to be given the family birthright even though his brother Esau was older. (See *Genesis 27*.)

▶ God called Samuel to be a prophet, even though he was only a servant to the prophet Eli. (See *1 Samuel 3*.)

▶ God chose Jeremiah as a prophet, even though Jeremiah protested that he did not know how to speak. (See *Jeremiah 1*.)

God calls all people to live in covenant friendship with him. It is always possible to say "yes" because God provides help in showing how to live in this relationship. Many figures in the Old Testament showed what it means to be in a covenant relationship with God.

✝ SCRIPTURE

GO TO THE SOURCE
Read **1 Samuel 3:1–10** and think about how you would respond if God called you like this.

LIVING OUT THE COVENANT

Noah
- ▶ With his family, he trusted that God would keep them safe through the flood.
- ▶ God made a covenant with Noah never to wash away all living creatures on earth again.

The Chosen People
- ▶ They were the descendants of Abraham and Sarah, and God promised to make of them a great nation.
- ▶ Even when they turned from God, they were forgiven and called back to the covenant.

Moses
- ▶ God saved Moses from his abandonment as an infant and raised him to lead Israel in rebellion against their Egyptian captors.
- ▶ Moses then led the people out of Egypt and through the Red Sea when God parted the water.
- ▶ God gave Moses the Ten Commandments as a sign of his covenant love.

Ruth
- ▶ Ruth was a Moabite who became part of the Chosen People through marriage.
- ▶ She became an example of self-sacrifice and good moral character through her gift of faith in God.

Solomon
- ▶ As King of Israel, Solomon was noted for a wisdom that reflected God's care for the people.

Susanna
- ▶ She trusted that God's wisdom in the prophet Daniel would prove that the accusations against her were false.
- ▶ She became a model of truthfulness for her family and all God's people.

Jeremiah
- ▶ Though at first he did not believe he was capable or worthy of being a prophet, he finally put his trust in God and answered the call.
- ▶ He constantly reminded the people that God would remove their hardened hearts and replace them with new hearts.

ACTIVITY

CONNECT YOUR FAITH List three responsibilities you have as part of your personal covenant with God.

my covenant with God calls me to:

GUIDED BY THE LAW

Focus How does the law help us live in God's image?

The law serves as God's way of helping us live out the covenant and grow closer to him because it helps us recognize evil.

The law is first of all based on nature because it is through human nature that people participate and share in God's goodness. Natural law is part of the spirit of every person and shows that each person created in God's image has a fundamental dignity. This dignity is the strong foundation on which all human rights and responsibilities are based. Natural law is the foundation for the rights and responsibilities all humans share.

NATURAL LAW:

helps humans distinguish between good and evil

shows the way to put that which is good into practice

is universal because it applies to every human being

varies in the way it is applied because humans are asked to use the gift of reason to make choices

is unchangeable and permanent throughout all of history

provides the basis for all other moral laws and rules

Laws of Love The revealed laws of God, like the Ten Commandments, guide us in making choices. Revealed law

▶ shows us the ideals toward which we strive to live

▶ sets before us the virtues (like faith, hope, and love) that make God's image real in our lives

▶ helps us to recognize what is evil and what creates separation or division from God and others

▶ gives us insight about how to make God's love a real part of our life

If human nature had remained perfect, humans would not have needed the laws of the Ten Commandments because these rules would have come from the heart and spirit of each person. The **Ten Commandments** are based on natural law, but have also been revealed by God as a way of instructing us in how to live a good life.

CHECK THIS OUT!

The Ten Commandments are also called the **Decalogue**, from a Greek phrase that means "ten words." The Decalogue applies to all human beings in matters that are serious and also in ways that are less serious but important. For example, everyone knows that killing is a most serious sin (Fifth Commandment). But the commandment also applies to hurting someone with abusive language.

God gave the Ten Commandments on Mount Sinai so that the people would have a guide for learning how to live in God's image and follow the covenant—through their love for God (commandments 1–3) and their love for each other (commandments 4–10).

The Ten Commandments come from the Old Testament, but the two versions given have some variations. (See *Exodus 20:2–17* and *Deuteronomy 5:6–21*.) Saint Augustine used the Ten Commandments to teach baptismal candidates and other members of the Church.

1. I am the Lord your God: you shall not have strange gods before me.

2. You shall not take the name of the Lord your God in vain.

3. Remember to keep holy the Lord's Day.

4. Honor your father and your mother.

5. You shall not kill.

6. You shall not commit adultery.

7. You shall not steal.

8. You shall not bear false witness against your neighbor.

9. You shall not covet your neighbor's wife.

10. You shall not covet your neighbor's goods.

ACTIVITY

LIVE YOUR FAITH With a group choose three commandments and explain them as positives ("You will . . .") to show how people your age can honor God's image in themselves and others.

IN SUMMARY

CATHOLICS BELIEVE

God made humans in his image and likeness so we could be in relationship with him.

▶ With a soul, reason, and free will, humans can set their priority and direction in life toward friendship with God. Jesus is the model for living out this relationship.

▶ God established a covenant with his people, promising to be faithful to them and to be their God. God calls each of us to be in relationship with him and to honor the covenant.

▶ The natural and revealed law—especially the Ten Commandments—guide people in what is good and evil, what is faithful living, and what it means to truly be an image of God.

PRAYER OF PETITION

Leader: Let us pray.

God,
we are not always sure why we are here.
We often see so many around us
who seem to be more talented,
more popular;
many who seem to have more success,
more friends,
or seem to have better luck.
Why were we born?
What is our purpose?

Reader 1: In the Bible,
we hear over and over again
about how we are "chosen,"
that we are "blessed,"
that we are each "called by name,"
that all of us have our part to play.

Reader 2: Help us to not get stuck,
but remember that you are our God,
and that you have a plan for us.

Reader 1: Help us to bless you,
and have faith in the dream for each and every one of us.
Even when we are stumbling and feel invisible.

Reader 2: Help us to be patient,
and have faith in believing that you have
called us all,
not just by any name,
but by our name,
to be your living image,
and to help others to know you.

Reader 1: We thank you God,
for not giving up on us,
and helping us to remember
that each of us is holy and chosen.

All: Amen.

 "Who Calls You By Name"
David Haas, © 1988, GIA Publications, Inc.

REVIEW

A **Work with Words** Circle the letter of the choice that best completes the sentence.

1. Your _____ is the spiritual principle that reflects God in you.
   a. intellect
   b. spirit
   c. soul
   d. body

2. _____ is the ability to choose and make decisions without being forced to choose or act in a certain way.
   a. Intellect
   b. Free will
   c. Free choice
   d. Covenant

3. A _____ is a sacred promise or agreement between God and humans involving mutual commitments.
   a. covenant
   b. contract
   c. vow
   d. commandment

4. Another name for the Ten Commandments is _____.
   a. Natural law
   b. Revealed law
   c. Decalogue
   d. Decalaw

B **Check Understanding** Complete each sentence with the correct term from the word bank at right.

5. Your _____ makes it possible for you to think, reason, and judge.

6. God chose _____ to lead his people out of Egypt and gave him the Ten Commandments.

7. The _____ helps people recognize the evil that leads them away from God.

8. _____ is universal because it applies to every human being.

9. _____, like the Ten Commandments, guides us in making choices.

10. The prophet _____ constantly reminded the people that God would take away their hardened hearts and replace them with a new heart.

Word Bank

natural law
Jeremiah
Solomon
spirit
Law
intellect
Moses
revealed law
Decalogue

C **Make Connections: Cause and Effect** Write a one-paragraph response to the questions.

Write about a relationship in which you have seen or experienced a human reflection of God's covenant love. How did that relationship illustrate God's love and commitment? What effect did that love have on you or the others involved?

OUR CATHOLIC FAITH

WHAT NOW?

★ Reevaluate your priorities.

★ Think about what it means to be God's friend.

★ Relax and think about the things that are good in your life.

★ Make a list of the ways that you think God has shown he cares for you.

★ Spend some time thinking about what your life would look like if God were not in it. Is it possible to think of life without God?

★ Thank the people in your life who show you what it means to be like God.

ACTIVITY

LIVE YOUR FAITH Imagine your life with no expectations or demands from others. You have to set all the expectations for yourself regarding your home life, school, friendships, and relationship with God; however, you could not set the expectations for how others interacted with you, took care of you, and so on. What expectations would you give yourself that would help you be an image of God to others?

In order to be a better image of God, here are my expectations of myself:

 Visit **www.harcourtreligion.com** for more family and community connections.

 **PRAYER**

I pray in thanksgiving for all those who have taught me to be a child of God.

Saint Marcella

Marcella knew she was created to be in relationship with God. She gave up many of the comforts of life to give herself to God and his work. Because of the way she lived in faith and sacrifice, Saint Jerome called her "the glory of the ladies of Rome."

Marcella was a wealthy Roman from a noble family. She married young, but she was widowed within her first year of marriage. The consul Cerealis, a leader in Rome, asked her to marry him. Marcella refused, choosing instead to live life humbly, with few material comforts. She invited a group of noble ladies to meet at her mansion. Together they lived a life of self-discipline and self-denial, giving themselves to the religious life. Her Aventine Hill mansion became a center of Christian activity.

Marcella wrote letters to Saint Jerome. Jerome gave much of his life to writing, and translated parts of the Bible. He gave guidance to the women by answering Marcella's questions about spiritual matters. Marcella learned from Saint Jerome, but was never afraid to stand up to him in arguments. She spent most of her time reading, praying, and visiting the shrines of martyrs.

When the Goths looted Rome in 410, they tortured Marcella. They wanted her treasure. But they let her go when they learned that she had given all her money to the poor. Marcella died shortly after from her injuries. She left no earthly wealth. But Marcella's relationship with God pointed her toward another treasure—a life rich in the Spirit of God.

▲ Saint Marcella, 325–410

GLOBAL DATA

Rome

- Rome is Italy's capital and largest city.

- Rome has a population of about 2.8 million people.

- Rome is the location of Vatican City.

- Many Christians were killed in the Roman Coliseum during large-scale persecutions of Christians.

- Rome is known for its art and architecture, including the Roman Forum, St. Peter's Square, and the Sistine Chapel.

 **PRAYER**   Make my faith stronger, Lord.

What does faith really mean?
Am I supposed to believe everything people say?
Sometimes I have questions about my faith
but am afraid to ask.

Charlita's brother had just left the naval base for six months on an aircraft carrier. When her friends asked about him, she told them what he had said as he left home. "He seemed so happy, even though there is so much danger around. He said that God will protect him and help him, no matter what happens. I told him I believed that, too."

"I'm not sure God can do much with all the violence that seems to be happening. Sometimes I wonder if God even cares about this stuff," Marvin said.

Duane just rolled his eyes, saying, "Whatever happens, happens. I just figure life is tough and we have to live with it."

"That sounds so sad," Charlita said. "If I didn't have faith, I'd be so depressed. I don't think I could handle all this without God helping me."

"Well, I was upset when my mother got sick last month," Marvin replied, "but the doctors healed her up and she's doing fine. We didn't need any faith or church to get through that."

"That's what I mean," Duane nodded, "we just get through it. It doesn't matter if God is around."

Charlita wasn't sure what to say, because she felt so strongly in her heart that God is part of the picture. She finally said, "You know, I don't see God doing magic, but somehow I think God has something to do with taking care of us. Can you really imagine the whole universe going on without God?"

ACTIVITY

LET'S BEGIN What is this story really about?

▶ **How would you have responded to Charlita when she told her friends about her brother and their faith? Have you ever been in a tough or scary situation when your faith helped you?**

_____

_____

_____

_____

_____

GOD MADE KNOWN

Focus Where do we find God's revelation?

We all have doubts and uncertainties at times, even about God and his presence in the world. Sometimes it's hard to have faith, especially when things aren't going very well. You might even wonder what it means to have faith, to believe in God and all that he has made known to us. Faith is a gift that God gives to each of us. We each can accept this gift of faith, or reject it. By following up on the questions or doubts we have, we can get to the bottom of things. We can understand our faith better.

Through Scripture and Tradition In order that the people would continue to hear the good news of God's love, Jesus asked his followers to tell others all about him. The Apostles did just that, and, inspired by the Holy Spirit, they passed on the Good News through their preaching, writing, and baptizing.

The newly baptized believers first relied on the stories and teachings of the Apostles and others who had known Jesus. They later turned to the letters of Saint Paul and other disciples, then to the Gospels recorded by Matthew, Mark, Luke, and John.

LOOKING BACK

The seven sacraments of the Church are an example of the way Tradition builds on Scripture because all of the sacraments flow from Jesus' life and teaching:

▶ **Baptism:** Jesus asked the disciples to go out to all the nations to spread the Good News and baptize new believers.

▶ **Confirmation:** Jesus promised to send his Holy Spirit as a guide.

▶ **Eucharist:** At the Last Supper, Jesus gave his followers his Body and Blood and asked them to share this meal in his memory.

▶ **Reconciliation:** Jesus constantly preached the forgiveness of sins, and he forgave those who were truly sorry.

▶ **Anointing of the Sick:** Jesus cured the sick and brought healing to many.

▶ **Marriage:** Jesus did his first miracle at the wedding feast of Cana and reminded the disciples that man and woman united show us the image of God.

▶ **Holy Orders:** Jesus commissioned his Apostles to share in his ministry and work in a special way as Church leaders.

As the Church grew, new leaders looked to the Scriptures, especially the Gospel stories about Christ, and they passed on what they had discovered. They helped Christians interpret the message contained in the Scripture. The living and true teachings of Jesus and his Good News of salvation are passed down in the Church from generation to generation, through **Tradition**.

Scripture and Tradition together are the one source of God's revelation to us. Scripture is the basis of Tradition, and Tradition helps us correctly interpret Scripture and apply it to the unique circumstances of our time. We use both to help us understand who God is and our relationship with him.

When have you talked with someone about what one of the stories in Scripture means to you?

Passing It On The Church strives to spread the message of God's revelation by finding just the right words and actions that will help people say "yes" to God. In this way, the Church continues to build on the Tradition that flows from the Word of God.

▶ In *doctrines*, the Church sets down in writing the important beliefs that are central for living a life of faith. An important example of this is a creed, or brief summary or statement of beliefs. We proclaim the Nicene Creed at Mass.

▶ In *worship*, like the Mass and the other sacraments, the Church comes together to give God thanks and praise.

▶ In the *life* of the members of the Church, we see the faith of Christians put into action, especially for those who are in need of God's help.

Tradition
faith
Church
councils
virtue
theological virtues

▲ Pope Benedict XVI

ACTIVITY

SHARE YOUR FAITH What's one thing about your faith that you feel is certain? What's one thing that you want more clarity about? Discuss this with another.

WE RESPOND IN FAITH

Focus What does it mean to have faith?

Most of us enjoy receiving a gift and hope it will be something we like. If we get something useless, we may pretend we like it, but then put it aside. The gift of faith that God gives to us is similar because he freely gives it. We may either accept or reject it.

Faith is a gift from God, but is also your response to God's invitation to share in his life. It is your acceptance of what God has made known through Scripture and Tradition, and by your willingness to let his love make a difference in your life. You show your faith through the things you think, the decisions you make, and your actions. Faith involves the whole of you, your heart, will, mind, and soul. Faith is a way of seeing life and the people around you as if through God's eyes.

Because people are imperfect, we need God's help to have faith. This is why Jesus poured out the Holy Spirit when he died. The Holy Spirit makes Christ present to us. With the Holy Spirit's help, it is possible for someone to have faith. But no one is ever forced to have faith. We are drawn toward faith by the work of the Holy Spirit in our hearts and lives. It is by God's grace—the free gift of his life—that we are able to believe.

Having faith and believing in God is always a free decision. And it takes work. We have to respond to the gift God has given us so that our faith can grow and mature. One way we can strengthen our faith is by reading the Scripture. Another is by asking Jesus to help us believe and increase our faith as one father did in the Gospel of Mark, "I believe; help my unbelief!" (*Mark 9:24*). And, we rely on the Holy Spirit to do both.

> ✝ **SCRIPTURE**
>
> **GO TO THE SOURCE**
> Read the healing of the boy with a demon in **Mark 9:14–29**. What did Jesus require of the sick boy's father?

? When have you caught yourself believing in something that did not seem possible?

Belief: An Act of the Church Not only is "believing" or having faith a human act, but it is also an act of the community of people who believe in the Trinity. The community of baptized believers who believe in God and follow Jesus is the **Church**. No one is alone when they have faith in God the Father, Son, and Holy Spirit. Our faith in God flows from the faith of the Church.

In turn, the faith of the Church offers us support and helps us to become stronger in faith throughout our lifetime. Saint Cyprian compared the Church to a mother who gives birth to our faith and who nourishes us always.

Everything that the Church does and teaches is part of Tradition, which flows from Scripture. This means that what the Church writes and passes down through the generations comes from God.

One of the ways that the Church passes on Tradition is by gathering bishops in **councils** to speak about the faith of the Church, its teachings, and important issues. The last council was the Second Vatican Council, or Vatican II, between 1962 and 1965. This council produced teachings on these topics:

▶ Revelation

▶ Liturgy and Worship

▶ Religious Freedom

▶ Ecumenism

▶ Missions

▶ Eastern Churches

▶ What the Church Is

▶ How the Church Lives in the Modern World

▶ Communications

▶ Bishops, Priests, Laity, and Religious Life

▶ Education

▶ Non-Christians

WHERE IT HAPPENED

THE SECOND Vatican Council took place in Vatican City, Rome, beginning in October 1962. The council of over 2,500 bishops met in St. Peter's Basilica, a magnificent church first built by Constantine, the first Christian emperor of Rome. Constantine chose the steep side of what was known as Vatican Hill, the site of an ancient Roman cemetery, because that is where Saint Peter is believed to be buried.

The Vatican is the smallest sovereign state in the world. It is about 109 acres (44 hectares) around, surrounded by ancient walls and the city of Rome. The Vatican was made independent in 1929, a feature that protects the pope from outside political interference.

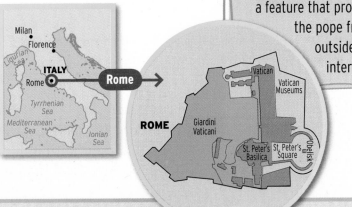

ACTIVITY

CONNECT YOUR FAITH Complete the diagram below to show the ways that the things you and your family believe and do as signs of your faith connect to what your parish believes and does.

MY FAMILY AND I

MY PARISH

WE LIVE BY FAITH

 Focus How does faith affect the way I live?

Faith is much more than belief in creeds and doctrines. If we look at some of the important people in the Scripture, we see that faith made a difference in the way they lived their lives:

▶ Abraham and Sarah were able to take the risk of moving to a foreign land because they believed that God would keep the promise to make them the parents of a great nation.

▶ David was willing to face the giant because he believed God would help him even though he was so much smaller than Goliath.

▶ The disciple Paul, after he converted to belief in Jesus, continued to preach the Gospel even when people tried to imprison and persecute him.

▶ Mary, the Mother of Jesus, had such faith in God and trusted in him so much that she said "yes" to the angel at the Annunciation.

▶ Peter identified Jesus' divinity first of all the Apostles, saying, "You are the Messiah, the Son of the living God" (*Matthew 16:16*).

We can see the Holy Spirit acting in the lives of these people, giving them the initial promptings to turn to God the Father. The Holy Spirit is in our hearts, too, guiding us to see and believe in what the Son has revealed.

We know from the Gospels that Jesus often healed or forgave someone because they had faith. He would tell them that their faith in him had saved them. Jesus' followers understood the importance of faith for life.

"The apostles said to the Lord, 'Increase our faith!' The Lord replied, 'If you had faith the size of a mustard seed, you could say to this mulberry tree, "Be uprooted and planted in the sea," and it would obey you'" (*Luke 17:5–6*).

 What do you think Jesus is telling his followers in this passage?

With Openness to God As a gift from God, faith is one of the theological virtues. A **virtue** is a strong habit of doing good that helps us make good moral decisions. Virtues guide our conduct and our emotions. The word *theological* is a combination of the two Greek words for "God" and "word."

The three **theological virtues**, faith, hope, and love (also called "charity") point us toward God. These gifts from God make it possible for Christians to live in relationship with one another and with God. They are the three virtues from which all other virtues flow. If a follower does not have them, it would be difficult to possess any other virtues. Saint Paul writes "And now faith, hope, and love abide, these three; and the greatest of these is love" (*1 Corinthians 13:13*).

▶ Faith helps us to see beyond what is purely human, to recognize the mystery of God in our hearts, in other people, and in all of creation.

▶ Hope sets our vision in the future, helping us realize that no matter what happens on earth, God will keep his promise to bring us to everlasting life. It helps us put our trust in God and his plan for us.

▶ Love makes faith and hope concrete—through love of God and others we join with the Church in showing the world that God's reign is beginning now.

✞ SCRIPTURE
GO TO THE SOURCE
Read **1 Corinthians 13:1–13**. Why do you think Paul says that the greatest of the theological virtues is love?

ACTIVITY

LIVE YOUR FAITH Choose one of the theological virtues and list the various ways that virtue can be seen in your life. Choose one that you want to develop and name some ways to do so.

IN SUMMARY

CATHOLICS BELIEVE

God reveals his love to us, and we are free to respond in faith by what we say and do.

▶ God's revelation is contained in his written word of Scripture and the lived Tradition of the Church passed down from generation to generation; together they make up one source of revelation, or deposit of faith.

▶ Faith is both a gift from God and a human choice and action. Faith is an individual act and act of the Church as a whole; the faith of the Church nourishes and strengthens the faith of each of us.

▶ Faith makes a difference in our lives; others can see by the way we live that we believe in God.

CELEBRATION OF THE WORD

Leader: Let us begin with the sign of our faith, the Sign of the Cross.

In today's reading, we hear the cry, "I believe; help my unbelief!"

A reading from the holy Gospel according to Mark.
Read Mark 9:14–29.

The Gospel of the Lord.

All: Praise to you, Lord Jesus Christ.

Leader: Lord, you alone provide the graces
to help us believe.
With all our heart, we pray to you:

All: Lord, increase our faith.

Leader: When we are in doubt,
when we feel weak,
when we feel you have abandoned us,

All: Lord, increase our faith.

Leader: When we want to make choices we know are wrong,
when we wonder whether or not you are real,
when we lose all our hope,

All: Lord, increase our faith.

Leader: When everything seems to be going right,
when we have more to be thankful for than to ask for,
when we need to remember that all our
    blessings come from you,

All: Lord, increase our faith.

Leader: When we have lost our way,
when it seems like our prayers go unanswered,
when we doubt ourselves,

All: Lord, increase our faith.

 "Lord, Increase our Faith"
David Haas, © 1997, GIA Publications, Inc.

26

REVIEW

A **Work with Words** Complete each sentence with the correct term from the word bank at right.

Word Bank

- Church
- councils
- Tradition
- canon
- virtue
- the Gospel
- inspiration
- faith

1. _____ helps us interpret Scripture and apply it to the circumstances of our time.

2. One of the ways that the Church passes on Tradition is by gathering bishops in _____ to speak about the faith of the Church, its teachings, and important issues.

3. _____ is both a gift from God and a free human response to believe in God.

4. The _____ is the community of baptized believers who believe in God and follow Jesus.

5. A strong habit of doing good that helps us make good moral decisions is known as a _____.

B **Check Understanding** Indicate whether the following statements are true or false. Then rewrite false statements to make them true.

_____ 6. Scripture and Tradition together are the one source of God's revelation to us.

_____

_____ 7. The Sacrament of Reconciliation is founded on the commissioning of the Apostles by Jesus to share in his ministry and work as Church leaders.

_____

_____ 8. In Scripture, the Church sets down in writing the important doctrines that are central for living a life of faith.

_____

_____ 9. The theological virtues—mercy, grace, and peace—are the three virtues from which all other virtues flow.

_____

_____ 10. Tradition and Scripture together ensure that what the Church writes and hands down through the generations comes from God.

_____

C **Make Connections: Draw Conclusions** Write a one-paragraph response to the questions.

Think of someone—described in the Bible or from your life—who has great faith. What role does faith play in that person's life? What do you learn from that person about your own faith?

OUR CATHOLIC FAITH

WHAT NOW?

★ Name some of the things or people you think might help you grow in your faith.

★ Share your beliefs with a friend.

★ Make a list of the questions you have about faith and talk to someone.

★ Have there been any times when faith has made a difference in a decision you made or an action you took?

ACTIVITY

LIVE YOUR FAITH Name some ways you can live by faith this week.

One way I am unique is _____.

I can thank God for _____

and I can thank a friend for _____.

I respected the dignity of _____ by _____

_____.

I plan to use the gifts of creation to _____

_____.

I can put my trust in God about _____

_____.

GO ONLINE Visit www.harcourtreligion.com for more family and community connections.

PRAYER

I thank you, Father, for the gift of faith.

Saint Thomas

History has named him Doubting Thomas. When we read the Gospels, it is easy to see why. Thomas was a doubter. But his doubt, his questions, did not disqualify him as a friend and follower of Jesus. This doubter became an Apostle who would, in the end, give his life for Christ.

Little is written about Thomas in the Gospels, but his personality is clear from the few stories we have. He was the one who questioned the words and actions of Jesus. When Jesus told the disciples he was going to Judea to visit Lazarus, Thomas said to his fellow disciples: "Let us also go, that we may die with him" (*John 11:16*). Before the Last Supper, Thomas questioned Jesus directly: "Thomas said to him, 'Lord, we do not know where you are going. How can we know the way?'" (*John 14:5*). But Thomas is best known for his response to reports of the Resurrection.

"Thomas (who was called the Twin), one of the twelve, was not with them when Jesus came. So the other disciples told him, 'We have seen the Lord.' But he said to them, 'Unless I see the mark of the nails in his hands, and put my finger in the mark of the nails and my hand in his side, I will not believe.' A week later his disciples were again in the house, and Thomas was with them. Although the doors were shut, Jesus came and stood among them and said, 'Peace be with you.' Then he said to Thomas, 'Put your finger here and see my hands. Reach out your hand and put it in my side. Do not doubt but believe.' Thomas answered him, 'My Lord and my God!' Jesus said to him, 'Have you believed because you have seen me? Blessed are those who have not seen and yet have come to believe'" (*John 20:24–29*).

Jesus responded to Thomas's statement with an invitation. Reach, touch, see for yourself—I am real. And Thomas turned from doubt to belief. Tradition says that Thomas, after Pentecost, was sent to preach to India. A large group there still call themselves "Christians of Saint Thomas." When Thomas came to the city of King Misdai, he converted the king's wife and son. For this, he was sentenced to death. He was led out of the city to a hill, and pierced through with spears by four soldiers. Thomas the doubter died a martyr, sure of his faith in Jesus.

▲ Saint Thomas, ?–72

GLOBAL DATA

India

- India is one of the oldest civilizations in the world, dating back at least 5,000 years.

- India has a population of over 1 billion people.

- India is home to two Eastern Catholic Churches, including the Syro-Malabar Catholic Church of the Chaldean Tradition, with approximately 4 million members.

- India is a mostly Hindu nation; over 80 percent of the people are Hindu.

- India is the largest democracy in the world.

CHAPTER 3 THE CHURCH Is Holy

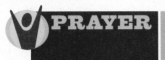 **PRAYER** Thank you for sharing your glory with all creation.

Can I really be holy?
Does holiness mean I have to pray all the time?
Some people really seem to make a difference.

"**H**ere, dear, let me help you with that." Brenda smiled as Mrs. Ebert took the scissors from her and expertly cut a shadow to fit behind the photo. "Wow. You're really good!" Brenda said as she looked up into Mrs. Ebert's face. "Yes, dear. I've had a few years of practice."

Brenda glanced around the rec room. All the other kids from Mrs. Warner's eighth-grade class at Holy Name school were scattered among the residents at tables at Fairview Senior Citizens' Center. She could hear the gentle hum of conversations and the occasional clank when scissors were set on the table.

Brenda hadn't been excited about the field trip. Her grandmother had died at a home for the elderly that smelled bad and the food looked gross. Brenda tried to be excited to visit her grandmother, but her joy felt forced and phony.

She didn't feel that way today. She was so busy working on a photo album of Mrs. Ebert's grandkids that she hadn't thought about funny smells or gross food.

Brenda heard her classmate Mike laughing. He seemed to be having a good time. Mike and the man he was supposed to be helping had stopped working with the photos. The man stood in front of Mike waving his arms back and forth. Mike was loving it. "Oh that's George," Mrs. Ebert said as she saw where Brenda was looking. "He loves to talk about the war."

"What war?" Brenda asked.

"Why, World War II, of course."

The hour flew by. It was time to say goodbye. Brenda looked at Mrs. Ebert. "Thank you for letting me help with your album. You have beautiful grandkids." Mrs. Ebert smiled. For a moment, Brenda thought she was going to cry. Then Mrs. Ebert took Brenda's hands in hers and said, "Goodbye, dear. You made my day."

Brenda felt so much love in that touch. She carried the feeling with her all the way back to school.

ACTIVITY

LET'S BEGIN Why do you think Brenda and Mike had such a good experience?

▶ **When have you had an experience where someone made you feel special and cared for? When have you done something to let another person know they are cared for?**

THE HOLINESS OF GOD

Focus How can we really be holy?

Sometimes people think that holiness is about hiding away in a monastery or spending the whole day in prayer. Very few people are able to do that. Holiness has something to do with the ordinary events of life. **Holiness** is becoming more God-like, living in his presence and with his love. Holiness can be doing normal things as if you were doing them with God. God calls every person to be holy in some unique way. If it wasn't possible for every person to be holy, God would not even ask us to be.

Sharing God's Glory On each of the six days of creation, God looked upon what he had made and said that it was "good." Everything reflected his own goodness and holiness. So all of creation is related because everything, including human beings, was created by God and shows his goodness.

God created the variety of creatures each with a different purpose and order. He made them to be interdependent. But God made human beings special. He created us in his image with an intellect and free will, and he set us over all creation to care for it. God wanted people to live in ways that would reflect his own goodness and holiness.

The writers of the psalms sung their prayers that acknowledge the awesome experience of being in friendship with God.

✝ SCRIPTURE

When I look at your heavens, the work of your fingers,
   the moon and stars that you have established;
What are human beings that you are mindful of them,
   mortals that you care for them?
Yet you have made them a little lower than God,
   and crowned them with glory and honor.
You have given them dominion over the works of your hands;
   you have put all things under their feet.

—Psalm 8:3–6

 How have you experienced God's friendship in a way that surprised you?

LOOKING BACK

In the second century, Saint Irenaeus wrote many works to explain what it means to be a Christian. One of his most well-known phrases is "the glory of God is the human person fully alive."

Holiness and happiness go together. God gave us the gift of life. Living life the way God intended us to—in ordinary holiness—brings you the deepest kind of happiness. The fully alive and holy person simply commits to go through life with God as the top priority, still going to dances, still playing cards, still trying to look good, still going to the movies, *and* still doing homework, cleaning your room, choosing right from wrong, watching your language, and going to Church. Irenaeus understood that all humans are capable of sharing in God's own holiness and goodness while still living life 24/7.

When the holiness of God is seen and communicated in creation and in humans, this is the glory of God. As we live on the earth, we have many chances to share in God's glory. We show others God's glory so that the whole human race will come to realize this gift of sharing in God's own holiness. When we live for the good of others, we show God's glory. And God promises that the fullness of glory will be ours when we finally arrive at his heavenly kingdom.

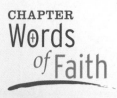
 What are some small ways for you to practice holiness?

From time to time God has sent messengers to make known and help people understand his plan for all of creation. These messengers are angels, spiritual beings that praise God and serve him. They can think and choose like humans, but they do not have bodies. The word *angel* comes from Greek and Hebrew words that mean "messenger from God." Although there are many angels in the stories of Scripture, three of them are named:

Gabriel ("the strength of God")
▶ helps the prophet Daniel to understand the mysteries and prophecies that God wants Daniel to communicate (See *Daniel 7* and *10.*)
▶ announces to Zachariah that he will have a son named John, who becomes John the Baptist and the cousin of Jesus
▶ announces the birth of Jesus to Mary at the Annunciation

Raphael ("the healing of God")
▶ appears by name only in the Book of Tobit (*12*) to heal Tobias of blindness and to help his wife struggle against evil

Michael ("who is like God")
▶ also appears with the prophet Daniel as the one who will help God's followers in their struggles, especially at the end of time (See *Daniel 10* and *12.*)
▶ is mentioned in the Letter to Jude as one who fights with the devil
▶ leads the battle in heaven that is recorded in the Book of Revelation (See *Revelation 12.*)

ACTIVITY

SHARE YOUR FAITH List three things you do as part of being fully alive, like a sleepover with a bunch of friends. Then name a way that you can do it with normal holiness. Compare your three examples with someone else.

1.

2.

3.

CATHOLICS TODAY

Just as God blesses us, we are a blessing for God. Our life, our actions, our thoughts, and our words give praise to God because we show God's goodness wherever we are. We bless God in prayer. Because God blesses us, we can return that blessing. When we share a blessing, we are really asking God, who is the source of all blessing, to bless. We can bless people, places, and things. Parents bless their children, teachers bless their students, priests and deacons bless parishioners, and we bless ourselves with the Sign of the Cross.

▼ *Christ Healing the Blind Man of Jericho*, by unknown artist (17th century)

THE HOLINESS OF THE CHURCH

Focus Who will help you grow in holiness?

Our world is covered with lakes and streams that are filled with life because water flows into one area and flows out somewhere else. Sometimes we find a stagnant body of water. Because there is no movement or outlet for the water, living organisms cannot survive.

It is much the same with the holiness of God that is given to every person and to the Church.

If we try to keep God's holiness for ourselves, we become lifeless. But when we share the goodness of God with others, we grow more and more in God's life. We are each called to holiness because the Church is called to be holy, as Christ himself is holy.

The Holiness of Jesus As the perfect and complete revelation of God, Jesus shows God's holiness

▶ by taking on our burdens

▶ by being the way to the Father

▶ by speaking with the voice of God

▶ by the way he lived the Beatitudes

▶ by reaching out to the lost, the needy, and sinners

▶ by being the perfect model of love

Being holy is one of the **marks of the Church**—the four essential or distinguishing characteristics of the Church: one, holy, catholic, and apostolic. The Church can be identified by these characteristics. Because the Church is the Body of Christ, the holiness of the Church comes from Christ. The Church is holy because the Holy Spirit gives us life and lives within us, guiding us as individuals and a community. The Church helps each of us to follow Jesus' example and to become holy, sometimes in small ways, sometimes in great ways.

PRAYER AND WORSHIP HELP US GROW IN HOLINESS

In the prayer and worship of the Church, Christians meet God in a personal way and are strengthened to grow in holiness. This is why the Church invites us to pray at all times and in all places.

▶ Initiation (Baptism, Confirmation, Eucharist) makes us members of the Church as God gives us new life and fills us with the Holy Spirit.

▶ Sacraments of Healing (Reconciliation and Anointing of the Sick) strengthen us in body and spirit when we have failed or when we are weakened by sickness.

▶ Feasts of the year remind us of events and people that are important models for holiness.

▶ Sacraments at the Service of Communion (Matrimony and Holy Orders) mark our commitment to follow God's call.

▶ Eucharist, or the Mass, is the central act of worship because we hear God's word, remember the death and Resurrection of Christ, and are intimately joined to Christ in Holy Communion.

▶ Personal prayer gives us an opportunity to speak with God in a way that relates to the circumstances of our own life.

▶ The Liturgy of Hours (prayed by ordained people, religious people, and many laypeople) makes every part of the day holy.

▶ Special devotions, like the Stations of the Cross, help us recall the presence of God in our lives and the help God offers at all times.

▶ Adoration of the Blessed Sacrament helps us remember and honor in a special way Jesus' unique presence in the Eucharist.

 What type of prayer or worship do you most enjoy? Why?

ACTIVITY

CONNECT YOUR FAITH Choose two ways Jesus modeled holiness for us. Think of two specific, concrete ways you can follow his example this week.

HOLINESS IN ACTION

Focus What does it mean to be holy?

Saint Paul tells us that a person without love is like a noisy gong or a clanging symbol. A person may do nice things and speak very persuasively, but if words and actions do not flow from love, that person is nothing. (See *1 Corinthians 13:1–2*.) Being holy means being in love with God and expressing that love of God through love for all creation and all people.

Prayer is an important part of being holy, but it is not the only part. Holiness that comes from love shows in your actions. Saint John taught this when he said that the way we can tell someone is in union with Christ is by the way that person lives like Christ. (See *1 John 2:5–6*.) One of the reasons Jesus criticized some of the religious leaders of his day was because they did not have love in their hearts. They upheld laws and rules, but they often did it to appear important. When the love of God and neighbor is the basis for a person's actions, that person is holy.

We Grow in Holiness When people are baptized, they receive the light of Christ, and the Church prays that the light of faith will always be bright. They also receive a baptismal garment, and the Church prays that the dignity of the baptized person will always be strong. The prayers of Baptism recognize that the gift of holiness develops and grows through a person's lifetime. Those prayers also recognize that sometimes people will face difficulties or evil as they learn how to grow in holiness and love.

The members of the Church help each other grow in holiness.

▶ They support and encourage each other.

▶ They pray together and learn together.

▶ They listen to the word of God and reflect on how to put God's word into practice.

▶ They remember God's mercy when they fail and find God's grace to help them become more holy.

✝ **SCRIPTURE**

GO TO THE SOURCE
Read **1 John 4:16–21**. How would you describe the relationship between love of God and love of our brothers and sisters?

ACTIVITY

LIVE YOUR FAITH Make a list of some of the ways the Church helps and supports you and some ways you help and support other members of the Church.

_____

_____

_____

_____

_____

IN SUMMARY

CATHOLICS BELIEVE

The Church is a sign of the holiness of God.

▶ Each of us is called to be holy in even the ordinary circumstances of our lives. God created humans to share in his glory, to be holy, and to be joined fully with him.

▶ The Church is holy because her founder is holy and because the Holy Spirit lives within her. The Church helps us grow in holiness, especially through prayer and worship.

▶ A life of holiness is built on love; the love that we have for our brothers and sisters is the way we see the love of God.

PRAYER

PRAYER OF SERVICE

Leader: Heavenly Father, over the centuries, women and men of faith
have served you in many ways.
We pray for guidance and assure you of our
longing to serve you in our day and in our time.

Let us pray.

Side 1: We know and believe that Jesus, your Son,
followed your plan and trusted in your will for his life.
We are here—we come to do your will.

All: We come to do your will.

Side 2: We know and believe that we are your children,
and that you want us to be happy
and to trust in your plan for us all.
We are here—we come to do your will.

All: We come to do your will.

Side 1: We know and believe that our world
is hurting, is wounded and in need of servants
who follow and respond to your voice;
servants willing to help and to heal
a weary and broken world.
We are here—we come to do your will.

All: We come to do your will.

Side 2: Heavenly Father,
send us your Spirit.
Give us the faith and the holiness needed
to be your people, your servants,
committed to you and to your will.

All: We ask this through Christ,
our Lord. Amen.

♪ "We Arise"
Michael Mahler and Tony Alonso, © 2004, GIA Publications, Inc.

REVIEW

A **Work with Words** Circle the letter of the choice that best completes the sentence.

1. _____ is becoming more God-like, living in his presence and with his love.
   a. Beatification   **b.** Justification   **c.** Holiness   **d.** Glorification

2. Human beings are created by God to be unique because we are made in his image with a(n)
   _____, and he set us over all creation to care for it.
   a. intellect   **b.** free will   **c.** challenge   **d.** both a and b

3. The word _____ comes from Greek and Hebrew words that mean "messenger from God."
   a. Messiah   **b.** savior   **c.** angel   **d.** Christ

4. Being holy is one of the _____ (the four essential or distinguishing characteristics of the Church).
   a. doctrines of the Church   **b.** marks of the Church   **c.** Traditions   **d.** characters of the Church

....

B **Check Understanding** Indicate whether the following statements are true or false. Then rewrite false statements to make them true.

_____ **5.** All of creation is related because everything, including human beings, has been created by God.

_____ **6.** The angel Gabriel leads the battle in heaven that is recorded in the Book of Revelation.

_____ **7.** The four essential or distinguishing characteristics of the Church are one, holy, catholic, and sacramental.

_____ **8.** Liturgy of the Hours gives special honor to Jesus' presence in the Eucharist.

_____ **9.** Holiness that comes from love is seen primarily in prayer and actions.

_____ **10.** Members of the Church grow in holiness as they listen to the word of God and reflect on how to put God's word into practice.

....

C **Make Connections: Interpret** Write a one-paragraph response to the questions.

Which type of prayer or worship is most meaningful to you? How do you encounter God through this experience?

OUR CATHOLIC FAITH

WHAT NOW?

★ Spend some time getting to know God by reading Scripture or in prayer.

★ Volunteer some time for a Church activity that helps people in need.

★ Do something to make the environment more beautiful.

★ Find someone you think is holy and talk with that person.

ACTIVITY

LIVE YOUR FAITH Name some people who you think model holiness for others. Think of someone younger than you, someone your age, and someone older than you. Write down a few words to describe each person.

Younger:

Your age:

Older:

▶ What do these three people have in common?

▶ Name something you can do to be more like each of them.

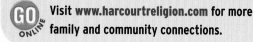 **Visit www.harcourtreligion.com** for more family and community connections.

 **PRAYER**

I want to be holy, Jesus. Please show me how.

Blessed Miguel Pro

As a child, Miguel Agustin Pro Juarez was a practical joker. Sometimes his jokes went too far and put him in danger.

One time, after an accident, Miguel asked for some "cocol" (sweet bread). "Cocol" became his nickname. And, later in life, it became the code name he used during his secret ministry. As a priest, he was persecuted. He lived a life of action, risking his own life for others.

Miguel was born on January 13, 1891, in Guadalupe, Mexico. He was the oldest son in the family. Much loved by his family, he was known as *Miguelito*. Miguel was very close to his older sister. When she entered a convent, he felt a calling to the priesthood. He could have had a good income managing his father's business. Instead, in 1911, Miguel chose to become a Jesuit.

In 1914, a wave of anti-Catholicism spread in Mexico. Miguel fled to the United States, through Texas and New Mexico, to California. From there, he traveled to Spain. From 1915 to 1924, Miguel studied in Spain. Finally, he was ordained as a priest in 1925. But Miguel had very bad stomach problems. After three operations, his health did not improve. So Miguel returned to Mexico in 1926.

Anti-Catholic feelings were still strong in Mexico. Churches closed and priests went into hiding. Miguel would spend the rest of his life in a secret ministry. He cared for the spiritual and physical needs of the people. And he took care of the poor in Mexico City. He moved about the city in disguise to carry out his secret ministry. In the middle of the night, he would dress as a beggar to baptize infants, bless marriages, and lead Mass. Dressed as a police officer, he would visit people in jail. Dressed in a suit with a fresh flower in his lapel, he would go to wealthy people to get items for the poor. He lived like a daring spy. But always, Father Pro lived a holy life and served Christ with joy.

Miguel became a wanted man. He was falsely accused of trying to assassinate a former Mexican president. The police arrested him, and he was sentenced to death without a trial. At his execution, Father Pro forgave the people putting him to death. He would not take a blindfold. As he died, he bravely said, "Viva Cristo Rey," which means "Long live Christ the King!"

▲ **Blessed Miguel Pro, 1891–1927**

GLOBAL DATA

Mexico

- Mexico was the site of some of the earliest and most developed civilizations.

- Mexico is just about three times the size of Texas.

- Mexico has a population of over 106 million people.

- Nearly 90 percent of the Mexican people are Catholic.

- Mexico celebrates los Dias de los Muertos (Days of the Dead) to remember family members who have died.

Faith in Action!

DISCOVER

Catholic Social Teaching:
Care for God's Creation

IN THIS UNIT you learned how much God has blessed you and that you were created to live in a loving relationship with God. This is half of God's covenant with us. The other half is being a blessing for others and for the earth, in return.

Care for Creation

Saint Francis of Assisi learned and lived these principles perhaps better than anyone else. As a young adult, he rediscovered an appreciation for the beauty of nature God had blessed him with in his youth. His response was to praise God through all the wonders of creation—sun and moon, mountains and rivers, trees and flowers, the wind and rain. And he called them his "brothers" and "sisters." We, too, are called to give God thanks and praise for all these beautiful gifts of creation.

But Francis also realized that God wants these gifts of creation to be available for everyone. He gave away all his things and money, renounced his inheritance, and began to care for lepers and beg for the poor. Like Francis, each of us is asked by God to be both charitable and just.

God wants us to take care of the goods God has given us, to be charitable in sharing them with others, and to support efforts to preserve the earth's resources for all God's children. Praying for help to Francis, who is the patron saint of ecology, you can promote recycling at home, at school, and in the community. You can help protect rain forests, rivers, soil, and endangered species, each of which is a revelation of God's wisdom, goodness, and beauty.

What most impresses you about the life of Saint Francis? How could you put this into practice in your own life?

WE ARE CALLED TO CARE
for God's creation. Let's look at how one parish's actions became a "Mission Possible."

"MISSION POSSIBLE"
PLANTING POSSIBILITIES

Learning and living Catholic social teaching is an integral part of the eighth-grade program at Holy Family Catholic Church in Irving, Texas. Last year when the theme was caring for God's creation, the youth were invited to create a potted plant that would represent how they would care for God's creation. At the first station, they decorated their clay pots with signs, symbols, and words that would remind them not only to care for their plant, but to care for creation in other ways as well. The students were also asked to put their name on their pot to remind them that they are also one of God's creations and that it is important to care for ourselves as well as others. At the second station, they each received their plant, which they put in their pot, along with a little additional topsoil.

At the conclusion of the activity, everyone was invited to share one thing they had learned from their creations. In listening to these discoveries, it was clear to Anne Keough, the adult leader, that the activity had hit home. Not only did these young people follow through on taking care of their plants, but a number of them also volunteered for "Mission Possible." This inter-parish youth service week provided these eighth-graders with the opportunity to expand their care for creation. Some of them helped to paint a house and plant a garden for an elderly Irving resident. Others planted flowers at a neighborhood social center. Still others worked at a local food bank, where they sorted canned goods and prepared "family packs" of food for individuals in need of help. Caring for creation doesn't stop with your own place or clay pot. It clearly goes into the community as well.

What part of your place and your community could use your caring "green thumb"?

SERVE   Your Community

SHARING THE GOODS OF CREATION WITH OTHERS

Make a list of the things you have (such as clothes, books, CDs, sports equipment, or other items) that you could give to others who don't have as much.

To whom could you donate these?

What could you give up occasionally to save some money (e.g., eating out, snacks, soda, name-brand clothes, movies, or video games)?

With whom could you share these savings?

Who else could you ask to help you in this effort?

THINGS TO SHARE

THINGS TO DO TO SAVE $

WHO TO HELP

PROTECTING CREATION

Identify with your classmates different aspects of creation that are in danger from human activity. Have individuals or teams research those that interest the class most and report their findings. Choose one and create a plan for protecting it.

Project Planning Sheet

Groups to present your project to

_____

Equipment needed

_____

Others who should be asked to help

_____

How to publicize your project

_____

Other specific tasks

_____

Your specific task(s)

_____

Calendar for completing the project

_____

When you think about all the people in the world who don't have what you have, who don't even have food or clean water, what do you think God wants you to do?

_____

_____

Why is it hard sometimes to give away things we like to others who need them? Or to make sacrifices so that we can share some of our money with others in need?

_____

_____

When you see or think about the forests that are being destroyed, the rivers that are being polluted, all the species of life that are becoming extinct every year, what do you think God wants you to do?

_____

_____

What do you do when you sometimes think "what's the use, the problems are too big and not that many people really care about it anyway"?

_____

What did you learn about the issue of caring for creation in doing the project?

_____

_____

What are you going to do differently the next time you try to make a difference in your family, school, or community about taking better care of creation?

_____

_____

What did you learn about yourself in doing each of these actions?

_____

_____

What did you learn about God and about your faith in doing them?

_____

List one thing that might be different about you after doing this project.

_____

REVIEW

A **Work with Words** Match the words on the left with the correct definitions or descriptions on the right.

_____ **1.** soul

_____ **2.** free will

_____ **3.** covenant

_____ **4.** Decalogue

_____ **5.** Tradition

_____ **6.** virtue

_____ **7.** angel

_____ **8.** marks of the Church

_____ **9.** natural law

_____ **10.** revealed law

A. another name for the Ten Commandments

B. rules for living that guide us in making choices

C. the four essential characteristics of the Church

D. from Greek and Hebrew words that mean "messenger from God"

E. spiritual principle that reflects God in you

F. a sacred promise between God and humans involving mutual commitments

G. this is universal because it applies to every human being

H. a strong habit of doing good that helps us make moral decisions

I. ability to choose and make decisions without being forced to act in a certain way

J. the living and true teachings of Jesus passed down in the Church from generation to generation

B Check Understanding Complete each sentence with the correct term from the word bank at right.

Word Bank

Adoration of the Blessed Sacrament
free will
Gospels
apostolic
theological virtues
Holy Orders
Scripture
holiness
Reconciliation
sacramental
Tradition
doctrines

11. _____ and _____ together are the source of God's revelation to us.

12. The Sacrament of _____ is founded on the commissioning of the Apostles by Jesus to share in his ministry and work in a special way as Church leaders.

13. In _____, the Church sets down in writing the important beliefs and teachings that are central for living a life of faith.

14. The _____, faith, hope, and love, are the three virtues from which all other virtues flow.

15. Human beings are created uniquely by God because we are made in his image with a(n) _____.

16. The four essential characteristics of the Church are one, holy, catholic, and _____.

17. _____ gives special honor to Jesus' unique presence in the Eucharist.

18. Members of the Church grow in _____ as they listen to the word of God and reflect on how to put God's word into practice.

C Make Connections Write a short answer to these questions.

19. **Synthesize.** God has a purpose for our lives: to know him, to love him, and to help others do the same. What does this purpose mean for your life? Write a purpose statement for your life that reflects your goals and desires as they are shaped by your relationship with God.

_____

_____

20. **Infer.** Jesus Christ was the fulfillment of God's own revelation. What aspects of God's character become more clear to you through the life of Jesus? Provide specific examples from Jesus' life to support your answer.

_____

_____

_____

JESUS Reveals the Trinity

*I'm so many different things to different people,
sometimes I forget who I am.
I can feel my relationship with my parents changing . . .
and that scares me a little!*

Joanelle stared blankly at the diagram. "In triangle *ABC*, *AB* = 25, *BC* = 16, and *AC* = 39. If *ABC* is rotated about its shortest side, what is the volume of the solid?" She sighed. Math was her nemesis. English, on the other hand, was easy for her. She felt sorry for some kids in her class who didn't get the difference between a simile and metaphor. "I guess the math geniuses feel sorry for me when they hear my sad questions," she thought to herself. Joanelle glanced quickly at the microwave clock. Her mom, the math whiz of the family, wouldn't be home to help with homework for another hour.

"I'm hungry," howled Jadon, her ten-year-old brother, as he hopped on one foot next to her chair. Joanelle called him the human food processor because he was always starving. She stopped herself from telling him to get his own snack, remembering the deal she had struck with her parents: take care of Jadon after school and they would double her allowance.

As she was fixing him a big plate of crackers and peanut butter, her best friend, Tania, called. Joanelle usually loved talking to her on the phone, but Tania had been in a two-day funk because of a boy. Joanelle was tired of listening to Tania talk about it. She couldn't just ignore her best friend when she needed help, but the call seemed to go on forever.

Maybe what Tania needs is experienced help, she thought as she hung up the phone. She decided to ask her dad and see if he could help. "Well," he said with a grin, "I had no clue about girls when I was your age." Picturing her dad as a clueless teenager made Joanelle smile.

Okay then, on to the next expert. Joanelle questioned her mom about Tania's problems. "All that's just normal teenage stuff," her mom said. Joanelle sighed. "Yes, but what can I do when Tania won't stop talking about it?" "I understand, honey. Listening can be tiring. But that's an important part of friendship. It might seem like you aren't doing anything, but what you are doing could be just the thing she needs."

ACTIVITY

LET'S BEGIN Discuss the events of the story. What are the different roles that Joanelle has in other people's lives? What roles does she want or need other people to assume in *her* life?

▶ **Draw a diagram of the network of relationships in your life (start with you in the center). How did those relationships come about and what are the connections between them?**

me

A UNIQUE VIEW INTO JESUS

 Focus What did the Transfiguration reveal about Jesus?

Sometimes we think we have someone figured out, a parent, a teacher, or a friend whom we've known for years. Then that person does something that surprises us, showing us a whole different side.

Just like all of us have different roles, Jesus does, too. His followers had seen him in action, preaching and healing. They knew he was special, but they had to grow in their understanding of who he really was.

✝ **SCRIPTURE**

The Transfiguration One day, Jesus took Peter, James, and John up a mountain to pray. His friends didn't expect anything out of the ordinary. However, they found out that Jesus was much more than simply their down-to-earth teacher and friend. As Jesus prayed, an incredible thing happened. Suddenly, his face changed and his clothes glowed whiter than anything imaginable. Then two men, also in shining clothing like an angel's, appeared out of nowhere and began talking with Jesus.

The disciples realized that the two men with Jesus were historic leaders of the Jewish people: Moses, the Lawgiver, and Elijah, the prophet, were standing before them, talking with their friend! The disciples had never seen this glorious side of Jesus before. They had walked many dusty miles with him and stayed in places that were far from heavenly. The unexpected experience was almost too much for the disciples. Then it became even more amazing when a cloud came and darkened the mountaintop, and they heard a voice from the cloud proclaim, "This is my Son, my Chosen; listen to him!" (*Luke 9:35*).

 How did the voice set Jesus apart from Moses and Elijah?

◀ *The Transfiguration*, by Giovanni Lanfranco (1582–1647)

A Glimpse into God Throughout Scripture, we find examples of God choosing to reveal important messages on mountaintops. In this particular mountaintop episode, the disciples witnessed the **Transfiguration** of the Lord, the event in which Jesus' divine glory was shown to them.

The Transfiguration not only revealed something about Jesus, but it also gave the disciples a glimpse into the Trinity. God the Father's voice was heard from the cloud, telling the disciples about the uniqueness of Jesus: He is not another prophet or Lawgiver, he is the Son of God, and they should listen to him. The cloud represented the Holy Spirit, as it had become a sign during Old Testament times of God's presence among his People.

As the voice finished speaking, the disciples looked around. The cloud was gone. Moses and Elijah were gone. Jesus alone stood before them. (See *Luke 9:34–36.*) The point was clear. The laws and prophets of the Old Testament had prepared the way for the coming of the Son of God. But now, Jesus is the Chosen One, the Person in whom we find the truth, the Person who reveals God to the world.

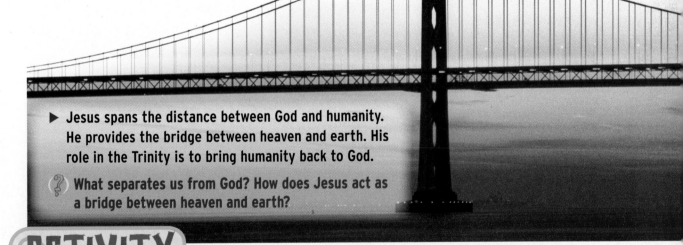

▶ **Jesus spans the distance between God and humanity. He provides the bridge between heaven and earth. His role in the Trinity is to bring humanity back to God.**

What separates us from God? How does Jesus act as a bridge between heaven and earth?

ACTIVITY

SHARE YOUR FAITH Are there times when you don't listen to someone you know you should listen to? What gets in the way of accepting what that person has to say? How can that person's words help you to make faith-filled decisions or to better live as a follower of Jesus?

_____

_____

_____

GOD'S GLORY REVEALED

Focus How does the Holy Spirit further God's work on earth?

Even your favorite class, with a fascinating subject and a dynamic teacher, can sometimes put you to sleep. No one can deny that life has its boring moments. But there are also glorious moments—totally exciting times that take your breath away:

▶ making the team

▶ going on the big class trip

▶ getting praise from someone you admire

▶ moments of understanding, discovery, or inspiration

In these moments, we have a glimpse of what glory feels like. It seems as if everything is coming together. We feel more deeply aware and alive. We realize, "Wow! Life *is* really worth it!" or "God *is* Good!"

Have you ever heard a mom speak to her child in a way that helps him or her learn the names of things around them, what they do, and how they look? "Hear that noise, Kevin? Look, it's a train! A big red train!" Just like a loving mother who takes time to point out things to her young children that they might otherwise miss, the Church helps us see and appreciate the glory of God just beneath the surface of life.

The Holy Spirit Gives Us the Church Jesus promised his Apostles that the Holy Spirit would come to them. The Holy Spirit would help them spread the Good News of Jesus' life to others once Jesus had ascended to his heavenly Father.

The Church was given to us on **Pentecost**, the day that the Holy Spirit descended on those first followers—so that all believers thereafter would have help like that of a loving parent, pointing out to them what is truly important in life.

The Church has the role of helping us recognize and give thanks for the many ways in which God reveals his glory. In the Church, the Holy Spirit prepares us to know and love Christ, to share his communion, and to transform us in Christ's saving work.

▼ *The Pentecost*, by Domenico Theotocopuli, known as "El Greco" (1541–1614)

❓ Apart from religion class or a parish youth group, when was the last time you talked about Jesus to another person?

❓ If you're shy about talking about your faith, how can you *show* your faith to others?

ACTIVITY

CONNECT YOUR FAITH What are some of your glorious moments? Make a list and then describe how the experience brought you closer to your family, friends, or God.

MOMENT OF GLORY		CONNECTION TO OTHERS
	···▶	
	···▶	
	···▶	
	···▶	

RELATING TO GOD

Focus How do you respond to God's gifts?

God does not leave it up to us to invent our relationship with him. He is always in relationship with us, waiting for us to respond. He gives us the Church to help us know and love him. God gives us the desire and the ability to know and love him as adopted sons and daughters. This gift is called **grace**.

Grace is God's free gift to us. We do not deserve it. We do not earn it on our own. God offers us this gift again and again in many different ways. He is generous; he is always giving us the possibility of a life lived as his sons and daughters.

But the choice is always ours. We are free to accept and respond to the gift of grace. When we do respond to grace, it makes our relationship to the Holy Trinity stronger and deeper.

Knowing the Father, Son, and Holy Spirit
In the Sacrament of Baptism we are baptized in the name of the Father, and of the Son, and of the Holy Spirit. As we get older, we are introduced to different ways of speaking about God. At Mass, at home, and in religion classes, we pray to God using different titles or names that reflect the various roles he has in our lives.

A favorite prayer addressed to Jesus is called the Jesus Prayer and uses two of his many titles, "Lord Jesus Christ, Son of God, have mercy on me a sinner!" When you speak of Jesus as "Lord," you are saying that you believe he is God.

CHECK THIS OUT!

Did you know that if there is great need, anyone can baptize another person? But only in an emergency situation and the person performing the Baptism must do it for the same reasons that the Church does. Water must be used, poured three times on the person's head, while the following words are said: "I baptize you in the name of the Father, and of the Son, and of the Holy Spirit."

Usually this sort of Baptism is celebrated when the person is in danger of dying without being baptized.

TO WHOM WE PRAY

▼ Prayer is usually addressed to the Father, although it can also be directed to Jesus and the Holy Spirit.

TO THE FATHER:

Lord God

Almighty God

O God

Heavenly Father

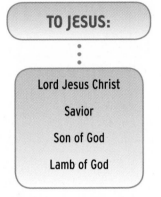

TO JESUS:

Lord Jesus Christ

Savior

Son of God

Lamb of God

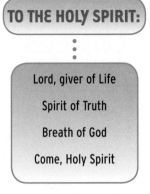

TO THE HOLY SPIRIT:

Lord, giver of Life

Spirit of Truth

Breath of God

Come, Holy Spirit

▲ Look at the titles to address God the Father, God the Son, and God the Holy Spirit. Choose one from each column and explain what it means to you to call God by that name.

ACTIVITY

LIVE YOUR FAITH When was the last time you were given a significant gift and simply set it aside, not using it? How would you feel if you gave someone a gift and he or she didn't seem to want it or like it?

▶ **How do you think God reacts when you don't accept or respond to his gift of grace?**

_____

_____

_____

IN SUMMARY

CATHOLICS BELIEVE

We relate to the three Persons of the Trinity in different ways. We are children of God the Father, brother and sister of Christ, and Spirit-filled.

▶ Jesus' Transfiguration revealed his divine glory as the Son of God, and shows us God the Father, Son, and Holy Spirit.

▶ The Holy Spirit is alive and active in the Church, who helps us recognize and give thanks for the many ways in which God reveals his glory.

▶ The gift of grace helps us to know and love God, to learn what it means to be his adopted children, and to grow in that role.

PROFESSION OF FAITH

Reader 1: We believe in one God,
The Father, the Almighty,
Maker of heaven and earth,
Of all that is seen and unseen.

Reader 2: We believe in one Lord, Jesus Christ,
The only Son of God,
Eternally begotten of the Father,
God from God, Light from Light,
true God from true God,
begotten, not made, one in being with the Father.

All: Yes, we believe.

Reader 3: Through him all things were made.
For us men and for our salvation
he came down from heaven.
by the power of the Holy Spirit
he was born of the Virgin Mary, and became man.

Reader 1: For our sake he was crucified under Pontius Pilate;
he suffered, died, and was buried.
On the third day he rose again
in fulfillment of the Scriptures;
he ascended into heaven
and is seated at the right hand of the Father.
He will come again in glory to judge the living and the dead,
and his kingdom will have no end.

All: Yes, we believe.

Reader 2: We believe in the Holy Spirit, the Lord, the giver of life,
who proceeds from the Father and the Son.
With the Father and the Son he is worshiped
and glorified.
He has spoken through the Prophets.

Reader 3: We believe in one holy catholic and
apostolic Church.
We acknowledge one baptism for the
forgiveness of sins.
We look for the resurrection of the dead,
and the life of the world to come.

All: Amen.

 "If You Believe"

Iona Community © 1991, Distributed by GIA Publications, Inc.

REVIEW

A Work with Words Circle the letter of the choice that best completes the sentence.

1. The event in which Jesus' divine glory was shown to his disciples on a mountaintop is the _____.

   a. Last Supper
   b. Transfiguration
   c. Sermon on the Mount
   d. Ascension

2. _____ is the free gift of God that enables us to be his adopted children.

   a. Courage
   b. Canon law
   c. Mercy
   d. Grace

3. The day the Holy Spirit came upon the disciples is known as _____.

   a. Easter
   b. Pentecost
   c. the Ascension
   d. the Transfiguration

4. Jesus promised the Apostles that the _____ would help them spread the Good News after his Ascension.

   a. disciples
   b. Bible
   c. Holy Spirit
   d. Church

5. The Transfiguration gave the disciples a glimpse into the _____.

   a. Word
   b. mercy
   c. salvation
   d. Trinity

B Check Understanding Complete each sentence with the correct term(s). You may use some words more than once.

6. The two men who appeared with Jesus at the Transfiguration were _____ and _____.

7. A role of Jesus in the _____ is to reveal God the Father to the world.

8. _____ is celebrated as the beginning of the Church.

9. In the Church _____ prepares us to love Christ and to share in his communion.

10. In the Sacrament of Baptism, we are baptized in the name of the _____, _____, and _____.

Word Bank

Father
Pentecost
Christmas
Trinity
Elijah
Holy Spirit
Moses
Matthew
Son

C Make Connections: Compare and Contrast Write a one-paragraph response to the questions.

List three different titles or names by which you address the Father, Son, and Holy Spirit in your prayers. Reflect on what those names or titles reveal about the various roles the Trinity has in your life. How are their roles the same? How are they different?

OUR CATHOLIC FAITH

WHAT NOW?

★ Think about what role God has in your life.

★ As you pray, become aware of which Person in the Trinity you are praying to.

★ Evaluate what you need most from God right now.

★ Decide on one small thing you think God is calling you to do and do it.

★ Name some roles you play in your life and reflect on what role you play when you pray.

ACTIVITY

LIVE YOUR FAITH Allow the Persons of the Holy Trinity to work for you in your prayer life. Think about which of the three divine Persons you need right now and why:

God the Father, protector and provider

God the Son, friend, Redeemer, and source of wisdom

God the Holy Spirit, guide, comforter, source of strength

▶ Write down how each Person could offer you the help you need in different situations.

▶ Because you were probably baptized when you were a baby and therefore don't remember it, call your parish and find out when the next Baptism will be celebrated. Sit as a member of the assembly and enjoy someone else's Baptism. Let that celebration be a touchstone for you in appreciating your *own* Baptism!

▶ Afterward, write about your experience. What did you see and hear? What were the highlights of the celebration? How did those present express their joy? What was the most interesting part of the celebration? What does this sacrament say to us about God? About the Church?

 Visit www.harcourtreligion.com for more family and community connections.

 **PRAYER**

Father, Son, and Spirit, be with me today and always.

Blessed Elizabeth of the Trinity Catez

Elizabeth Catez had a cheerful personality, even though she lost her father at a very young age. As a girl, she attended family gatherings in her hometown of Dijon, France, and played the piano brilliantly for guests. She spread joy to many through her music.

One day Father Valee, a Dominican, had a long conversation with Elizabeth. He explained to her that the Blessed Trinity dwelt in her soul. She was immediately inspired to live a life of praise and homage to God dwelling in her. She began to focus on her mission and her place in the society in which she lived. She visited the sick and taught catechism to the children.

Prayer became the center of Elizabeth's life. She would start each day praying before daybreak. Adoration of the Blessed Sacrament, the Holy Rosary, and the Way of the Cross were her special prayers. She did penance and even wore a rough hair shirt. But Elizabeth wanted to feel more strongly that she was sacrificing all for God, so she prayed to suffer the Crown of Thorns. She wanted to experience the same pain that Jesus had suffered. She began to have terrible headaches. After two years, the headaches disappeared at the command of Elizabeth's spiritual director. She lived by the following rule: "In order to have peace, one must forget about oneself."

Elizabeth entered the Carmelite Convent in 1901. There she received the name of Sister Elizabeth of the Trinity. She devoutly referred to the Trinity as "My Three." She understood that a Carmelite lives a life of prayer and penance offered for souls. She spent long hours, sometimes days, in contemplation of the Blessed Mother and the suffering of Our Lord.

Toward the end of her life, Sister Elizabeth wrote on a wide variety of religious subjects. In 1906 she became incurably ill with what is believed to have been Addison's disease. However, she continued to pray and write rather than stay in bed. On August 31, 1906, Sister Elizabeth died at the age of 26.

After her death, the letters and retreat notes of Blessed Elizabeth of the Trinity were studied and commended by a number of leading theologians. Some have even said that her ability to express theology and her talent for writing "rivals that of Saint Paul." Among her best-known writings was her "Prayer to the Trinity." She was beatified by Pope John Paul II in 1984.

▲ **Insignia of the Carmelite Order, which Blessed Elizabeth joined in 1901.**

GLOBAL DATA

France

- France is the largest nation in Western Europe, about the size of Texas.

- France is the only nation in Europe that borders both the Atlantic Ocean and the Mediterranean Sea.

- France is about 90 percent Catholic.

- Avignon, in southern France, was the Holy See for seven popes from 1309 to 1377.

5 WE ARE Christ's People

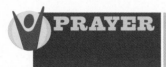

PRAYER O God, give me wisdom to know where I belong and to go where you lead me.

I want to do different things and make some new friends. Why are my parents so protective? How can I make my own choices?

Tracy felt like an orange that someone had squeezed all the juice out of. At first, the invitations had thrilled her, but who would've thought that being invited to two parties would end up being so high pressure?

It started when Shelly had stopped her in the hall after fourth period. Tracy felt flattered; Shelly was in the popular crowd. "I'm having a party next Saturday. Everyone's going to be there. Do you want to come?" Tracy felt her heart skip a beat. "I'd love to come!" she blurted out. A reminder flashed across the back of her brain, but she ignored it. She wondered what her mom would say; she probably wouldn't approve of Shelly's crowd.

Tracy's best friend, Felicia, called after dinner. "You remember about Saturday, right?" Tracy felt a brief flutter. "No." She tried to keep her voice steady. "What about Saturday?" "How could you forget?" Felicia asked, "We're going to Brad's birthday party." Oh no. Tracy tried to talk, but the words got stuck in her throat. She mumbled a quick "Oh yeah. Of course," then hung up.

"I'm dead!" she yelled at the wall. No matter what party she went to, she was going to hurt somebody's feelings. She sat staring at her U.S. history book. There was a quiz on the Monroe Doctrine the next day, but Tracy's mind kept grinding away on the party question.

For a moment, Tracy felt angry at Felicia, Brad, and her group of friends. "Why did they have to plan Brad's birthday party for Saturday?" Then she felt embarrassed about her anger— Saturday *was* Brad's birthday. The truth was she didn't want to admit to herself how badly she wanted to hang out with Shelly and her friends.

But she couldn't shake off how sad and disappointed Brad and Felicia would be if she blew them off. The knot in her stomach was still there when she drifted off into a restless sleep.

ACTIVITY

LET'S BEGIN Discuss what could happen in this story. If you were in Tracy's shoes, which party would you go to and why? What might help Tracy make a decision?

▶ **Are you friends with different groups of people or are most of your friends in the same group? How do your school, family, and community contribute to who your friends are?**

_____

_____

_____

_____

WE BELONG TO THE CHURCH

 Focus How does the Church help us develop our faith?

Throughout life, we belong to a variety of groups. We are part of a family, a class, a school, a parish, a team, a circle of friends. We are born into some communities. We choose to belong to others. And other groups choose us.

We can belong to many groups at one time, but some groups are more essential to who we are. For example, we don't stop being part of our family because we are part of a sports team or a community group. And, as Catholics, we are part of God's People, his Church.

From "No People" to "God's People" From the time of Abraham and Moses, God called the Israelites and later the Jews to be his Chosen People. He is their God; they are his People. But with the coming of the Son of God, those who believed in him became part of the new People of God in Christ, his Church. We are Christ's Church because he is with us always, present among us as we pray and worship him, acting through us to continue his mission in the world. No longer do you have to be Jewish to be part of God's People. What you need to have is faith in Jesus. You do not have to be born into God's Chosen People; you have to be born anew through Baptism. Peter tells us:

 SCRIPTURE

"But you are a chosen race, a royal priesthood, a holy nation, God's own people, in order that you may proclaim the mighty acts of him who called you out of darkness into his marvelous light.

Once you were not a people,
   but now you are God's people . . ."

—*1 Peter 2:9–10*

SCRIPTURE

GO TO THE SOURCE

Read **1 Peter 2:1–5** and think about his image of Jesus as a "living stone," the cornerstone of a building made of all believers. What does Peter say we must cut from our lives so that we might be built into this spiritual house?

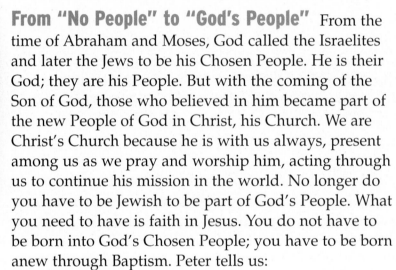 **What is the holy nation of Christians called to do?**

The People of God If we are called to be part of God's People, how does that happen? Are some called and others not? No, God invites everyone to be a part of his family, and he does it through the Church itself. The Church is the Bride of Christ: He loved her and gave himself for her. Jesus has purified her by his death and made her the fruitful mother of all God's children.

Through the work of the Church, the Good News of Jesus is brought to people everywhere. Those who have faith and choose to be baptized become members of God's People. In fact, the Church is like an international household of faith. Though members speak all different languages and represent many cultures, we are all united through Baptism. We form one family of faith, one People of God.

We cannot underestimate the importance of faith. Yes, it's a free gift from God, but it's also our choice. We don't have to have perfect faith to be baptized; in fact, faith before Baptism is young faith that needs to mature and grow. Our faith grows as we learn and experience life, with the help of our family, the example of other Catholics, our teachers and catechists, prayer, and sacraments.

salvation
domestic Church
offices of Christ

GLOBAL DATA

- There are over 1.1 billion Catholics in the world.
- That's more than 17 percent of the world's people.
- Here's where they live:
  ▶ 143 million, in Africa
  ▶ 122 million, in China
  ▶ 277 million, in Europe
  ▶ 477 million, in Latin America
  ▶ 79 million, in North America
  ▶ 8 million, in Oceania
- The Catholic Church is found in 235 countries—more than any other religion.

ACTIVITY

SHARE YOUR FAITH Describe a time in your life when you witnessed a faithful act of someone—something that showed his or her trust and belief in God. Then describe a time you witnessed or experienced a faithful act of God—a time when God revealed his care of you or another of his People.

GOD'S PLAN FOR THE CHURCH

 Focus How does the Church bring us together?

The Church exists to spread the Good News of Jesus Christ. The job of the Church is to reach out and let everyone know about salvation—that our sins have been forgiven and our friendship with God is restored through Christ.

God's plan is that all women and men come to know him. He uses the Church as a way to keep his plan in motion. Building the Church is also a goal of God's plan. As both the means and the goal of God's plan, the Church is

▶ a planned part of his good creation

▶ started by the Old Covenant that was given to Abraham and Moses by God

▶ founded in the words and actions of Jesus Christ

▶ fulfilled by Jesus' death and Resurrection

▶ revealed in the outpouring of the Holy Spirit upon the Apostles

▶ perfected in the glory of heaven

Together as the Church, we help one another. As diverse as we are, we are all in it together. The spiritually strong, the weak, those suffering in mind and body, young and old, the poor and the persecuted, are all the Church.

What is God's plan for the Church? How do you think you are part of that plan?

We Are Family The Christian family is the center of faith, the **domestic Church**. This means that your home is a smaller version of the larger Church. Parents carry the primary responsibility for educating and bringing up their children in the faith of Jesus Christ.

Just like your family comes together, the Third Commandment tells us, the Church, to come together to observe the Lord's Day, Sunday. The most important way we do this is by participating in the Mass.

Why is it so important to take part in the celebration of the Mass every week? We are nourished by the word of God and by the Eucharist when we gather together. We need this spiritual food often—just as a person needs physical food. Otherwise, we will starve and our faith will become weaker. We won't be growing strong because we will have separated ourselves from one of God's sources of strength and growth, the family of the Church.

❓ **What do you think it means that we call the family the domestic Church?**

❓ **Why do we compare the Church to a family? How is the Church like a family? How is it different?**

ACTIVITY

CONNECT YOUR FAITH Design a mural or create a collage of words and images that portrays the People of God, the Church, today. What kinds of changes do you think the Church faces in the future as it grows?

HIS WORK IS OURS

 Focus How does Jesus accomplish what his Father set out for him?

When you hear the word *office*, you probably think of a place where someone works. The word has other meanings, too. For instance, the office of president would refer to a position of authority, trust, or duty given to someone. An office is also a function or role given to someone.

During the time of the Israelites and Jews before Jesus' time, men were appointed to be *priests* to offer sacrifices to God to keep the covenant, *prophets* to speak God's word and call the people to live faithfully, and *kings* to rule God's people. These were their offices, and they were anointed and sent by God to do his work.

Then God the Father sent his own Son to us. The Father anointed Jesus with the Holy Spirit as shown at his Baptism and established him as *the* priest, *the* prophet, and *the* king. These roles are called the three **offices of Christ**. They describe his mission and work among God's people.

As priest, Jesus offers the most amazing sacrifice, doing something no other can do. He gave his life so that all can be reconciled with the Father. He intercedes with the Father for us.

As prophet, Jesus completes the Law and prophecy that had come before him. He gives us the words of truth and life that no one else can.

As king, Jesus leads by example, teaching his People to give of themselves for the needs of others. Jesus was not the ruler the people had expected. He was not concerned with earthly kingdoms or politics, but with God's kingdom. He shows us the true meaning of leadership: service.

 What kind of ruler do you think people expected Jesus to be for them? How did he end up leading his people?

We Share in Jesus' Mission When we were baptized, we were united with Christ and his mission. We, too, were anointed to be priest, prophet, and king to the world. We live out these offices, or roles, in our daily lives at school, at home, in sports practice, at work. We can show others what it means to follow Christ and to live for God's kingdom.

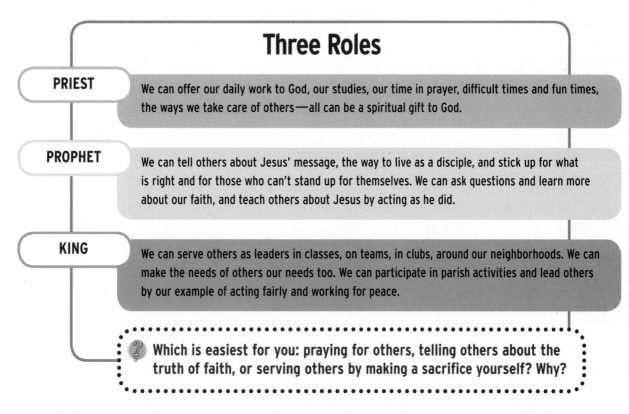

Three Roles

PRIEST
We can offer our daily work to God, our studies, our time in prayer, difficult times and fun times, the ways we take care of others—all can be a spiritual gift to God.

PROPHET
We can tell others about Jesus' message, the way to live as a disciple, and stick up for what is right and for those who can't stand up for themselves. We can ask questions and learn more about our faith, and teach others about Jesus by acting as he did.

KING
We can serve others as leaders in classes, on teams, in clubs, around our neighborhoods. We can make the needs of others our needs too. We can participate in parish activities and lead others by our example of acting fairly and working for peace.

Which is easiest for you: praying for others, telling others about the truth of faith, or serving others by making a sacrifice yourself? Why?

ACTIVITY

LIVE YOUR FAITH Meet with two leaders in your parish and ask them about their roles in the Church. Ask each of them which of the offices they feel called to perform most often in their work: priest, prophet, or king? What does performing that role involve? Take notes and share your results in class.

IN SUMMARY

CATHOLICS BELIEVE

As the People of God, all the Church's members have an important relationship with God and a role in spreading his message.

▶ We belong to the People of God through belief in Christ, which matures as we grow and experience more, and Baptism.

▶ The Church is part of God's plan for all people to come to know him and love him, and the Christian family has a special role in this plan as the domestic Church.

▶ Through Baptism, each of us shares in Jesus' mission as priest, prophet, and king. We offer our lives and prayer to God, show others the Good News through our words and actions, and serve and lead others.

CELEBRATION OF THE WORD

Leader: We gather here this day
in the name of the Father,
and of the Son,
and of the Holy Spirit. Amen.

Reader 1: Let us be attentive to the wisdom of Saint Paul's first letter
to the Corinthians.

Read 1 Corinthians 12:12–14, 27–31.

The Word of the Lord.

All: Thanks be to God.

Leader: O God of all,
before we were even born you formed us
and shaped us as one like you.
On the day of our birth, you claimed us as your own.
On the day of our Baptism, your Church welcomed us
into the family of believers,
who claim Christ, your Son, as Lord.

How good it is to know that we have always belonged,
that we are never alone,
that there are others out there just like us,
that we are chosen members of something greater than ourselves!

Help us to understand what a gift it is to be members of a community
that chooses Christ in times of trouble,
that chooses Christ in times of joy and excitement,
that chooses Christ in times of worry and decision making,
that chooses Christ to lead us each and every day.
May all that we do
and all that we say
be done in the name of Christ Jesus.

All: Amen.

♪ "We Are Many Parts"
Marty Haugen, © 1980, 1986, GIA Publications, Inc.

REVIEW

A **Work with Words** Circle the letter of the choice that best completes the sentence.

1. Each Christian family is called to be a(n) _____.
   - **a.** domestic office
   - **b.** ekklessia
   - **c.** domestic Church
   - **d.** parish

2. When our sins are forgiven and our relationship with God is restored, we receive _____.
   - **a.** salvation
   - **b.** abba
   - **c.** heaven
   - **d.** prudence

3. In scripture, the word for Church *ekklessia*, means _____.
   - **a.** chosen people
   - **b.** those called together
   - **c.** people of God
   - **d.** people of the Word

4. Jesus' roles as priest, prophet, and king are known as the _____.
   - **a.** new covenant offices
   - **b.** fulfillment of God's law
   - **c.** Old Testament offices
   - **d.** three offices of Christ

B **Check Understanding** Indicate whether the following statements are true or false. Then rewrite false statements to make them true.

_____ 5. The Church is like an international household of faith, all united through Baptism.

_____ 6. The Church exists to spread the Good News of Jesus Christ.

_____ 7. From the time of Abraham and Moses, God called the Israelites to be his Chosen People.

_____ 8. Through the Sacrament of Reconciliation, we share in Jesus' roles as priest, prophet, and king.

_____ 9. The First Commandment requires us to come together on Sunday to observe the Lord's Day.

_____ 10. Jesus showed us that the true meaning of leadership is service.

C **Make Connections: Identify** Write a one-paragraph response to the question.

As a baptized member of the Church, how can you more fully live out your role as a prophet, a priest, or a king?

OUR CATHOLIC FAITH

WHAT NOW?

- ★ Go to Mass every Sunday.
- ★ Pray for others in need.
- ★ Speak about faith in Christ to others.
- ★ Support the ministries of the Church through financial contributions.
- ★ Do good for another without expecting anything in return.
- ★ Read and reflect on Scripture by yourself or in a group.

ACTIVITY

LIVE YOUR FAITH Imagine you are a reporter who has interviewed a Catholic person. Create a name, age, and gender.

This person spoke of

- ▶ being part of God's family, and of being part of an international Church
- ▶ reasons it is important to attend Mass regularly
- ▶ how each Catholic is called to act as priest, prophet, and king

▶ **Choose one of these topics and reread the section on it in the previous pages.**

▶ **Write a newspaper article based on your "interview" on your chosen topic.**

 Visit www.harcourtreligion.com for more family and community connections.

 **PRAYER**

Thank you for the people who worship, lead, and serve in my parish.

Mechthild von Magdeburg

The later Middle Ages in Europe were a time of violence, disorder, and a breakdown of leadership and unity. Nations as we know them today didn't exist. Most of the European people lived under a system known as *feudalism*. People depended on powerful lords and their fortified castles for protection from roving bands of warriors. The only places of order existed within the monasteries and nunneries—almost the only places where learning occurred.

Among Christ's People who had been called to communicate his message during the Dark Ages, Mechthild (Matilda) of Magdeburg, Germany, was one of the most eloquent.

At an early age, Mechthild felt close to God. When she was twelve years old, she said she was greeted by the Holy Ghost. This went on daily throughout the rest of her life. She entered a nunnery at the age of twenty and, under the guidance of the Dominican Order, she led a life of prayer and self-denial. She experienced visions and received Divine inspiration.

Coming from an educated family, Mechthild was among the minority of people at that time who could read and write. On the orders of her Confessor, she used her gifts to write down her visions. Later, from these writings, she created a lasting body of work that has been translated as *The Flowing Light of the Godhead*. The writings that made up the seven volumes of her work contain her visions, love songs, praises to God, and descriptions of how she envisioned heaven and hell.

At that time, nuns had to take their orders from priests rather than from the superiors of their religious orders. Women had few, if any, rights and were not supposed to speak out on spiritual matters. Mechthild was different. She spoke out anyway and wrote about what it was like to be one of Christ's Chosen People. She also did not hesitate to criticize members of the clergy who she felt were straying from the path Christ had chosen for them.

Following her death in 1280, *The Flowing Light* was translated into a number of other languages and widely circulated. It is one of the best-written accounts of religious life during the Middle Ages. The Italian poet, Dante Alighieri, is believed to have used her visions of the afterlife as models for his most famous work, *The Divine Comedy*.

▲ **Relief sculptures on the Cloister in Magdeburg.**

GLOBAL DATA

Germany

■ Germany is located in north-central Europe between the Rhine River and the Baltic and North seas.

■ Germany has a population that is 34 percent Catholic.

■ Germany is the home nation of the current Pope, Benedict XVI.

■ Following the downfall of the Roman Empire, Germany became the center of Western Christianity.

CHAPTER 6 TEMPLE of the Holy Spirit

PRAYER O God, help me hear what you are telling me to do.

When I see people in need, sometimes I want to turn away. I think I feel the Holy Spirit leading me, but how can I be sure? I want to help people, but I never know what to do.

Connor's stomach felt heavy, as if all his dread and reluctance had sunk to the bottom there. But because it had been his idea, he knew he had to wear a brave face.

It had started when Connor saw a documentary about the poorest county in his state. The camera panning slowly across images of kids in ragged clothes and roofs with gaping holes made him feel an ache in his heart. That night at the leadership meeting for the parish youth group, he told the others about it. After he finished, everyone grew quiet. Then Connor blurted, "Why don't we go there this summer?" His friend, Chris, stared at him. "And do what?" The ideas came slowly, but by the end of the evening, they had hammered out how they'd rent a bus; get permission to sleep in a high school gym; and raise money to buy paint, brushes and rollers, and hammers and nails.

But now, as the bus slowly navigated the potholes in the road, the true face of poverty threw ice water on their excitement. It looked like a war zone: dilapidated cars in yards, broken windows, and dirt everywhere—on the kids, the sidewalk, and in the air. "We can't fix this," Connor said to himself.

After supper, Sheila, their youth minister, passed out their schedules and a list of teams and projects. By day, they would do simple repair work and painting. In the evening, they would gather to share thoughts and prayers about their day.

By mid-morning the following day, all of Connor's good spirits had drained down to the bottoms of his ruined shoes. He had been scraping paint off the side of a ramshackle house for hours. Sweat dripped off his forehead and stung his eyes. His arms ached.

The following afternoon, Connor finished rolling a coat of white paint on the back of the house when it hit him that he had stopped thinking about his aching arms and the sweat. "Not bad," he thought, looking at the fresh coat of paint shining in the sun.

Each evening after supper, the group prayed, sang, and shared. Then each team gave a brief progress report. Home by home, they were making a difference.

Connor remembered how he had felt watching the documentary and realized that the feeling in his heart had changed from sadness to joy.

ACTIVITY

LET'S BEGIN How did Connor's feelings change from his first idea, to when he actually arrived in the town, to when he was done? How do you think this experience changed Connor?

▶ **Have you ever felt physically exhausted and yet excited at the same time? How can this be? What's the difference between people doing good things because of their faith versus people who just do good things?**

SOMETHING MORE

Focus How do the body and the soul work together in God's plan?

We are given our bodies by God. We care for and nourish them by eating and drinking properly. We also care for our bodies by exercising and keeping our bodies strong. Souls are similar. Just as a body can be undernourished or weak, a soul can be malnourished and weak.

Everyone has a soul, which God created in them. You cannot point to your soul or examine it like the parts of your body. But your soul is there, inside, spiritual and everlasting. Your soul is an essential part of who you are—your body and soul together make you who you are.

✝ SCRIPTURE

Temple of the Spirit In his letters to the people of Corinth, Paul describes how the soul resides within the body. He uses the image of a temple and applies it to our body and soul. Paul says,

". . . [D]o you not know that your body is a temple of the Holy Spirit within you, which you have from God, and that you are not your own? For you were bought with a price; therefore glorify God in your body" (*1 Corinthians 6:19–20*).

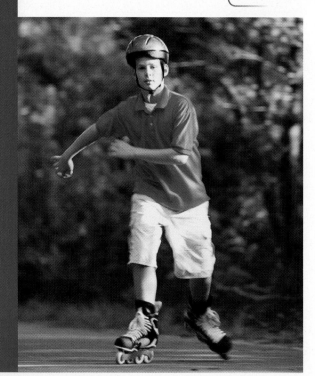

Faithful people pay attention to their souls. Caring for and paying attention to your soul is the flip side of caring for and paying attention to your body. Care of your soul and care of your body are two sides of the same coin of nourishing yourself. You can't take care of the world around you unless you first take care of yourself. Soul-nourishing and soul-building are important tasks if you are going to grow and mature.

❓ **What are some of the ways you have already learned that are good for nourishing your Christian soul?**

THE TEMPLE IN JESUS' DAY

In Jesus' time, and for about 40 years after his crucifixion (before Paul's letter to the Corinthians was written), the Temple in Jerusalem was the main focus for Jewish religion. Paul was Jewish before he was baptized as a Christian.

The Temple was where devout Jews offered sacrifices to God. This was the third Temple to stand on this spot, a sign of God's presence among his Chosen People. It was *the* place that symbolized their entire religious practice. It was so significant that every male Jew was required to visit the Temple once a year to make a sacrifice to God of a dove, a sheep, or an ox. This understanding of temple must have been in Paul's mind when he told us that we are the temple of the Holy Spirit. (See *1 Corinthians 6:19*.)

▲ **A model of the Temple in Jerusalem.**

ACTIVITY

SHARE YOUR FAITH Reread the Scripture from 1 Corinthians. Spend a few minutes meditating on it. Then draw a picture of yourself that conveys the meaning of this Scripture.

SOUL FOOD

Focus What gifts does the Holy Spirit give us?

You need to eat right to be right. The right kinds of food promote healthy growth in our bodies. Balanced meals include all the vitamins, minerals, and other nutrients our bodies need.

Ours souls are nourished by God's grace. Grace comes to us in a variety of ways, most importantly in Baptism, the Eucharist, and the other sacraments. Baptism is the gateway into the life of the Holy Spirit. In Baptism, we are set apart as belonging to Jesus Christ by being marked with a permanent spiritual seal called a **character**. This seal strengthens us to be Christ's witnesses in the world. Other sacraments that confer a lasting seal are Confirmation and Holy Orders.

The Gifts of the Holy Spirit
What helps us to be witnesses of the Good News? The Holy Spirit does. In Baptism, throughout life, and most especially in Confirmation, he gives us seven special gifts to guide us.

▶ wisdom—to develop a deep understanding of God and life

▶ understanding—to see truth and live faithfully

▶ counsel—to judge good and evil and avoid sin

▶ fortitude—to act with confidence, strength, and courage

▶ knowledge—to understand the Word of God

▶ piety—to worship and respect the Lord

▶ awe, or fear of the Lord—to love and honor God

These gifts are referenced in Isaiah 11:1–2

How is Confirmation celebrated in your parish? How are people prepared for Confirmation?

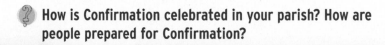

76

Maturity Since Baptism, we have received many gifts from God. We have been growing in faith, hope, and love. At Confirmation, we are again anointed with the Holy Spirit, who first entered our lives in Baptism. Through Confirmation, our relationship with God is strengthened and deepened.

Why does your relationship with God need to deepen? Because your world expands as you grow older. You will meet new people, and go beyond your family and household. Every day you will meet new challenges. Therefore, you need the Holy Spirit and his gifts so that you can

▶ connect on a deeper level to Jesus

▶ grow as a member of the Church

▶ become more involved with the activity, ministry, and mission of the Church

▶ be strengthened to witness the Christian faith by the things you say and do

In many ways, the Gifts of the Holy Spirit you receive play an important role in your maturing as a Christian. Like other kinds of learning and growing, we all need to use the Gifts of the Holy Spirit for them to have a lasting impact on our lives.

What are some ways you can become more involved in the work of the Church?

What are some ways that have you been involved recently?

Each person, cooperating with the Holy Spirit, shows Christian maturity in unique ways. All Christians should strive to put into practice the example of Christ's life and his teaching. The Church also names twelve ways in which a mature Christian shows that he or she is bearing fruit in the Spirit—
   The Fruits of the Holy Spirit
   (See Galations 5:22–23)

▶ charity

▶ joy

▶ peace

▶ patience

▶ kindness

▶ goodness

▶ generosity

▶ gentleness

▶ faithfulness

▶ modesty

▶ self-control

▶ chastity

ACTIVITY

CONNECT YOUR FAITH With a partner, choose two or three Gifts of the Holy Spirit. Discuss situations in which people your age could rely on these gifts. Then role-play the situations with two different outcomes: one in which the person relied on the gift and one in which the gift did not seem present.

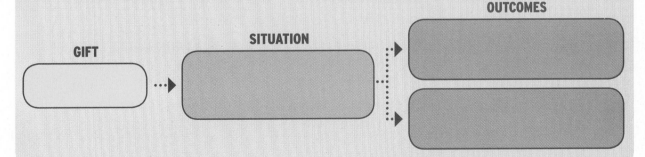

GIFT → SITUATION → OUTCOMES

A TEMPLE NOT BUILT BY HUMAN HANDS

Focus What plan does the Holy Spirit have for the Church?

The Church is truly a mystery, visible and spiritual at the same time. The Church is both a structured organization of members with a variety of roles, and the Body of Christ. The Church is a visible community and a spiritual one. This visible organization needs buildings and structures. Parish churches, along with schools, hospitals, monasteries, convents, shelters, centers, halls, and office buildings, make up the bulk of our buildings. But just as we are more than our bodies, the Church is more than just the visible organization or its property.

What the Church Is The Church is the **Mystical Body of Christ**. The Church unites all believers through the Holy Spirit into one holy people, with Christ as their head and themselves as the body, or members. The same Spirit unites members to one another as brothers and sisters in the faith.

Just as our own bodies have a soul, the Holy Spirit is like a "soul" for the Church. In other words, the Mystical Body is not just a collection of human beings who happen to believe the same thing or belong to the same community. Together they are the Church because the Holy Spirit lives in them, giving them energy and life, helping them be the People of God.

✝ SCRIPTURE The Holy Spirit makes this promise of God real:

". . . For we are the temple of the living God; as God said, 'I will live in them and walk among them, and I will be their God, and they shall be my people . . . and I will be your father, and you shall be my sons and daughters, says the Lord Almighty.'"

—*2 Corinthians 6:16–18*

The Holy Spirit builds up this true spiritual temple. The Holy Spirit gives life to the Church and makes it holy. He helps us relate to God in this world.

The Spirit Leads Us Where We Would Not Go

Everyone seeks to be comfortable, protected from the dangers of the world. No one wants to be hungry, homeless, and hurting. The Church, urged on by the Holy Spirit, follows Christ in his mission of outreach to those who are poor and in need. The Church goes to every part of the world where healing and hope are needed. The Holy Spirit leads us. We go!

ACTIVITY

LIVE YOUR FAITH Who or what in your neighborhood or city could use help or healing?

_____

_____

▶ **Describe some ways that you and your parish could help.**

_____

_____

_____

IN SUMMARY

CATHOLICS BELIEVE

God the Holy Spirit lives within each of us as individuals and in the Church as a community. We are temples of the Holy Spirit as is the Church.

▶ Our souls and bodies united make us who we are, and we need to take care of our souls like we take care of our bodies.

▶ The Gifts of the Holy Spirit help us to give witness to Christ and live faithful lives, and the Fruits of the Holy Spirit are the results of the gifts working in our lives.

▶ The Church is both a visible, structured organization and the Mystical Body of Christ, in which the Holy Spirit lives uniting the Church, guiding her and giving her life.

MEDITATION ON THE HOLY SPIRIT

Leader: Let us begin with the Sign of the Cross.
Place yourselves in Jesus' presence.
Close your eyes and turn to that place deep within your heart,
where you and God are one.
Take a deep, relaxing breath, and enter into the meditation:
(read the following, slowly and meditatively)

Spirit of God,
Open my eyes to see all the beauty before me.
Open my eyes to see the beauty within me.
Open my eyes to see the needs of those around me.

(pause for reflective silence)

Spirit of God,
Open my ears to hear the Gospel call before me.
Open my ears to hear your guiding voice within me.
Open my ears to hear the cries of those around me.

(pause for reflective silence)

Spirit of God,
Open my heart to receive the love that's here before me.
Open my heart to know your presence deep within me.
Open my heart to comfort the broken ones around me.

(pause for reflective silence)

Sprit of God,
Open my hands to welcome your people here before me.
Open my hands to feel your healing touch within me.
Open my hands to serve the poor ones all around me.

O Spirit of God,
Come and dwell deep within me.
With every step I take, guide me.
With every word I speak, teach me.
With every prayer I make, hear me.
With every breath I take, love me.
Spirit of God I am yours.

(pause for reflective silence)

 "Spirit of God"
James Moore, © 2002, GIA Publications, Inc.

REVIEW

A **Work with Words** Circle the letter of the choice that best completes the sentence.

1. Your _____ is your spiritual principle that is an essential part of who you are.
   a. intellect
   b. body
   c. character
   d. soul

2. In Baptism, we are marked with a permanent spiritual seal called a _____.
   a. soul
   b. Confirmation
   c. character
   d. mystery

3. In _____ we are again anointed with the Holy Spirit, who first entered our lives in Baptism.
   a. Confirmation
   b. Holy Orders
   c. Mass
   d. Church

4. The Church is the Mystical Body of Christ because in it the Holy Spirit _____.
   a. cannot be seen
   b. unites believers to Christ as one holy people
   c. gives us hope
   d. celebrates Mass

B **Check Understanding** Complete each sentence with the correct term(s). You may use some terms more than once.

5. According to Paul, our bodies are temples of the _____.

6. Through the _____ our souls are nourished by God's grace.

7. _____ is the gateway into the life of the Holy Spirit.

8. The Church is both a structured organization of members and the _____.

9. The _____ guides the Church in its mission to help those who are poor and in need.

10. Charity, joy, and peace are examples of the _____ of the Holy Spirit.

Word Bank

law
fruits
priesthood
Holy Spirit
sacraments
Baptism
Body of Christ
Trinity

C **Make Connections: Synthesize** Write a one-paragraph response to the question below.

Create a spiritual food pyramid of things that would nourish your soul. Based on your pyramid, how healthy is your soul today?

OUR CATHOLIC FAITH

WHAT NOW?

Respect your body:

★ Provide for your physical health.

★ Promote your mental and emotional health.

★ Refrain from using the body in selfish ways.

★ Avoid violent acts.

Respect your soul:

★ Allow the Church to influence your words and actions.

★ Pray every day.

★ Gather with others to share faith.

★ Receive Holy Communion each week and allow this nourishment to guide you.

★ When you need help, seek the advice of a priest or other wise member of the Church.

ACTIVITY

LIVE YOUR FAITH Identify one item from each of the above lists that you want to work on further. Write down three action steps in pursuing these two goals.

▶ **List the ways in which your parish reaches out to the poor. Can you think of other practical ways in helping the poor or needy?**

_____

_____

_____

_____

_____

GO ONLINE Visit www.harcourtreligion.com for more family and community connections.

PRAYER

Come, Holy Spirit, fill me with your gifts.

Blessed Cyprian Michael Iwene Tansi

▲ **The Church of the Holy Trinity in Onitsha, Nigeria**

When Our Lord speaks of the "Temple of the Holy Spirit," it means recognizing that God is within you. You honor your body and your mind as a holy place in which the spirit of God dwells. You are like a church within yourself, so wherever you go you take the Church with you.

The Blessed Father Cyprian Michael Iwene Tansi embodied this Holy Spirit within himself. From the tropical rain forests of his native Nigeria, to his pilgrimage to Rome, to his final home at a monastery in England, Father Tansi shared the love of the Holy Spirit with everyone with whom he came in contact.

Today Nigeria is the most populous nation on the African continent, with large cities and modern conveniences. However, many Nigerians live in the interior. No roads connect them. People traveling between villages do so on foot along narrow trails.

Father Tansi was born in 1903 when Nigeria was still a British colony. Though his parents were non-Christian, they sent the boy to live with and be educated by a Christian uncle. He was baptized in 1912 and given the name Michael. After completing his studies, he taught at several Catholic schools in Nigeria and entered a seminary there. For thirteen years he was a parish priest for several small villages, traveling widely on foot to minister to his parishioners.

Many of the villages in which Father Tansi preached didn't have churches. From the Temple of the Holy Spirit within himself, he taught the Word of God in small and large gatherings. He also labored alongside the villagers to build churches. Nearly everyone was impressed by his holiness, his humility, and his devotion to Christ. Many called him a "living saint."

Father Tansi made his pilgrimage to the Holy See at Rome in 1950. Not long afterward, he became a Trappist monk at a monastery in England and took on the name Cyprian. He died there in 1964. During a visit to Nigeria in 1998, Pope John Paul II praised his work and beatified him, taking the first step toward Father Tansi's canonization.

GLOBAL DATA

Nigeria

- Nigeria is the most populous nation in Africa with more than 130 million people.

- Nigeria is about 50 percent Muslim, 40 percent Christian, and the other 10 percent native religions.

- Nigeria became independent from Great Britain in 1960.

- Despite having rich oil deposits offshore, much of Nigeria is still poor, and it has been ruled by military dictators for most of its time since gaining independence.

Faith in Action!

DISCOVER

Catholic Social Teaching:
Life and Dignity of the Human Person

IN THIS UNIT, you learned about being a child of God, a brother or sister of Jesus, and that you belong to a community that includes all people, not just those like yourself.

Life and Dignity

Every person is created in the image and likeness of God, equally precious in the eyes of God. He wants all of us, not just some of us, to be with Him forever. Every person is his child, so we are all sisters and brothers. In 1979, the Catholic Bishops of the United States wrote a pastoral letter entitled *Brothers and Sisters to Us*. They reminded us that people of every racial and cultural group are equal in dignity. To treat any person or group as less than fully equal to ourselves is a sin. Racism is one of the worst possible sins because it "divides the human family" and denies God's plan to make us all one family.

Racism has a terrible history in our nation. It began with killing many Native Americans and stealing their land. It increased with the slavery of Africans. Then other people of color were brought here to do hard labor under brutal conditions. And racism continues today in unequal treatment and lack of equal opportunity. Look at who is in prison, who runs corporations, who makes decisions about education and other services, who lives in suburban homes, who goes to private schools. Possessions, privileges, and power in this country are mainly in the hands of white Americans. But these sinful inequalities contradict the equal dignity of all God's children. Therefore, the Church calls everyone to challenge these sinful inequalities, even eighth graders.

 What has been your own experience of racism?

TO LIVE IN PEACE IS A WAY of life. Let's look at a group of young people who taught this in a public way.

WE SHALL OVERCOME
JUNIOR HIGH YOUTH IN ACTION

Noel Hall-Niemann was youth director at Peace Lutheran Church in Charlotte, Michigan, in the 1990s. At a workshop on racism for families and youth, he related an inspiring story of his own youth group. On a Saturday afternoon the previous year, a group of Ku Klux Klan members assembled on the steps of the state capital in Lansing. They broadcasted their message of hate to anyone willing to stop and listen. An article about this hate rally appeared in the Sunday newspaper. When Noel brought the article to his youth group that Sunday evening, several of them were quite angry about how such a small group of negative people could get such wide media coverage. So they decided to act.

On the following Saturday, twelve members of Peace Lutheran youth group brought buckets of water, soap, and scrub brushes to those same capital steps, where they scrubbed the steps clean. They wanted to symbolize cleansing the "dirt" of the message that the Klan members had brought to those steps. After the symbolic cleansing, the youth group sang songs of caring and inclusion, concluding with "We Shall Overcome." The group had invited members of the media to be present for their action. That Sunday's newspaper featured a message of love and acceptance.

For decades individuals and groups fighting racism and hate have drawn strength from that banner song from the civil rights era. Yes, "Deep in my heart, I do believe that we shall overcome someday . . . We'll walk hand in hand . . . We are not afraid . . . We shall overcome someday." Now it's your turn to follow in the footsteps of Rosa Parks, Martin Luther King, Jr., César Chávez, and thousands of others, including the youth from Charlotte, Michigan.

If you had been in Lansing on both those Saturdays and had happened upon the two demonstrations, what would you have done in each case?

▼ **Martin Luther King, Jr. (above) and César Chávez (below) worked to end racism and discrimination in the United States.**

SERVE Your Community

PERSONAL DECISIONS ON RESPECTING DIGNITY

Whether you are white or a person of color, write down a time when you chose to avoid, exclude, or say or do something mean about someone from another race or culture.

Then write down a time when you did the opposite—when you chose to be with someone from another race or culture and defended that person when others were saying or doing something mean.

A time when I

avoided . . .

defended . . .

MAKE A DIFFERENCE AS A CLASS

Research, with your classmates, places or situations where people of color are treated unfairly or are not included in your community. It could be in your school, parish, on local TV shows, in textbooks, magazine or TV ads, movies, on the covers of greeting cards, featured in kids' toys, or pictured disrespectfully in cartoons or on sports teams' logos. Present these to the entire class. Choose one of these situations and create a plan for challenging it.

Project Planning Sheet

Others who should be involved

How to publicize your findings

Other specific tasks

Your specific task(s)

Calendar for completing the project

REFLECT On Your Experience

Did you remember more times when you avoided, excluded, or hurt others than times when you did the right thing?

What did you learn about yourself in doing the personal decisions activity?

What did you learn about racism (and the need to include people of different ethnicities in your life) as you did this project?

What did you learn about yourself in doing it?

What did you learn about God and about your faith in doing it?

List one thing that might be different about you after doing this project.

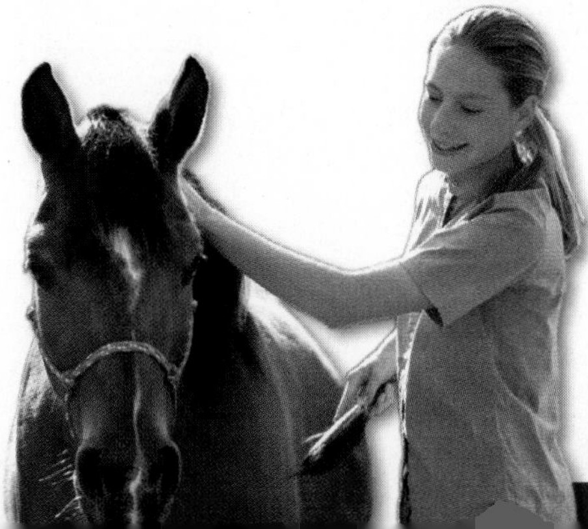

REVIEW

A **Work with Words** Match the words on the left with the correct definitions or descriptions on the right.

_____ **1.** Transfiguration

A. forgiveness of sins and restoration of our relationship with God

_____ **2.** grace

B. your spiritual principle that is an essential part of who you are

_____ **3.** Pentecost

C. word for Church that means "those called together"

_____ **4.** salvation

D. free gift of God that enables us to be his adopted children

_____ **5.** domestic Church

E. the coming of the Holy Spirit upon the disciples

_____ **6.** ekklessia

F. event in which Jesus' divine glory was shown to his disciples

_____ **7.** soul

G. believers united by the Holy Spirit as one holy People

_____ **8.** Mystical Body of Christ

H. Christian families are called to be this

B **Check Understanding** Indicate whether the following statements are true or false. Then rewrite false statements to make them true.

_____ **9.** The Ascension gave the disciples a glimpse into the divinity of Christ.

_____

_____ **10.** The Holy Spirit prepares us to love Christ and share in his communion.

_____

_____ **11.** The Paschal Feast is celebrated as the beginning of the Church.

_____

_____ **12.** Jesus reveals God the Father to the world.

_____

_____ **13.** People who have faith and are baptized, become members of God's People.

_____

_____ **14.** From the time of Peter and Paul, God called the Israelites to be his Chosen People.

_____

_____ **15.** When we are confirmed, we are anointed to share in Christ's role as priest, prophet, and king.

_____

_____ **16.** According to Paul, our bodies are temples of the Holy Spirit.

_____

_____ **17.** Prayer is the gateway into the life of the Holy Spirit.

_____

_____ **18.** Charity, joy, and peace are examples of the Fruits of the Holy Spirit.

_____

C **Make Connections** Write a short answer to these questions.

19. Draw Conclusions. Think about the roles of each Person in the Trinity. Which Person in the Trinity do you tend to relate to the most? Which do you relate to the least? What do your answers reveal about your view of God?

_____

_____

_____

_____

20. Compare. Your body is a temple of the Holy Spirit. Use this analogy of a temple or house where God lives to describe the condition of your heart. What would God see as he walks through your temple? What might he ask you to move or change?

_____

_____

_____

_____

CHAPTER 7 JESUS' Relationships

INVITE

PRAYER Help me see as Jesus saw.

I feel so uncomfortable when I don't "fit in" with a group. Some people seem to get along with everybody. Did Jesus act differently with different people?

Anna knew her sister meant well, but what she described wasn't making her feel any better about going to high school. Luisa was two years older, a sophomore. Anna would be a freshman in just a few months.

"High school is very different," Luisa warned. "You need to figure out who your real friends are going to be." Anna wondered how that was possible. She hadn't even met most of the other students yet. They'd be coming in from schools all over the city.

Luisa continued. "There are a lot of cliques at our school and some of them will try to put a label on you. Because you are an athlete, they will try to drop you in the 'jock' category. Or because you are an *A* student, they might try to tell you that you would only fit in with the computer club."

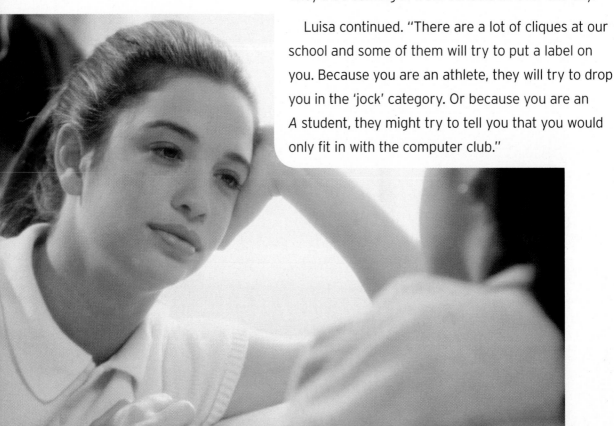

"I could fit in lots of places! I plan to try out for the basketball team *and* keep up my grades."

Luisa said, "Right. That's what you should do. But cliques don't respect kids for who they are. When I was a freshman, I thought that if I wanted to be popular, I couldn't be 'too smart'—or hang out with the computer club. . . . "

"Why not?" Anna blurted. "My friend Clem is a genius—she helped me make my Web site last year . . . of course I'd still hang out with her! I have 'athletic' friends who helped me improve my jump shot. I have 'musical' friends who are in marching band, and 'trendy' friends who know what color lip gloss won't clash with my nail polish."

"See, that's what you have to watch out for: The cliques have labels and sometimes kids are afraid to cross lines to hang out with anyone who is different," said Luisa.

"Does that mean I can't make any new friends?" asked Anna.

"Of course not!" said Luisa. "Some students don't care about being part of a clique. They are friends with all sorts of people. Being part of a clique could mean losing more than the activities you like to do. You might lose your best friends and your true self. Just be yourself, and you'll avoid the whole clique mentality."

Anna promised. She walked upstairs thoughtfully. It wasn't even spring break yet, and she was already praying for help with September.

ACTIVITY

LET'S BEGIN Why did Luisa insist that Anna keep an open mind about different kinds of friends at high school? Do you think Anna can stay friends with different types of people if she tries?

▶ **When have you felt trapped by a label? How free are you to be friends with different types of kids, or are the cliques too powerful at school?**

▶ **What advice would you give to someone who wanted to change the clique situation he or she is in?**

THE PEOPLE JESUS MET

Focus How did Jesus treat people equally?

Many schools have cliques that define friendships. In some places, an actor from the spring musical would never have lunch with an athlete from the soccer team or a clarinet player from the marching band. It's as if there are these invisible walls between groups, and the pressure is on to stay on the right side of the wall.

Jesus ran into this kind of pressure. He was criticized for the kinds of people he spent time with. Being judged and facing the pressure not to be with a certain kind of person is not fun. Jesus is an example of how to rise above that kind of thinking.

Think of these words, found in the middle of the Lord's Prayer

"Your kingdom come
  Your will be done, on earth as it is in heaven."

Bringing the ways of the kingdom from heaven to earth is exactly what Jesus did. In heaven, everything is perfect. All are in complete happiness, and no one is left out. When we take care not to leave anyone out, that's one way of living the kingdom here on earth.

Jesus encountered many different people in his ministry. He saw their need and called them to have faith. He called out the names of some, not caring how other people treated them or labeled them. He spent time eating with them, asking them to believe and to change their lives.

SCRIPTURE

Why does he eat with tax collectors and sinners? **Mark 2:16**

▼ *The First Shall Be Last*, by James Jacques Joseph Tissot (1836–1902)

Jesus called some people to be his **Apostles**, his closest followers, to travel with him and share in his work and ministry in a special way. Jesus asked these people to believe in his Good News and his message of the coming Kingdom. Still others were his friends who did not go on the road, but were with him when he traveled through their towns. They welcomed him and the Apostles in their homes and at their tables.

DIFFERENT PEOPLE, SAME MESSAGE

Bartimaeus, a blind man, sat by the roadside begging . . . "My teacher, let me see again."
—*Mark 10:51*

There was a man there who had a withered hand . . . "Stretch out your hand. He stretched it out . . ."
—*Matthew 12:13*

She was bent over, completely incapable of standing erect . . . "Woman, you are set free from your ailment . . ."
—*Luke 13:12*

Zacchaeus, a tax collector, was not trusted by many Jews because he worked for the Romans. People grumbled when Jesus called him by name and invited himself to Zacchaeus's home. "Zacchaeus, hurry and come down; for I must stay at your house today."
—*Luke 19:5*

A woman known as a sinner wept on Jesus' feet, dried them with her hair, and anointed them with ointment from an alabaster jar. The Pharisee who invited Jesus to dinner was annoyed that Jesus would let this happen. Jesus told him that the woman had treated him better than he had! "Therefore, I tell you, her sins, which were many, have been forgiven; hence she has shown great love."
—*Luke 7:47*

✝ SCRIPTURE

GO TO THE SOURCE
For more on these stories, read **Mark 10:46–52, Matthew 12:9–14, Luke 13:10–17, Luke 19:1–10,** or **Luke 7:36–50.**

What connects all of these different people who were part of Jesus' life? The obvious answer is Jesus, but it's more than that. Jesus met each of these people where they were in life. Many ordinary people loved Jesus for his open heart—not only because he made them better physically or emotionally, or brought them the peace of forgiveness. They also loved him because he cared about them. He took the time to acknowledge them and show them God's love. With Jesus, they mattered. They were important.

ACTIVITY

SHARE YOUR FAITH Think about the different people in your life: acquaintances, close friends, or classmates. How are you different from them? How are you the same? What are some ways you could be more open and accepting of them all, like Jesus?

_____

_____

_____

JESUS' CLOSEST FRIENDS

 Focus How did people become friends with Jesus?

Close friends are the people we feel most comfortable with. People we love like family—people we can pour our hearts out to. We learn from the Gospels that Jesus had such friends.

The Apostles Peter, James, and John were Jesus' closest friends. They were the only ones who

▶ saw Jesus' Transfiguration. (See *Mark 9:2–8*.)

▶ entered Jarius' home when Jesus raised his daughter from the dead. (See *Luke 8:40–56*.)

▶ came with Jesus when he went off to pray alone on the night before he was arrested. (See *Mark 14:32–42*.)

Mary Magdalene also was a close friend. She was

▶ at the cross when Jesus died. (See *Matthew 27:55–56*.)

▶ the first person Jesus appeared to after he rose from the dead. (See *John 20:11–18*.)

Peter or Mary You might think that I was Jesus' favorite because he called me "The Rock." I'm also the only Apostle who walked on water!

But I have to be honest. When push came to shove, I was not his most faithful friend. Mary Magdalene was. When they arrested him, I ran. I told people I didn't know who he was. Three times I pretended not to be his friend. I didn't stick with him.

But Mary did.

She was right there, at the foot of the cross, giving him comfort and support at the most agonizing moment of his life.

Not me. Mary.

And when he rose from the dead, whom did he appear to first?

Not me. Mary.

❓ What would you ask Mary Magdalene?

❓ If you could ask Peter anything, what would it be?

▲ Saint Mary Magdalene

✝ **SCRIPTURE**

GO TO THE SOURCE
What you just read about Peter and Mary is true. Read the following passages to learn more:
Matthew 28:1–8, **Mark 16:1–11**, **Luke 24:1–12**, and **John 20:1–18**.

▲ Saint Peter

Friends from Bethany Lazarus, Martha, and Mary were a brother and two sisters who lived in Bethany. They were also close friends of Jesus.

▶ Jesus settled an argument between them when Martha was busy doing housework while Mary just sat at Jesus' feet, listening to him and not helping her sister. (See *Luke 10:38–42*.)

▶ Jesus brought Lazarus back to life after he had been in the tomb for four days. (See *John 11:1–44*.)

There were other women, besides Martha and Mary of Bethany and Mary Magdalene, who followed Jesus and provided for him out of their own resources. Joanna and Susanna are also named (see *Luke 8:3*), as well as the mother of James and John (see *Matthew 27:56*).

ACTIVITY

CONNECT YOUR FAITH If Jesus asked you to pick three of your friends to be his Apostles, which of your friends would you pick? Write down the initials of each friend and the reason(s) why you selected that person.

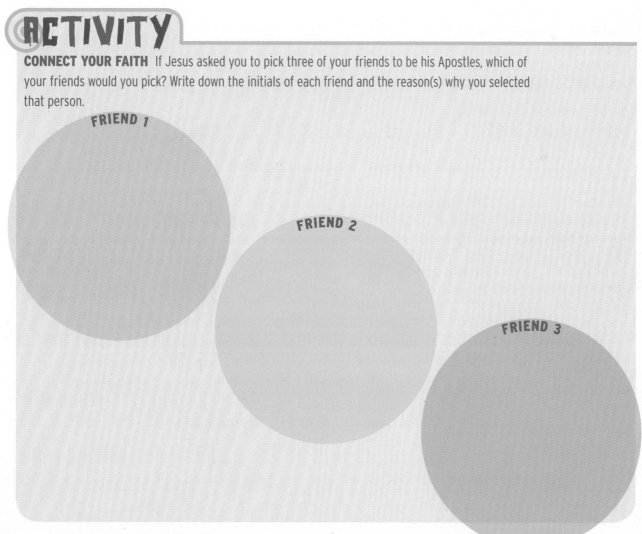

FRIEND 1

FRIEND 2

FRIEND 3

In Milwaukee, every fall, a group of teenagers from different Christian churches comes together to learn about issues related to violence in the city. Teenagers give presentations about prejudice, solving conflict peacefully, and forgiveness. They pray together and resolve to be peacemakers.

The first year, they had a balance scale, with big rocks on one side and a few tiny pebbles on the other side. Things such as drive-by shootings, gangs, and rape are like gigantic boulders. We feel like tiny, powerless pebbles. What can one pebble do?

But many pebbles of peace can outweigh boulders of violence.

That's what they call themselves now—"Pebbles of Peace Outweighing Boulders of Violence."

Every year after their fall gathering, the students plan projects to promote peace.

When we of faith come together, we can make the world a better place. We can bring the kingdom of heaven to earth.

THE FIRST CHURCH MEMBERS

Focus What can we learn from the early Christians?

Have you ever had to say good-bye to a close friend that you will probably never see again? If so, then you know that it is a very sad, lonely feeling.

That's how Jesus' followers and friends must have felt after his **Ascension**, when he returned in glory to his Father in heaven. They watched him go up into heaven. Jesus had promised that they would not be alone, that the Holy Spirit would come upon them. They would be strengthened to be Jesus' witnesses throughout the world. But they probably felt lost, not knowing how they could possibly keep his message alive.

Then the Holy Spirit came to them on Pentecost. Wind, tongues of fire, and an inner strength came from God that made them a changed group of people, filled with courage and understanding.

▶ They became a united community.

▶ They looked after each other.

▶ They opened their homes to each other; they discussed Jesus' teachings together and motivated one another to tell others about him and his message.

▶ They broke bread together.

▶ They shared their money, their food, and their possessions.

In short, they helped each other out in every way possible. Their community showed us what solidarity looks like, sharing more than material things by providing for one another's spiritual needs, too. These women and men demonstrated what true Christian friendship was all about: trust, loyalty, generosity, hospitality, concern, joy, and hope. If we follow their example, we will embrace everyone who wants to become a part of God's family, no matter whether they are from different backgrounds and have different kinds of personalities.

WHO WERE THEY?

Peter
- the first to speak after receiving the Holy Spirit (See *Acts Chapters 2* and *3*.)
- was imprisoned, but escaped when an angel caused the doors to open and the chains to fall off (See *Acts 12:1–19*.)

Stephen
- one of the first seven deacons or assistants to the Apostles (See *Acts 6:1–7*.)
- the first martyr, the first person to give up his life for believing in Jesus (See *Acts 7:55–60*.)

Saul, also known as Paul
- persecuted the disciples and was present when Stephen was stoned to death (See *Acts 7:58* and *8:1*.)
- changed his life after he was temporarily struck blind and heard the voice of Jesus asking him why he persecuted Jesus (See *Acts 9:4–5*.)
- wrote many of the letters of the New Testament and was a great leader

Lydia
- was a businesswoman, a dealer of purple cloth, in Philippi (See *Acts 16:14*.)
- offered her home to Paul and Silas; when they left prison, they returned to her home (See *Acts 16:40*.)

Priscilla and her husband Aquila
- were tentmakers, as was Paul; they spent time working together, while Paul stayed with them at their home in Corinth (See *Acts 18:1–3*.)
- used their home as a church center for the faith community (See *1 Corinthians 16:19*.)

Phoebe
- a woman who served the church at Cenchrae (See *Romans 16:1*.)
- was a friend of Paul; he recommended that she be received "in a manner worthy of the holy ones" (See *Romans 16:2*.)

ACTIVITY

LIVE YOUR FAITH List two or three things you need to do to be a better friend, one that reflects the kind of friend Jesus was. Pray for the Holy Spirit's help in developing strong friendships.

IN SUMMARY

CATHOLICS BELIEVE

As members of the Church, we look to Jesus as an example of respect for others and friendship.

- Jesus met many people in different circumstances. Even though his interaction with them varied, he welcomed them all, urged them to believe, and encouraged them to change their lives.

- Jesus had close friends that he trusted and depended on. Sometimes they let him down, but he still loved them.

- The first members of the Church demonstrated true Christian friendship by the way they worshiped together, followed the example of Jesus, and took care of each other.

CELEBRATION OF THE WORD

Leader: We know and believe when two or more gather,
Christ is with us.
Let us take this time to listen to all he has to say to us
through the Scripture reading.

Reader 1: A reading from the holy Gospel according to Luke.
Read Luke 19:1–10.
The Gospel of the Lord

All: Praise to you, Lord Jesus Christ.

Reader 2: As Jesus welcomed and called Zacchaeus down from the tree,
help us to welcome and seek out all those among us
who sit on the outside of our circle of friends,
who are different,
and who are in need of comfort and friendship.

Reader 3: As Jesus welcomed and healed the man who was born blind,
help us to welcome and comfort all those among us who are sick,
disabled, and in need of a friend.

Reader 4: As Jesus, who on the day of his death,
welcomed the criminal into paradise with him,
help us welcome and forgive all who have hurt us.

Leader: Gracious Father,
send the Holy Spirit to walk with us and guide us in all our choices.
Be with us in the times when it is easy to serve you
and in the times when the pressures around us
make it seem almost impossible.
Help us to know that you love us.
Remind us always and often
that you are the God who welcomes all.
We ask this prayer in the name of Jesus our
brother and friend.

All: Amen.

♪ "All Are Welcome"
Marty Haugen, © 1994, GIA Publications, Inc.

98

REVIEW

Ⓐ Work with Words Circle the letter of the choice that best completes the sentence.

1. Jesus called _____ "The Rock".

   a. Jesus   **b.** Peter   **c.** John   **d.** Mary

2. Jesus brought _____ back to life, after being in the tomb for four days.

   a. Mary   **b.** Martha   **c.** Jairus   **d.** Lazarus

3. Jesus' _____ were his closest followers who shared in his work and ministry in a special way.

   a. friends   **b.** disciples   **c.** Apostles   **d.** companions

4. Peter was arrested, put in jail, and set free by _____.

   a. the disciples   **b.** a tornado   **c.** an angel   **d.** none of the above

5. _____ was the first martyr, the first person to be killed for believing in Jesus.

   a. Stephen   **b.** Peter   **c.** Paul   **d.** Timothy

. . . .

Ⓑ Check Understanding Indicate whether the following statements are true or false. Then rewrite false statements to make them true.

_____ **6.** Matthew, James, and John were the only disciples who came with Jesus when he went off to pray alone on the night before he was arrested.

_____

_____ **7.** Peter was the first person Jesus appeared to after he rose from the dead.

_____

_____ **8.** The Holy Spirit came as tongues of fire and made the disciples a united community.

_____

_____ **9.** After the Holy Spirit came on the disciples, they shared their money, their food, and their possessions.

_____

_____ **10.** Priscilla was a businesswoman in Philippi, who offered her home to Paul and Silas.

_____

. . . .

Ⓒ Make Connections: Draw Conclusions Write a one-paragraph response to the question below.

Think about someone you know who might feel left out—someone at school, at church, or in your community. How would Jesus respond to that person and what do you learn from his example?

OUR CATHOLIC FAITH

WHAT NOW?

★ Notice the people who often go unnoticed.

★ Put time and effort into your closer relationships.

★ Consider what gifts you bring to all your friendships.

★ Try to model your friendships after those of the first Christians.

★ Pray for your friends, and pray about important issues in the world and in your city.

★ Remember that your "one pebble" counts in outweighing big boulders.

ACTIVITY

LIVE YOUR FAITH Time to turn the tables. What would you need to do in order to be recommended by a friend as an Apostle? Write it down here.

_____

_____

▶ Think about your own school or community. What groups of people are considered bad or should be avoided? Why do people believe they should be avoided? Are any of those stereotypes? What would Jesus think about these people? What can you do?

_____

_____

_____

_____

 Visit www.harcourtreligion.com for more family and community connections.

 PRAYER

Dear Jesus,
Please make me worthy
of my friends.

Saints Prisca and Aquila

During Jesus' life on earth, he placed great value on friendships and relationships. In the years of his ministry, he traveled among the people. He formed many different kinds of relationships, but all of them were in the spirit of sharing. He shared his blessings and the blessings of his Father with them, and many of them shared their homes and their possessions with him.

Many years later, when Saint Paul was traveling throughout the Mediterranean region spreading the Gospel of Jesus, he, too, relied on friendships and hospitality. Among those who shared their home and hospitality with him were Prisca (Priscilla) and her husband Aquila.

Prisca and Aquila lived in Corinth, Greece. They were Jews who had lived in Rome but had been banished by the Emperor Claudius because of their faith. Aquila and Paul were both tentmakers by trade and they worked together during the time Paul stayed in Corinth. It is probable that Prisca and Aquila converted to Christianity around this time because the Scriptures (*1 Corinthians 16:19–20* and *Romans 16:3–5*) speak of them having a church in their home. Paul also speaks of them risking their lives for him, although he doesn't specify how they did this. In the spirit of Jesus, Prisca and Aquila opened their hearts to Paul in friendship, for which he was deeply grateful. He expressed his thankfulness for them in letters he sent to his other followers.

Paul stayed with Prisca and Aquila in Corinth for about a year and a half, making many converts among the Jews living there. When he set sail for Syria, the couple sailed with him. When they reached Ephesus, in what is now Turkey, Paul left them there. We hear no more about Prisca and Aquila in the Scriptures after that, but it is believed they returned to Rome and were martyred there.

For their devotion to their faith and the friendship they showed to Paul, Prisca and Aquila were both canonized.

▲ **Prisca and Aquila were tentmakers.**

GLOBAL DATA

Corinth

- ■ Corinth is a city of 150,000 people in southern Greece that sits on a narrow isthmus divided by a canal.

- ■ Corinth is the site of the ruins of the Temple of Apollo, one of the great architectural wonders of the ancient world.

- ■ Corinth was home to the famous Greek philosopher Diogenes in the fourth century B.C.

- ■ Corinth was a host city for Saint Paul during his travels and is the namesake for two books of Scripture—*1 Corinthians* and *2 Corinthians*.

8 CHRIST Offers Life

PRAYER Dear Lord, help me make good choices.

I think I understand how people can ignore good advice and hurt themselves instead.
I really want to change, but I keep falling into the same behaviors.
How can believing in Jesus make my life different?

Becky was Emily's best friend. Emily just got back from a weekend retreat with her parish youth group, and she came to school Monday with a "Jesus Is the Good News!" button on her book bag.

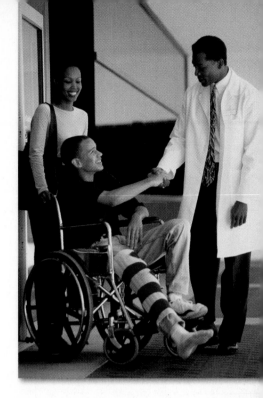

Becky was waiting for Tyler to notice it. She knew he would have something to say about it. Finally, he pointed to the shiny blue circle.

"Hey nice button, Em. So what's the 'good news' about Jesus?"

"'Good News' is what the word Gospel means. Like Matthew, Mark, Luke, and John. Hello?"

Great answer, Becky thought.

But Tyler wasn't through. "Ever think it's more like bad news? Church is just a long list of 'don't do this' and 'don't do that!' All red lights. No green lights."

Next he turned to Becky. "Beck, you followin' me on this?"

She froze. But Emily was all over it. "Yeah, Tyler, when you go to a doctor, and you find out why you're not feeling well, you might not think that's good news. But the doctor doesn't just tell you what *not* to do. He or she will tell you what to do to get well. So the Gospels tell us what can make us sick and what can make us well. Everything the New Testament tells us is Good News, whether it's what we shouldn't do or what we should do. You followin' me?"

ACTIVITY

LET'S BEGIN Why do you think Becky had trouble thinking of a response to Tyler? Why do you think Emily stepped in to continue the conversation with Tyler?

▶ **When have you struggled to explain your beliefs? When have you found them easy to explain? Was it because you had given it a lot of thought beforehand or was it more like the words came from out of nowhere?**

_____

_____

_____

_____

Some people say that the world has become a very dark place . . . that we have all forgotten what citizenship and good neighboring is all about. The late Pope John Paul II labeled the violence, hatred, fear, and anger in society as part of the "culture of death."

He challenged Catholics to live in and create a "culture of life"—to live as "children of light" and to bring about a transformation of our culture. For example, instead of seeking revenge, we can show forgiveness whenever we are wronged. Instead of accepting violence in movies or video games, we can turn away from it and choose other entertainment. Instead of being afraid of people who are different, we can look for ways to appreciate those differences.

"For once you were in darkness, but now in the Lord you are light. Live as children of light—for the fruit of the light is found in all that is good and right and true." (*Ephesians 5:8–9*).

THE PROMISE OF LIFE

Focus How do I know who Jesus is?

It's hard to imagine a friend who never calls you on the phone, never sends you an e-mail, or never goes to the movies with you. How would you know anything about the person? Why would you even call that person a friend?

Jesus Tells Us about His Relationship with Us

How do we get to know Jesus? Well, in the Gospels of Matthew, Mark, Luke, and John, we find out a lot about who Jesus is. We discover what he says about his relationship with the Father and with us. The Gospels tell us about the wise teachings Jesus gave us while he was on earth. They remind us that Jesus loves and understands us, knows our needs, and wants to give us what only God can give: life.

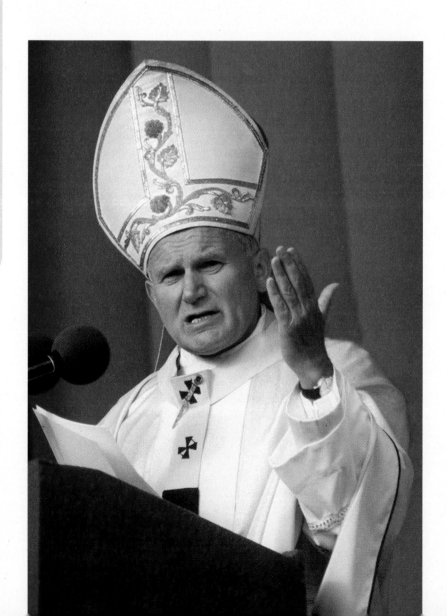

IN HIS WORDS

"I am the vine, you are the branches" (*John 15:5*).

Jesus is the source of life. Think of yourself as bringing good and healthy fruit to others through your actions.

"I am the good shepherd. I know my own and my own know me" (*John 10:14*).

Jesus is the caring shepherd who knows what you need and takes care of you.

Think about some things you might do that would show your care and concern for family, friends, or neighbors.

✝ SCRIPTURE

GO TO THE SOURCE

The Old Testament prophets and psalmists had spoken of Israel as a vineyard and a vine. The Jews of Jesus' time would have understood the analogy Jesus was making. Read **John 15:1–10** to find out how to remain a disciple.

"I am the bread of life. Whoever comes to me will never be hungry, and whoever believes in me will never be thirsty" (*John 6:35*).

Jesus gives us spiritual life the way food and drink nourish our bodies. Think of what you can do to increase your spiritual life, to nourish your soul.

"I am the light of the world. Whoever follows me will never walk in darkness but will have the light of life" (*John 8:12*).

Jesus is your companion in life, shining a light on the path so you know where to walk.

If you follow his teachings, they will show you the way to respect the dignity of life—yours, and that of everyone else you meet.

ACTIVITY

SHARE YOUR FAITH In a group of two or three, imagine talking with Jesus. What do you think he would say about the way the "culture of death" is influencing young people? What advice do you think he would give you about living the "gospel of life?" What questions would you have for him?

MADE JUST AND RIGHT

Focus How does Jesus affect your life?

Because Jesus is the Light of the World, the Bread of Life, and the Vine, what are we? We are the followers on the path who sometimes stumble in darkness, we are the spiritually hungry and needy, we are the branches that are connected to Jesus and give witness to him by all that we say and do. And as the Church, we are all in this together.

These images of Jesus remind us that Jesus offers life, but how do we respond? How are we to live now so that we can know the happiness of living forever with God? We learn from the New Testament letters that doing what is just and right, and standing up for what is good, is a big part of our response.

"But if Christ is in you, though the body is dead because of sin, the Spirit is life because of righteousness" (*Romans 8:10*).

Justification and Righteousness

"Just" and "right" are good qualities. We say someone is "just" if he or she acts fairly. We say something is "right" if it is correct. Our spiritual life needs to be just and right. The Church uses concepts like *right*eousness and *just*ification to help us understand the role of Jesus in our lives.

Justification is the forgiveness of sins and the return to the goodness for which humans were first created. Justification goes beyond our sins being pardoned. It involves being made holy and being renewed spiritually.

Jesus has "justified" humans by becoming one of us and showing us how to live—including how to suffer and die. What does it mean to be justified? The word *justify* means, "to demonstrate or prove to be just or right" and "to declare free of blame or to absolve." So, by the act of his becoming human, dying, and rising to new life, the Son of God has made it possible for people to be just and right once again with God. All we need is to believe.

When we are justified, we

▶ are motivated by the Holy Spirit to see what is not right in our lives and to turn away from the things, people, and actions that keep us from God

▶ grow in our love for God, by the choices we make, the people we spend time with, and the ways we pray

▶ accept forgiveness and live **righteous** lives—to live in accordance with God's will, free from guilt or sin

▶ receive grace (God's favor and help) and grow in holiness

▶ are refreshed, replenished, and made like new. We want to avoid sin

▶ belong to God and want to continue to improve our relationship with Jesus

Free to Us Justification was earned for us by the Passion of Christ and is given onto us when we are baptized. God makes us just by the power of his mercy. Being justified brings us to praise and give glory to God for our gift of eternal life.

Eternal life is God's free gift! We cannot buy it, and we do not earn it. God rewards us with eternal life because he freely chooses to share it with us. In order to gain this free gift of eternal life, we must first respond to God's grace and cooperate with his ways. After this initial turn toward God prompted by the Holy Spirit, we can achieve eternal happiness if we act in ways that reflect God's love and his laws. We do this by the help of the Holy Spirit who inspires us and moves us to live as Jesus' followers. He lives within us and influences us to live right and just lives.

ACTIVITY

CONNECT YOUR FAITH Write about a part of your life that is going well. What are you grateful for? Think of something in your life that is not going so well. Write about how following Jesus more closely could help you improve things so they become more "just" and "right."

_____

_____

_____

_____

_____

MAKING A CHANGE

Focus What is conversion?

The world is full of stories about people who used to perform sinful actions, but changed their lives around and now do good. Perhaps you have heard or read about

▶ someone who used to be in a gang that injured people and destroyed property, but now spends time helping other gang members get out and find support

▶ someone who used to be a computer hacker, illegally accessing people's personal information, who now volunteers with nonprofit agencies making their networks more secure

▶ someone who used to be very prejudiced against certain groups of people, who now speaks out whenever he or she hears a racial joke or comment

In their own ways, each of these people experienced a conversion.

Conversion implies a change. From a faith perspective, it's a turning away from what keeps us from growing in God's love. It includes turning away from evil, wanting to change one's life, following the path of renewal, and being moved by God's grace.

Sometimes we make big conversions, and sometimes we make smaller ones. Conversion doesn't happen overnight or just once in our lives. It's ongoing.

As we are exposed to new and different challenges, sometimes we don't make the best choices or do the right things. But our faith really is Good News because God is merciful and forgiving! The Holy Spirit works in us, helping us appreciate that conversion must be part of our lives.

A sin always involves failure. If we recognize what we did wrong, and ask for forgiveness, we can learn from it and change our ways. Our sins may get more serious if we keep doing them over and over again without improving or growing spiritually.

Conversion in Action Once we recognize that something we have been doing is sinful, then we need to

▶ be sorry for that sin

▶ reject our past sins

▶ decide to try to avoid sin in the future

We know that God is merciful and forgiving, and that gives us hope and a share in his life. The original grace that leads us to conversion is a free gift from God. We cannot buy it, and we didn't earn it. The Holy Spirit moves and inspires us. This brings us closer to eternal life.

ACTIVITY

LIVE YOUR FAITH When have you heard or seen a conversion story—a story about a person who overcame a particular sin and turned into someone who "lived in the Light" of what was just and right? Write out that story in your own words—it can be a true story or a fictional story. You could also write a personal story about one of your own conversions.

IN SUMMARY

CATHOLICS BELIEVE

God offers us forgiveness, holiness, and renewal.

▶ Jesus is the Vine, the Bread of Life, the Light of the World who offers eternal life to those who believe.

▶ We are justified by Jesus. We are forgiven and made whole again. We don't earn our own righteousness; it is God's free gift.

▶ Conversion is a continuing process. The Holy Spirit helps us recognize our past sinfulness and helps us overcome sin in the future.

CELEBRATE

REFLECTION ON JESUS

Leader: We know and believe when two or more gather,
Christ is here and present among us.
Let us take this time to pray
in the name of the one who loves us and calls us each by name.

Let us pray . . .

Leader: Jesus said, "I am the bread of Life."

Reader 1: This I know and believe.
Jesus offers his life to us in the Eucharist.
With Jesus, I know I will never go hungry.

Leader: Jesus said, "I am the light of the World."

Reader 2: This I know and believe.
Jesus lights the path when I am confused and need direction.
With Jesus, I can find the right way to live.

Leader: Jesus said, "I am the gate for the sheep."

Reader 3: This I know and believe.
Jesus opens the door when I need to be welcomed.
With Jesus, I know I have an open invitation.

Leader: Jesus said, "I am the good shepherd."

Reader 4: This I know and believe.
Jesus keeps me safe; Jesus keeps me in line.
With Jesus, I know I will be well taken care of.

Leader: Jesus said, "I am the resurrection and the life."

Reader 5: This I know and believe.
Jesus raises me up every time I fall.
With Jesus, I know something better awaits me.

Leader: Jesus said, "I am the way, the truth and the life."

Reader 6: This I know and believe.
Jesus is the right and true path for me.
With Jesus, I know I will have a good and full life.

Leader: O Father,
we know and believe in Jesus your Son.
Help us to know that we can call on him
and talk with him in any place and at any time.
We ask this through Christ our brother and friend,
Amen.

♪ "I Am the Resurrection"
David Haas, © 1988, GIA Publications, Inc.

110

REVIEW

A **Work with Words** Complete each sentence with the correct term from the word bank at right.

Word Bank

- conversion
- disciples
- Christmas
- righteous
- Pentecost
- justification
- holiness
- culture of life
- Lent

1. _____ is the forgiveness of sins and the return to the goodness for which humans were first created.

2. When we are _____, we want to live in accordance with God's will, free from guilt or sin.

3. _____ means turning away from what keeps us from God and turning back to him.

4. The season of _____ helps us focus on what would make our lives more just and right.

5. By showing forgiveness, we can help create a _____.

B **Check Understanding** Indicate whether the following statements are true or false. Then rewrite false statements to make them true.

_____ **6.** Jesus is the Light of the World and the Bread of Life.

_____

_____ **7.** The word *justify* means "to declare free of blame or to absolve."

_____

_____ **8.** When we are baptized, we are joined to the righteousness of God who justifies us.

_____

_____ **9.** Conversion is a change that happens once in our lives when we are baptized.

_____

_____ **10.** The original grace that leads us to conversion is a free gift from God, but the Holy Spirit moves us closer to eternal life.

_____

C **Make Connections: Evaluate** Write a one-paragraph response to the following.

Name and explain Jesus' "I Am" statements presented in this chapter. Create some modern "I Am" statements that might share the same message as the ones Jesus gave us.

OUR CATHOLIC FAITH

WHAT NOW?

★ Decide to spend time getting to know Jesus and his teachings better.

★ Read Scripture. Pray, fast, and give alms.

★ Pay attention to the way the Holy Spirit might be calling you to act.

★ Keep checking to see where you need to make some small or big conversions.

★ Find people—friends and trustworthy adults—who can help you grow spiritually and ask for their help.

ACTIVITY

LIVE YOUR FAITH

▶ Think of your childhood.

▶ Think of your current life.

▶ Remember several times when you recognized your sinfulness and changed your way of acting.

▶ When you were a child, what was it like to be sorry? How did you "decide not to sin again"?

▶ What is it like for you to be sorry now?

▶ How have you grown and matured in your ability to recognize sinfulness, make good decisions, and follow through?

_____

_____

_____

_____

_____

 Visit www.harcourtreligion.com for more family and community connection.

 **PRAYER**

Lord, As I go through my day, let me be the person you have created me to be.

Blessed Victoria Rasoamanarivo

During his lifetime, Our Lord Jesus Christ offered the blessings of life to those around him: compassion, holiness, spirituality, and forgiveness. The example he set has carried down through the ages. For over two thousand years, holy men and women have sought to be more like him.

Victoria Rasoamanarivo was an embodiment of the Spirit of Christ during her lifetime. She was born into a prominent family on the island of Madagascar, off the southeastern coast of Africa in 1848, and baptized into the faith at the age of fifteen. A year after her conversion, Victoria married a man who was an alcoholic. Through her Christ-like gifts for patience, understanding, and compassion, she tried to help him overcome his addiction.

A virtuous lay woman, Victoria founded the Catholic Action movement in Madagascar. This organization, with branches around the world, focuses on improving the conditions of the people in the nations in which they are located. Madagascar, at that time, was a kingdom made up of many tribes. They all spoke different languages and had a wide variety of religious customs. Malagasy people were a mixture of many cultures because the island bridged southern Asia and southern Africa. By Western standards of the time, it was thought to be primitive and backward, even though it had a thriving culture of its own.

There were few priests on the island, so Victoria assumed much of what they would have done. She ministered to the people, teaching them about the blessings they would receive through acceptance of Jesus as Lord. She helped the poor and promoted the rights of women.

Following an accident in 1888, Victoria's husband died. She baptized him as he lay dying. She continued her spiritual work among the Malagasy people until her death in 1894. Two years later, Madagascar became a French colony and more of its people converted to Catholicism.

During his visit to the Madagascar capital of Antananarivo on April 30, 1989, Pope John Paul II beatified Victoria Rasoamanarivo. Nearly 500,000 people attended the mass held by his Holiness in which she was declared Blessed. Less than two years later, the tension and civil unrest that had plagued the country for many years came to an end.

▲ Madagascar, where the Blessed Victoria Rasoamanarivo lived, is an island off the southeastern coast of Africa.

GLOBAL DATA

■ Madagascar is located off the southeastern coast of Africa in the Indian Ocean.

■ Madagascar is the world's fourth largest island with a population of 18 million.

■ Madagascar was a French colony from 1896 until independence in 1960.

■ Madagascar is about 20 percent Catholic, with 52 percent of the people following indigenous beliefs, followed by other Christians at 20 percent and Muslims at 7 percent.

9 THE CHURCH
One in Christ

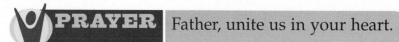

PRAYER Father, unite us in your heart.

People seem so different. What can they have in common with me? Can people believe the same thing but show it in different ways? All Christians must have something in common, right?

Juanita didn't want to move.

She loved her friends at Blessed Sacrament school, and she wanted to stay with them until they graduated from eighth grade together. Juanita begged her parents to stay when they told her they had to move far away. She was upset for weeks. But it was no use. She had to leave the place she called home and move to a place where she knew no one.

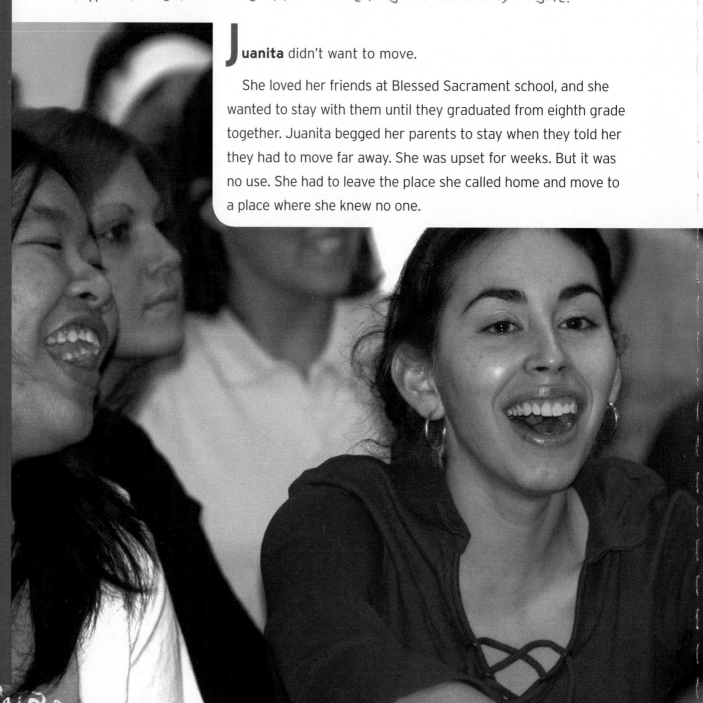

When she got there, Juanita found out everything was so different! The music was different. The slang was different. Nobody was like her friends at home. Nobody laughed at her jokes. Back home, everyone got all her jokes. Here—well, nothing was funny here.

And back home, she knew what to wear. Back home, she was part of it all. Here—well, honestly, she was nobody.

"This is home," her parents told her. But it just wasn't true.

Then they took her to the new parish for Mass. She wanted it to look and feel like the one she'd always gone to. But even their new church looked different. Back home, there were beautiful statues and colorful stained-glass windows. Here, everything was made out of cinderblock. Juanita felt like she was in somebody's unfinished basement instead of in church.

Then the music started. The opening song was one of her favorites. At last! Something she could relate to! She saw all the teens who had seemed so different singing the same song she and her old friends had sung together. Maybe they weren't so different after all. Juanita grabbed a songbook and sang like she used to back home. "It still looks different," she thought, "but at least I can feel like home when we are at Mass!"

ACTIVITY

LET'S BEGIN What part of being Catholic was Juanita experiencing? What could she do to help her parents better understand her feelings? What could Juanita do to help herself?

▶ Think of a time when you did not see what different people had in common. How did you learn that the people were united by something? What did they have in common? What do all young people have in common? What do all people—young and old—have in common?

DIFFERENT BUT THE SAME

Focus What unites the Catholic Church?

We all want to belong. We all like to feel comfortable with where we are and with the people around us. Most of the time our friends like the same music we like or the same kinds of movies or the same kinds of sports. But sometimes you wind up in a group of people you don't know. You might be sitting with fans of the other team at a game, or go to a party with a friend and discover you don't know anyone else there.

What you often find is although new acquaintances may be different, there are things you share in common. You follow the same sport, or you have some of the same friends. And the more you get to know new people, the better chance you have of discovering that you have even more in common than you first thought.

Expressing the Same Beliefs The first disciples of Jesus were from different backgrounds, but their faith in him brought them together. At his Last Supper Christ prayed for all of his followers to be one. (See *John 17:20–26.*) He wanted them to put aside their differences to know that they all belonged to God and were loved by God.

✝ SCRIPTURE

GO TO THE SOURCE

". . . so that they may be one . . ." Jesus was praying these words about his Apostles, but this is a prayer for all of us. Read the rest of **John 17:20–26** to see what else Jesus said at the Last Supper, the night he was arrested.

So what unites us as the Catholic Church—no matter where we live?

▶ We proclaim one Lord, Jesus, and profess the same creed. That means we all believe what's contained in the Apostles' and Nicene Creeds.

▶ We celebrate the seven sacraments. The details of how we celebrate might be different, but we all baptize in the name of the Father, Son, and Holy Spirit. Through the Eucharist we are given life and are united by the same Holy Spirit. We become the one Body of Christ, the Church.

▶ We are apostolic. We fall under the same Church hierarchy led by the pope. Through the unbroken line of bishops and popes, we can trace our history back to the Apostles. We are served by the ordained ministry of bishops, priests, and deacons.

▶ We are committed to justice. Serving the poor and standing up against injustice have always been characteristics of Catholicism.

This unity is one of the marks of the Catholic Church. The Church has diverse people from many different cultures and with a variety of gifts. That great richness of diversity doesn't get in the way of our unity. Diversity makes our customs and experiences richer and deeper. Even though different Catholic parishes have their own styles, being Catholic is the same everywhere you go. And all kinds of different people, with all their favorite ways of praying, are welcomed.

ACTIVITY

SHARE YOUR FAITH How many different Catholic churches have you visited? Try to remember what differences you have seen. Talk to your friends and ask them what differences they have noticed in other Catholic churches. Make a list of all the examples you can think of that demonstrate different ways to celebrate our one united faith. Which of the characteristics of being Catholic listed above means the most to you? Explain. What questions do you have about any of them?

UNITED BUT UNIQUE

Focus How are Eastern and Roman Catholics alike and different?

You might have heard someone say she was Roman Catholic and wondered what that meant. Isn't it enough to say "I'm Catholic"?

There is one Catholic Church, but as it grew and spread during its early history, the people in different places expressed their Catholic belief in their unique customs, language, and favorite ways of praying. That's why there is more than one Church in the Catholic Church. The different Churches developed under the leadership of the Pope, the Bishop of Rome, and continue under his authority.

There are two overarching Churches: the Latin or Roman Catholic Church and the Eastern Catholic Church.

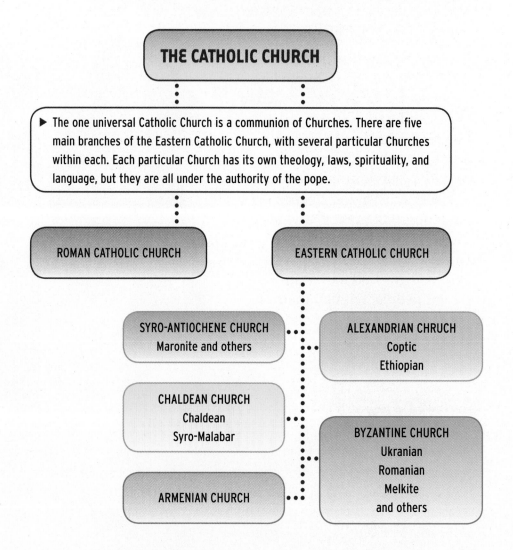

THE CATHOLIC CHURCH

▶ The one universal Catholic Church is a communion of Churches. There are five main branches of the Eastern Catholic Church, with several particular Churches within each. Each particular Church has its own theology, laws, spirituality, and language, but they are all under the authority of the pope.

ROMAN CATHOLIC CHURCH

EASTERN CATHOLIC CHURCH

SYRO-ANTIOCHENE CHURCH
Maronite and others

ALEXANDRIAN CHRUCH
Coptic
Ethiopian

CHALDEAN CHURCH
Chaldean
Syro-Malabar

BYZANTINE CHURCH
Ukranian
Romanian
Melkite
and others

ARMENIAN CHURCH

Roman Catholics and Eastern Catholics have different ways of worshiping, but their worship is a sign of the same mystery of Christ. Their sacraments may be celebrated differently, but they share the same grace with those who receive them. What the Churches have in common (creed, sacraments, and leadership under the pope) and what they hold unique show the true nature of the universal Church. The universal church is one Catholic Church. We all worship the one Triune God. Our unity comes from the unity of the Blessed Trinity: Father, Son, and Holy Spirit are three divine and distinct Persons, but they form one united God.

Have you ever been to worship in a Catholic Church that follows a different Tradition than your own? If so, what did you see that was new to you there?

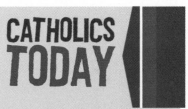

CATHOLICS TODAY

In the Eastern Catholic Church, babies are baptized, then confirmed, and then given Eucharist by the priest all during the same celebration. This emphasizes the unity of all three Sacraments of Initiation—Baptism, Confirmation, and Eucharist.

In the Roman Catholic or Latin Church, priests baptize babies, but Confirmation usually comes later. The local bishop administers the sacrament. This shows that Confirmation makes the recipient's bond to the Church stronger.

The celebration of Confirmation is one example of how the Eastern and Roman Churches celebrate the same beliefs but in different ways.

At the Sacrament of Confirmation, the minister lays hands on the person and anoints the forehead with oil. In the Byzantine Tradition, other sense organs like the eyes, ears, and hands are anointed as well.

The words spoken are very similar:
▶ "The seal of the gift that is the Holy Spirit" (Byzantine Tradition of the Eastern Church) and
▶ "Be sealed with the Gift of the Holy Spirit" (Roman Church).

ACTIVITY

CONNECT YOUR FAITH Write down how you might describe one of the Sacraments of Initiation (Baptism, Confirmation, or Eucharist) to a person who has never seen Catholic sacraments take place.

_____ ┈┈▶ _____

(Sacrament) _____

_____

_____

BROTHERS AND SISTERS IN CHRIST

 Focus How do we come together?

You might walk into a Christian church, see a bishop in vestments, hear about Jesus, and pray familiar prayers, and still discover that you are not in a Catholic church! "How can that be?" you wonder. "Aren't Catholics Christians?" Yes, Christians are people who believe in and follow Jesus the Christ, the second Person of the Blessed Trinity. All Catholics are Christians. But not all Christians are Catholic. Some Christians are Baptist, some are Presbyterian, Lutheran, Methodist, Episcopalian, Pentecostal, or Disciples of Christ.

Some Christian churches call their leaders "bishops" and "priests"; others do not. Some have worship services that include a sharing of bread and wine; others do not. Some have married male and female ministers; others do not.

 Have you ever visited a Christian church that is not Catholic? If so, what was it like?

The Christian Family History Right now, all of these are separate Christian churches. The Christian churches of the world can be spoken of as a world Christian family. But how did all of these churches come to be?

For the first millennium, Christians were, for the most part, united as one Church under the leadership of the bishop of Rome, the pope. Then, in A.D. 1054, because of arguments among Church leaders about Church authority, practices, and teaching, many in the Eastern Church split from the Western (Roman) Church. This is known as the Great Schism. The word *schism* means "division" or "cutting." Many Eastern Churches in Eastern Europe, the Middle East, and in Asia became known as the Eastern Orthodox Church.

Then, in the 1500s, the Western Church experienced another split. In A.D. 1517, a priest named Martin Luther spoke out, or protested, against what he saw as abuses and errors in the Church. Although he began calling for reforms, his actions led to the Protestant Reformation, in which Luther and several other Christian leaders and groups separated from the Catholic Church and the authority of the pope. The unity, or full communion, of the Western Church was broken.

Those who left the communion of the Catholic Church became known as Protestants, and those who remained became known as Roman Catholics.

Christians Today The Catholic Church (Roman and Eastern) is the one that is governed by the successor of Peter (the pope), and all the bishops in communion with him. The Church of Christ subsists in the Catholic Church; through her alone can the fullness of the means of salvation be found. However, in many ways, all baptized Christians are joined together, even though they do not share all the beliefs of the Catholic faith, and their churches are not in perfect communion with the pope.

This separation of Catholic and Protestant was a tragedy from many centuries ago. No one church was totally responsible for this. In spite of the separation, much holiness and truth are still found in other churches outside of the Catholic Church. We hope some day that all Christian churches can be united together.

But we do more than hope for the unity of Christians. We work toward building community with all Christians. The effort toward unity among all Christian people is called **ecumenism**. Ecumenism requires a lot of communication and cooperation among people of all Christian faiths. We do this by praying together, discussing what we have in common, respecting one another, and learning more about what others believe.

 Have you ever asked your Protestant friends what their faith or their church is like? If so, how did they respond?

ACTIVITY

LIVE YOUR FAITH Write a prayer expressing the hope that all Christian churches can come together and be united some day.

IN SUMMARY

CATHOLICS BELIEVE

The universal Catholic Church is united by common beliefs and practices.

▶ The Church is made up of diverse people from different cultures who express their common faith in different ways.

▶ The Catholic Church is made up of Eastern Catholics and Roman Catholics who are united by a common creed, the seven sacraments, and the leadership of the pope.

▶ A unity exists among all baptized Christians, and we pray and work toward the full unity that Christ desires for all his followers.

PRAYER FOR UNITY

Leader: Let us be attentive to the wisdom of Saint Paul's letter to the Ephesians.

Reader 1: Lead a life worthy of the calling to which you were called,

Reader 2: With all humility,

Reader 3: With gentleness and patience,

All three: Bearing with one another in love,
making every effort to maintain the unity of the Spirit,
in the bond of peace.

Reader 1: There is one body,

Reader 2: There is one Spirit,

Reader 3: There is one baptism,

All three: There is one God and Father of all.

Reader 1: Who is above all, through all, and in all.

Reader 2: Living the truth in love,

Reader 3: We should grow in every way into him who is the head, Christ.

Reader 1: So be imitators of God,

Reader 2: As beloved children,

All three: And live in love

Reader 3: As Christ loved us.

—Based on 4:1–7, 15, 5:1–2.

Leader: Guide us, O God, in your ways,
so that we will learn to love others.
We seek to live in the love
Your Son showed us.
We ask this in Christ, our Lord.

All: Amen.

 "One Lord"
Lori True, © 2004, GIA Publications, Inc.

REVIEW

A Work with Words Complete each sentence with the correct term.

Word Bank

- the pope
- ecumenism
- apostolic
- just
- diversity
- creeds
- Byzantine
- reformation
- Martin Luther

1. The Catholic Church is _____ because, through the unbroken line of bishops and popes, we can trace her history back to the Apostles.

2. _____ makes Catholic customs and experiences richer and deeper.

3. The different Churches within the one Catholic Church formed under the leadership of the _____.

4. The five Eastern Catholic Churches are _____, Chaldean, Syro-Antiochene, Alexandrian, and Armenian.

5. The movement toward building unity and community among all Christian people is called _____.

B Check Understanding Circle the letter of the choice that best completes the sentence.

6. At the Last Supper Christ prayed for all of his followers to be _____.
   - **a.** happy
   - **b.** priests
   - **c.** one
   - **d.** perfect

7. As Catholics, we are united by our creeds, our sacraments, and our _____ ministry.
   - **a.** ordained
   - **b.** traditional
   - **c.** long
   - **d.** Latin

8. The two main Churches are the Latin or Roman and the _____.
   - **a.** Armenian
   - **b.** Byzantine
   - **c.** Eastern
   - **d.** Chaldean

9. The split between many in the Eastern Church and the Western Church in 1054 is known as the _____.
   - **a.** Ecumenical Movement
   - **b.** Reformation
   - **c.** Great Divide
   - **d.** Great Schism

10. Martin Luther called for reforms in the Church that led to the _____.
    - **a.** Ecumenical Movement
    - **b.** Protestant Reformation
    - **c.** Great Divide
    - **d.** Great Schism

C Make Connections: Compare and Contrast Write a one-paragraph response to the question.

Think about someone you know who is a Christian but not a Catholic. What parts of your faith do you have in common? What beliefs are different?

123

OUR CATHOLIC FAITH

WHAT NOW?

★ Memorize the Nicene Creed. It is the core statement defining our Catholic belief.

★ Don't assume that you can't be united with others who are different!

★ Learn more about your own Catholic faith—your beliefs, sacraments, and history.

★ Be open to learning about other Christian churches.

★ Respect all people and their religious customs.

ACTIVITY

LIVE YOUR FAITH

Try to make two Catholic lists:

▶ The things that all Catholics have in common

▶ The ways we might be different

Try to make two Christian lists:

▶ The things that all Christian churches have in common

▶ Some of the ways that Protestant churches might be different from our Catholic churches

GO ONLINE Visit www.harcoutreligion.com for more family and community connections.

PRAYER

I pray with your servant, "I believe; help my unbelief!"

Mark 9:24

Venerable Samuel Mazzuchelli

The Church has always welcomed the many different peoples of the world. Our faith teaches us that we are "one in Christ" and that he loves us all despite our differences.

When Father Samuel Mazzuchelli was assigned to preach among the Native American tribes of the upper Great Lakes region of the United States in 1830, he brought with him the virtues gained from the example of Our Lord. When he arrived on Mackinac Island between Lake Huron and Lake Michigan, he was the only priest in the region. He gained the confidence and affection of the Native American tribes as he recognized their plight and sympathized with it, as Jesus might have done.

The Native Americans of the Great Lakes region and the American Midwest were being forced to move from their ancient homelands. Treaties were made with the American government, and then broken. During the War of 1812 between the United States and Great Britain, many Native Americans sided with the British. They had hoped the British would protect them against the steady encroachment of American settlers moving westward. When the war ended and British troops withdrew, many of the native peoples moved farther westward, across the Mississippi River, and out of the path of the white American settlers. Others stayed where they were and tried to make the best of the situation with the Americans.

Father Mazzuchelli was one of the few individuals bold enough to speak out for Native Americans. In a letter to a friend in 1836, he wrote, "I am convinced that most of our Indian wars are the natural and unavoidable consequences of the misconduct of the whites. Most of our Indian treaties are badly planned by individuals, unfairly ratified and shamefully executed. Individuals make their fortune at the expense of justice."

Father Mazzuchelli continued to speak out against the injustices he saw. His accomplishments while ministering to the region were many. He founded the first Catholic school in Wisconsin, established and designed many churches throughout the region, and founded the Saint Clare Academy in Sinsinawa, Wisconsin, a frontier school for girls that today has grown into Dominican University.

Father Mazzuchelli also founded the Congregation of the Dominican Sisters of the Holy Rosary of Sinsinawa. By the time of his death in 1864, he had laid the foundation for the modern Church in the Great Lakes and upper Midwest.

▲ Venerable Samuel Mazzuchelli, 1806–1864

GLOBAL DATA

United States

- The United States is the fourth largest country in the world in area and third largest in population.

- The United States is about 24 percent Catholic, with more than 72 million members.

- The United States became a haven for Catholics fleeing persecution in England in the 1630s.

- The United States contains more than 19,000 parishes in 32 Latin Catholic Archdioceses, 146 Latin Catholic Dioceses, 2 Eastern Catholic Archdioceses, and 15 Eastern Catholic Dioceses.

- The United States has 13 cardinals. The Church has more than 30,000 diocesan priests, 15,000 priests vowed to a specific order, 75,000 sisters, and 5,600 brothers. There are 150,000 Catholic schoolteachers, teaching 2.7 million students.

Faith in Action!

DISCOVER Catholic Social Teaching:
Rights and Responsibilities of the Human Person

IN THIS UNIT you learned about how Jesus embraced human differences and befriended everyone. He challenges all of us to be open to human differences and to be loving of all.

Rights and Responsibilities

The dignity of each person is the basis for human equality and basic human rights. These basic human rights start with the right to life and the basic necessities of life—food, shelter, clothing, health care, education, and work, but they go further. Every person has the right to dignity. This means being respected and appreciated for one's uniqueness. It also means developing mutual relationships with people—learning from them as well as helping them. Just as you like to be treated as a responsible person and not a helpless child, so too the people you visit in the nursing home or the elderly in your parish want you to treat them in the same way.

The third area of human rights revolves around the right of people to participate in the decisions that affect their lives. Governments especially must respect this fundamental human right and create the conditions for the full political involvement of their peoples. Everyone has the right to be heard by those in authority, but too often their voices are silenced. The Church calls us to be the voice of the voiceless victims of injustice. Jubliee Campaign was created many years ago to amplify the voices of caring people around the world on behalf of those voiceless victims falsely imprisoned by their own governments. In the U.S., the organization lobbies Congress on behalf of those suffering persecution. Every government, even our own, has a tendency toward totalitarianism—to silence those who criticize it. Disciples of Jesus are called to bring the light of the Gospel to bear on these unjust situations. We have a responsibility to speak up for these prisoners of conscience.

How can you become a "voice" for voiceless victims of injustice?

GOD CALLS HIS FOLLOWERS to protect the rights of every human person to the goods of his creation. Let's look at how one group puts those beliefs into practice.

"VOICES THAT CHALLENGE"
SPEAKING UP FOR SOCIAL JUSTICE

Amanda Stanley was in the sixth grade when two students at Columbine High School in Littleton, Colorado, killed eleven schoolmates, a teacher, and themselves. She was especially bothered that the shooters were considered outcasts and apparently had some racist feelings. So Amanda got her middle school in Tidewater, Virginia, to take the Pledge of Nonviolence and a Pledge Against Racism.

But Amanda was also concerned about making a difference outside of her school. As a high school freshman, she became one of the founding members of Voices That Challenge (VTC), a group of youth in her area and the Outer Banks, North Carolina, working for social justice according to the principles of Catholic social teaching. They have done many projects to improve the environment and help the poor, but all of them have a similar theme—the right of every human person to the goods of creation and the responsibility of everyone to work with those who don't.

In summer 2004, she and nine other VTC youth went on a "Borderlinks" trip to the border of Arizona and Mexico to learn about the plight of the Mexican people who were traveling through the desert for two or three days with only one gallon of water to reach the United States. They met caring Christians, who told them how they leave out water bottles for the migrants and invite them into their homes despite it being against the law.

Because of this experience, according to Katie Schwermer, one of the VTC youth leaders from St. Pius X Church in Norfolk, they are working on legislative advocacy to help both the poor in Mexico and Mexican immigrants to the United States. They have written letters about making NAFTA (the North American Free Trade Agreement) fairer and about supporting the DREAM Act, which will help undocumented students go to college. And they continue to pray for their new friends.

? Do you think immigrants to our country deserve the same rights as citizens who have been here for a long time?

? Why do you think in the Bible that God tells us more than 50 times not to mistreat "orphans, widows, and aliens"? Who are "aliens"?

▼ A trip to the U.S.-Mexican border spurred youth from Voices That Challenge to become advocates for poor immigrants.

MUTUAL RELATIONSHIPS WITH THOSE YOU "SERVE"

Make a list of the people you, your parish, your school, or your family are serving in some way, especially people who need your help.

Which word would you use to describe each relationship—"mutual" or "one-way helping"?

Choose one of those relationships that is more "one-way helping" and decide one thing you can do to make it a more mutual relationship (e.g., asking an elderly person to teach you something).

Carry out your decision and tell someone you trust about the experience.

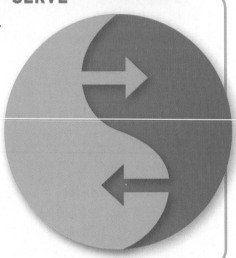

GIVING "VOICE" TO THE VOICELESS

In addition to researching the situation of immigrants in your community, your class might also research some of Jubliee Campaign's and the Catholic Campaign for Human Development's (CCHD) current projects in your area. CCHD is committed to funding projects where the recipients of aid have a direct voice in how the project is organized and carried out.

Share the results of your research and decide whether to create a single class project or divide the class into several projects.

Create a plan for carrying out the project(s).

Project Planning Sheet

Groups to speak to about the project

Possible actions to ask others to do in support of the project(s)

How to publicize the project(s)

Other specific tasks

Your specific task(s)

Calendar for completing the project

What did you learn about yourself from doing the mutual relationships activity?

_____

_____

_____

What did you learn about Jubliee Campaign or the Catholic Campaign for Human Development from doing the class project?

_____

_____

_____

What did you learn about yourself in doing the project?

_____

_____

_____

What did you learn about Jesus and about your faith in doing it?

_____

_____

_____

List one thing that might be different about you after doing this project. How will your life be different because of these actions?

_____

_____

_____

"You shall not oppress a resident alien;
you know the heart of an alien, for you
were aliens in the land of Egypt."
—*Exodus 23:9*

REVIEW

A **Work with Words** Use the clues below to complete the crossword puzzle.

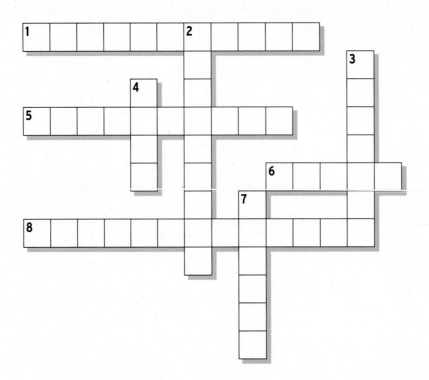

Across

1 Movement started by Martin Luther

5 Turning away from what keeps us from God and turning back to him

6 Disciple Jesus called "The Rock"

8 Forgiveness of sins and the return to goodness for which humans were first created

Down

2 The Catholic Church is this because the popes and bishops trace their leadership back to the Apostles.

3 One of the two main branches of the Catholic Church

4 Season that helps us focus on what would make our lives more just and right

7 Lazarus' sister and a close friend of Jesus

B **Check Understanding** Circle the letter of the best answer to complete the following statements.

9. _____ was the first person Jesus appeared to after he rose from the dead.

   a. Peter

   b. John

   c. Mary Magdalene

   d. Martha

10. Peter, James, and _____ were the only disciples who came with Jesus to pray the night he was arrested.

   a. John

   b. Matthew

   c. James

   d. Mark

11. _____ was a businesswoman in Philippi, who offered her home to Paul and Silas.

   a. Priscilla   **c.** Ruth

   b. Lydia   **d.** Naomi

12. The word _____ means to "declare free of blame or to absolve."

   a. sanctify   **c.** righteous

   b. conversion   **d.** justify

13. When we are _____, we are joined to the righteousness of God who justifies us.

   a. baptized   **c.** forgiven

   b. converted   **d.** holy

14. _____ is the process of turning away from sin and toward God that happens throughout our lives.

   a. Justification   **c.** The Eucharist

   b. Salvation   **d.** Conversion

15. When we are _____, we live in accordance with God's will, free from guilt or sin.

   a. traditional   **c.** righteous

   b. diverse   **d.** prayerful

16. As Catholics, we are united in our belief of one Lord, Jesus, and by the celebration of _____.

   a. Pentacost   **c.** Eucharist

   b. doctrines   **d.** Baptism

17. The five parts of the Eastern Catholic Church in the United States are _____, Chaldean, Syro-Antiochene, Alexandrian, and Armenian.

   a. Byzantine   **c.** Latin

   b. Alexandrian   **d.** Roman

18. The movement toward building unity and community among all Christian people is called

_____.

   a. reform   **c.** apostolic

   b. ecumenism   **d.** none of the above

ⓒ Make Connections Write a short answer to these questions.

19. Interpret. Imagine you are one of the disciples at Pentecost—the day the Holy Spirit first descended. What is happening around you? What are your thoughts and reactions?

20. Infer. Jesus is the Light of the World, Bread of Life, and the Vine. Select one of these images. What does this image mean in terms of relationship with God?

10 THE CHURCH Is Apostolic

 **PRAYER** | Lord, teach me.

How are things we think and do today connected to people from the past? Why should I care about what happened years ago?

"I don't want to go, why don't *you* go with Mom today" Gigi said to her brother as she looked at the clock above the T.V. "I don't want to miss the rest of my show and I want to go see a movie today with Katie."

"You know I can't go, this lunch is only for the women in our family, so that pretty much rules me out," said Tony.

It's a family tradition for the women in Gigi's family to get together for lunch once a month at Grandma Pat's house. All of her Aunts and cousins would come to talk, cook, and eat together. It was a way for her Mom and Aunts to spend time

together in Grandma Pat's kitchen, they way they used to when they were little girls. Now Gigi and all of her cousins could learn how to cook like Grandma Pat, the way she learned from her Grandmother.

"It's totally not fair that I have to go to this mother-daughter family lunch every month. I know we have a lot of women in the family, but do all of us have to go?" asked Gigi.

"Well, you can always ask Mom if you can stay, but I think it's pretty cool that you all get to hang out and eat everything Grandma Pat and Aunt Nina cook. Maybe one day you will cook for everyone like they do," Tony replied.

"Yeah, I guess, I just wish I could stay home today and do what I want, but I know it means a lot to Mom," Gigi answered.

Gigi started thinking about the time one of her cousins stayed at home because she was sick and couldn't come to the lunch. She thought about how much she missed her cousin being there that time. She also thought about how much her mom really looked forward to these lunches and how disappointed she would be if Gigi didn't go. What would happen if everyone decided not to go today? Grandma Pat would probably be really sad.

"I'll just catch the re-run, besides, I don't want to miss Grandma Pat's latest recipe," she said as she turned off the T.V.

ACTIVITY

LET'S BEGIN Why do you think Gigi decided to go to the mother-daughter lunch? Why would her Mom be disappointed if Gigi stayed home? Why do you think Gigi's family started this tradition? How is it being passed on?

▶ **Think about some traditions that have been passed on in your school, family, or parish. Which ones seem most important to you? How do people know about them?**

_____

_____

_____

UPON THIS ROCK

Focus How has the Catholic Church kept the faith of Jesus after so many centuries?

People like to follow traditions that have been passed down from generation to generation. Maybe it makes us feel connected to the people who came before us—or helps us see that we are part of something important. Or, it might be that following the tradition identifies us as a group.

Many things identify us as Catholics. And, although some things have changed since Jesus called his first disciples nearly two thousand years ago, the Catholic Church has always kept the same faith and proclaimed the same Gospel. It's our Tradition.

Peter the Apostle As Jesus began his public life, he called many followers. From among those disciples, he chose twelve to be his Apostles. He taught them everything he could. He sent them out to share in his mission to tell others the Good News he brought and to build up God's kingdom. Jesus gave his Apostles and their successors the power to act in his name.

Jesus chose the Apostle Simon, who was a fisherman, to be the leader of the Apostles and his Church. Jesus gave him the name "Peter." This was a play on words—the word *Peter* means "rock."

✝ SCRIPTURE "And I tell you, you are Peter, and on this rock I will build my church, and the gates of Hades will not prevail against it. I will give you the keys of the kingdom of heaven, and whatever you bind on earth will be bound in heaven, and whatever you loose on earth will be loosed in heaven."

—*Matthew 16:18–19*

Once Jesus ascended to heaven to sit at the right hand of the Father, he was no longer visible to us. So he gave the Church a visible head, Saint Peter, who was his Vicar, or representative on earth. Jesus formed the Apostles into a permanent gathering or assembly (also called a "college"), which together leads the Church. The power given to that college of Apostles with Peter at its head has stayed with the Church ever since.

✝ SCRIPTURE

GO TO THE SOURCE

What qualities did Jesus see in Peter that made him a "rock"? Read **Matthew 16:13–19** to find out. What qualities do you think Church leaders need today?

SCRIPTURE The twelve Apostles gathered in the Upper Room after Jesus ascended to heaven.

"When the day of Pentecost had come, they were all together in one place. And suddenly from heaven there came a sound like the rush of a violent wind, and it filled the entire house where they were sitting. Divided tongues, as of fire, appeared among them, and a tongue rested on each of them. All of them were filled with the Holy Spirit and began to speak in other languages, as the Spirit gave them ability."

—Acts 2:1–4

apostolic succession

magisterium

infallible

diocese

Birth of the Church All of the Apostles were present as the Church was born that day. Their successors, the pope and bishops, are present to lead the Church today.

The pope is the successor to Saint Peter as bishop of Rome and as the leader of the entire universal Church. He is also called the "Vicar of Christ," the Church's visible head. Another title the pope has received from Saint Peter is "Pastor of the universal Church." Jesus not only gave Peter power over the Church, but he also told Peter to be a pastor, or shepherd, and to "feed my sheep" (*John 21:17*).

Jesus gave all of the Apostles power to lead the Church under Saint Peter. This power has been handed down directly from the Apostles to the pope and bishops of the Church today. This is called **apostolic succession**. We can trace the leadership of the Church all the way back to Jesus, Saint Peter, and the Apostles. This is a big part of our Tradition.

WHERE IT HAPPENED

JUST OUTSIDE the Zion Gate of the old city in Jerusalem is an ancient building known as the Cenacle. Jesus and the Apostles ate the Last Supper in the Upper Room of the Cenacle. Fifty days later, the Apostles and Mary were gathered in the Cenacle when the Holy Spirit came upon them.

Harrod's Gate
Lion's Gate
Damascus Gate
Golden Gate
Church of the Holy Sepulchre
Dome of the Rock
New Gate
As-Aksa Mosque
Western Wall
Jaffa Gate
Jerusalem
Zion Gate

ACTIVITY

SHARE YOUR FAITH Read the parable in **Matthew 7:24–27**. Do you think Jesus might have had this parable in mind when he called Simon a "Rock"? What kinds of floods and storms has the Church had to endure? What kind of strength do you think Jesus knew the Church would need in the future? Share your thoughts with one another or draw a picture symbolizing the Church built on a rock, standing up against powerful forces.

TEACHING FROM THE APOSTLES

 Focus Where do the Church's teachings come from?

Someone somewhere had to create or come up with the important things we say or do. This is especially true about our Tradition, which all starts with one person—Jesus.

Jesus taught the Apostles about God's kingdom while he was with them. After his Resurrection and Ascension, Jesus sent the Holy Spirit to continue teaching them. Everything Jesus entrusted to them, the Apostles handed down to the whole Church by their preaching and writing. Until Christ returns at the end of time, the Church faithfully hands down his teachings to all generations.

The living teaching authority of the Church is called the **magisterium**. It is the authority held by Peter and all the Apostles, and passed on to each pope and bishop down through the generations. The magisterium authentically and faithfully interprets God's Word as it is given to us in Scripture and Church Tradition. To this day, the college of bishops in union with the pope, as bishop of Rome, are the authentic teachers who pass on the faith to the People of God and make pronouncements on moral questions.

The most important teachings from the Church are **infallible**, free from error. That is, when the pope, as head of the magisterium, speaks officially on a matter of faith or morals that is to be believed by everyone in the Church, his teaching is infallible. This infallibility also extends to the full body of bishops when they teach, in union with the pope, about faith and morals, most especially in ecumenical councils. We can trust that it comes from Christ because he has handed on his teaching authority and sent the guidance of the Holy Spirit to the pope and bishops today through the ages from the Apostles. This is why we say that one of the marks of the Church is that it is apostolic.

 What are some ways you have benefited from the teaching office of the Church?

Creeds From the beginning of the Church, believers have professed their faith using summaries called *creeds*. The word *creed* comes from a word meaning "to give my heart to." The early Church professed faith using the Apostles' Creed, which represents the teaching of the Apostles. The Apostles' Creed is said during some Masses with younger children, and a version of it is used in the Sacrament of Baptism.

The other main creed is the Nicene Creed, which was written at the Council of Nicaea in A.D. 325. The Council of Constantinople added even more detail to the Creed later, in A.D. 381. We profess the Creed at Sunday Mass.

Unity Amid Diversity

The Christian churches of the world can be spoken of as a world Christian family. But not every Christian is a member of the Catholic Church. There are Christian denominations that are not in union with the pope, but they share some of the same important beliefs about Jesus. Only the Catholic Church contains all the teachings of Christ handed on directly to us from Peter and the Apostles to the pope and the bishops. But we hope for and work toward unity among all Christians. We do this by praying together, discussing what we have in common, respecting one another, and learning more about what other Christians believe.

Of course, down through the ages, the Church has grown to be a worldwide community, and there is a lot of diversity in the ways people worship and express their faith. How can we be sure that a particular group professing to be Christian is in union with the Catholic Church? We can look to the group's fidelity to apostolic Tradition: Is it in union with the pope and bishops? Does it carry on the faith and the sacraments that came from Christ through his Apostles? If a Christian community does all of this, it is in union with the Catholic Church.

LOOKING BACK

Why is the Nicene Creed so much longer than the Apostles' Creed? At the time the Nicene Creed was written (A.D. 325), there were heresies (false teachings) being spread that Jesus was not really a man, but was God who made himself look like a man; or that Jesus did not exist before he was born.

The pope and bishops met together in several councils at Nicaea and Constantinople expressly to answer these heresies. They declared that Jesus Christ is both true God and true man. The councils wrote the Nicene Creed with very clearly defined details, which stated this belief once and for all.

ACTIVITY

CONNECT YOUR FAITH Choose two or three statements of faith from the Nicene Creed on page 301, and think about how you can demonstrate these beliefs in your everyday life. How can you show them this week?

CATHOLICS TODAY

THE WORK OF THE APOSTLES

Focus How do ordained ministers continue the work of the Apostles?

As the Church grew, the Apostles ordained more bishops who later ordained priests, deacons, and more new bishops. The line of succession from the Apostles has never been broken. People still come to faith in Christ through the pope, bishops, priests, and deacons.

Saint Paul reminds us that God wills that everyone be saved, but it cannot happen unless someone is sent to preach the Good News:

✝ SCRIPTURE "For, 'Everyone who calls on the name of the Lord shall be saved.' But how are they to call on one in whom they have not believed? And how are they to believe in one of whom they have never heard? And how are they to hear without someone to proclaim him? And how are they to proclaim him unless they are sent?"

—Romans 10:13–15

The Sacrament of Holy Orders is "the sacrament of apostolic ministry." The mission Christ gave to his Apostles continues in the Church until the end of time through this sacrament. We speak of *orders*, instead of just one order, because Holy Orders are conferred in three degrees: bishops, presbyters (priests), and deacons. All three are necessary for the Church's mission to be carried out.

 What would be missing in the Catholic Church today if we didn't have each of these orders?

Bishop The bishop receives the fullness of the Sacrament of Holy Orders. He was first ordained a deacon and then a priest. Under the authority of the pope, he is the visible head of the particular Church entrusted to him.

The bishop is the chief teacher, shepherd, and priest for his particular Church, called a **diocese**. Each diocese is divided into smaller faith communities called "parishes." The bishop acts as Christ's representative.

He oversees the celebration of all seven of the sacraments and confers Holy Orders on deacons, priests, and other bishops.

Priest Presbyters, or priests belong to the second degree of Holy Orders. A priest can celebrate most of the sacraments; however, he cannot confer the Sacrament of Holy Orders. Under certain circumstances, a priest can confirm.

Priests share the dignity of priesthood with their bishops, but they also depend on the bishops to delegate them to act as priests in the diocese. Priests are called to be the bishops' co-workers. Each priest receives the charge of a parish or some other ministry.

Deacon Deacons belong to the third degree of Holy Orders. A deacon is ordained for tasks of service to the Church. They have a special role in the ministry of the Word (Scripture), the worship of the Church, works of charity and service, and outreach to the community. A deacon can preside at the Sacrament of Baptism and witness at Matrimony.

🔹 **To which diocese do you belong? Who is your bishop?**

🔹 **Who are some priests and deacons you know?**

ACTIVITY

LIVE YOUR FAITH Does your own parish have a full-time pastor or does your parish share a pastor with another parish? Do you have more than one priest in your parish? Make a list of the ways priests serve your parish. Write a question you would like to ask your priest about his role.

IN SUMMARY

CATHOLICS BELIEVE

The Church is apostolic, continuing the mission Christ gave to his Apostles.

▶ Jesus named Peter to be head of his Church and gathered the rest of the Apostles as a united "college" to help lead it. The pope is the direct successor of Peter as head of the Church, and the bishops are direct successors of the Apostles.

▶ The Church continues to teach the truth of Christ and his Church through the magisterium—the pope, and bishops in union with him, guided by the Holy Spirit.

▶ Particular Churches, or dioceses, are led by bishops, who appoint priests to be pastors and deacons to perform important works of service.

CELEBRATE

PRAYER FOR HELP

Leader 1: Let us take this time to allow the Holy Spirit to enter our hearts,
and lead us as children of light.

All: Call us to hear the voices that challenge!

Leader 1: Father of us all,
through your Son, Jesus,
you called friends and disciples,
servants and teachers, to spread your word,
your "good news," and your mission.
We want to be called
to reach out to others and serve in your name.

All: Call us to hear the voices that challenge!

Leader 2: Lord,
through those saints and leaders who have gone before us,
your story continues
to heal, to teach, to spread hope through all the world.
We want to be called
to keep sharing the message of your love and your care.

All: Call us to hear the voices that challenge!

Leader 1: Father,
you have chosen us to be your "Church,"
a living, breathing, spirit-filled community,
that challenges all to live with passion and joy,
care and compassion,
and to spread the good news and hope
that you bring meaning to life.
Call us to be your voices that challenge,
like your Son, Jesus,
and those who follow him,
and keep the story alive.

We ask this through your Son, Jesus,
our Lord. Amen.

 "Voices That Challenge"
David Haas, © 1990, GIA Publications, Inc.

REVIEW

A Work with Words Circle the letter of the choice that best completes the sentence.

1. The most important Church teachings about faith and morals are _____, free from error.
   - **a.** apostolic
   - **b.** infallible
   - **c.** Papal law
   - **d.** Tradition

2. The living teaching authority of the Church is called the _____.
   - **a.** magisterium
   - **b.** Tradition
   - **c.** Scriptures
   - **d.** apostolic succession

3. The particular Church that is led by a bishop is called a _____.
   - **a.** vicar
   - **b.** presbyter
   - **c.** parish
   - **d.** diocese

4. _____, or priests, belong to the second degree of Holy Orders.
   - **a.** Presbyters
   - **b.** Deacons
   - **c.** Bishops
   - **d.** Cardinals

5. Because of _____, we can trace the leadership of the Church all the way back to Jesus, Saint Peter, and the Apostles.
   - **a.** tradition
   - **b.** Scripture
   - **c.** Papal infallibility
   - **d.** apostolic succession

B Check Understanding Complete each sentence with the correct terms from the word bank at right.

6. The pope, as the successor to Saint Peter and the leader of the entire universal Church, is called the _____.

7. To this day, the _____ in union with the _____ are the authentic teachers who pass on the faith to the People of God and make pronouncements on moral questions.

8. From the beginning of the Church, believers have professed their faith using summaries called _____.

9. A _____, a position of honor, is a part of a college that elects a new pope.

10. _____, who are ordained for tasks of service to the Church, belong to the third degree of Holy Orders.

Word Bank

cardinal
College of Bishops
creeds
presbyters
Vicar of Christ
pope
Tradition
Archbishop
deacons

C Make Connections: Explain Write a one-paragraph response to the question below.

What is the importance of apostolic succession to the Church and to you personally?

141

OUR CATHOLIC FAITH

WHAT NOW?

★ Take time to learn about the teachers of the Church, the pope, bishops, and priests in your area.

★ Think about the elements of the Creed and pray for guidance to live these beliefs.

★ Learn and live by the teachings and guidance that the Church offers.

★ Pray for vocations and pray for those in leadership of the Church.

ACTIVITY

LIVE YOUR FAITH Look up the story of one of the great popes of the past. You might try Pope John Paul II, Pope Paul VI, Pope John XXIII, or Pope Saint Pius X. When did this pope live? What did he teach the Church? In what special way did he lead the Church?

_____

_____

_____

_____

▶ Get an issue or two of your diocesan newspaper. What does it tell you about the universal Church? About your diocese? List some information you gathered about the bishop and the diocese. Is there anything in the paper about your parish or a parish near you?

_____

_____

_____

_____

 Visit www.harcourtreligion.com for more family and community connections.

 **PRAYER**

Jesus, may the wisdom of your Church guide my actions each day. Amen.

Saint Peter Damien

By the eleventh century A.D., the Church was a thousand years old. It had begun to experience "growing pains." Significant changes were taking place within its structure, its practices, and how it defined its role in society. This was the time of the Great Schism, when the Eastern and Western branches of the Church went their separate ways. The issue of priestly celibacy was being defined, and corrupt practices within the Church were open and widespread.

Saint Peter Damien was among those seeking to keep the Church focused on its mission of continuing the work begun by our Lord and carried on by his Apostles, despite the changes that were taking place.

As a young adult, Peter Damien became a Benedictine monk. He lived a strict, self-sacrificing life spending his time in prayer and learning. He spent most of his life in and around Ravenna, Italy, a worldly seaport on the Adriatic Sea.

Peter Damien saw ordinary people and church officials engaged in practices that violated Church principles. He lashed out in writings and speeches at corrupt practices, especially simony, buying and selling high Church official positions. He also defended celibacy at a time when many priests and bishops were married and had families. One of his best-known quotes is "Let us faithfully transmit to posterity the example of virtue which we have received from our forefathers."

He preferred a secluded, monastic life, but Peter's intelligence and gifts for diplomacy and organization made several popes ask for his help. He was often called upon to mediate disputes between religious orders, government officials, and within the Church structure itself. Rival cities questioned the authority of Rome. Peter was sent as a papal legate to persuade them to acknowledge the Pope as the Church's head.

A prolific writer, Peter Damien wrote about the saints and important topics. He also wrote poetry. He was appointed Cardinal of Ostia in 1057. He continued to resolve disputes among clergy and keep the Church intact during a time of schism.

In 1072, after preventing the excommunication of Ravenna's citizens for rebelling against Church authority, Peter Damien died. Although never formally canonized, he was declared a Doctor of the Church in 1828.

▲ **Saint Peter Damien, 1007–1072**

GLOBAL DATA

Ravenna, Italy

- Ravenna dates back to the second millennium B.C. and was the base for the Roman fleet under Emperor Augustus.

- Ravenna was home to St. Vitale Church, one of the best preserved examples of early Byzantine architecture.

- The great poet Danté lived there after his exile from Florence and he died there in 1321.

- Ravenna has a population of about 140,000 today.

11THE CHURCH Is Catholic

INVITE

 **PRAYER** Lord, give me the right words to say.

Why can't I just keep my religious beliefs private? Sometimes I'm really uncomfortable telling somebody what I believe about God and the Church.

"**G**reat game, Carly!" bellowed Mike. "You're going to the end-of-the-season party, aren't you?"

It seemed like the whole soccer team was waiting for Carly's answer. "I can't," she mumbled. All week she had dreaded saying this to her friends. It's not that she minded that much, but she didn't want to hear all their arguments and comments. Maybe they'd let it go without any questions.

Right. The questions started flying. "Are you grounded?" "Are you mad at us?" "Do you have something better to do?"

As a matter of fact, Carly *did* have something better to do. "I'm serving the 5 o'clock Mass. It's for my Aunt Julia."

"Bummer!" Aaron groaned. "Can't you get out of it?"

"I don't want to get out of it," Carly replied. "It's a way of praying for my aunt."

"I don't get it," said Carly's best friend, Annie. "She's already dead. Why keep saying prayers? And if you have to pray, why does it have to be today at that Mass?"

"Catholics always pray for the dead. Especially at Mass. We pray for the living, too," Carly explained. "But I really loved my aunt and I miss her. I believe my prayers will help her."

Annie didn't respond, but she looked serious as she listened to her friend.

"Go for it, then," said Mike. "And say a prayer for me!" he grinned.

"Hey, you need more than prayer. You need a *miracle*," teased Aaron.

ACTIVITY

LET'S BEGIN Why did Carly dread telling her friends she was missing the party? How do you think her friends felt about what she said?

▶ **When have you tried to explain something about your Catholic faith to one of your friends? What was it like? Hard? Easy? Did the other person understand?**

_____

_____

_____

_____

BELIEVERS SPREAD THE GOOD NEWS

◎ Focus Am I willing to tell other people about Jesus and his Church?

Sometimes talking about your faith is easy and natural. Sometimes it feels awkward. Sometimes it feels competitive—or preachy. When it comes to talking about your Catholic faith, speak simply and from your heart. When you speak from the heart about what you believe, like Carly did, others tend to respect it—whether they get it or not. Talking about God comes with being a disciple.

Evangelists The four authors of the Gospels—Matthew, Mark, Luke, and John—are called "the Four Evangelists." They were certainly bearers of the Good News, and that is what it means to be an evangelist.

Did you know that one of the very first evangelists was a woman? Before any of the Gospels were written, she brought an entire town to meet Jesus. She was willing to share what she knew, even though many of the townspeople did not like her very much.

She became known as the Woman at the Well, a Samaritan woman Jesus met while he was traveling. (See *John 4:4–42*.) She was a woman with a bad reputation. Jesus knew all about her, and he told her so. He also told her he was the Messiah who could give her life-giving water. An important thing about the Samaritan woman at the well is that she became an evangelist.

▼ *Christ and the Woman at the Well,* by Annibale Carracci (1560–1609)

✚ SCRIPTURE

GO TO THE SOURCE

What did Jesus say to the Samaritan woman? Read **John 4:13–26** to find out.

✚ **SCRIPTURE** "Many Samaritans from that city believed in him because of the woman's testimony, 'He told me everything I have ever done.' So when the Samaritans came to him, they asked him to stay with them; and he stayed there two days. And many more believed because of his word. They said to the woman, 'It is no longer because of what you said that we believe, for we have heard for ourselves, and we know that this is truly the Savior of the world.'"

—*John 4:39–42*

The Samaritan woman believed what Jesus told her and she told others about him. And they came to believe too.

If Jesus came to stay with you, what would you want to ask him and learn from him?

An Urgent Mandate Jesus sends his disciples out with urgency. He says, "For God so loved the world that he gave his only Son, so that everyone who believes in him may not perish but may have eternal life" (*John 3:16*). After his Resurrection Jesus told his Apostles to make disciples of all nations. The Church is the sign of salvation and new life sent by God to all nations in all times to bring the saving message of Jesus to everyone. Salvation can only come through faith in Christ and his Church, so the Church *must* spread the Gospel everywhere. This is her **missionary mandate**.

Christ did not send only the leaders to spread the Gospel. He sent the whole Church. This means he also sent and continues to send *each of us*. There is no other way for us to truly be disciples of Jesus. He expects us to be evangelists.

We might doubt our ability to spread the Good News or be afraid of how people will receive us. Jesus reassures us: "And remember, I am with you always, to the end of the age" (*Matthew 28:20*). He has stayed with his Church down through the ages. He is with us now.

missionary mandate

▶ **Spend time figuring out what you know and believe about your Catholic faith.** *This will make it easier for you to explain it later.*

▶ **Pay attention to when you have felt closest to God.** *This helps you talk from your heart.*

▶ **Make mental notes about the questions you still have.** *This shows that you still want to grow and that you don't have all the answers.*

▶ **Don't try to *sell*, but explain *what* you believe and *why*.** *This will show your respect for others.*

▶ **Ask questions of others.** *This will help you better understand how much your beliefs are different or the same.*

ACTIVITY

SHARE YOUR FAITH Make a list of ways people can tell that you are a Catholic. Think of other Catholics you know. Make a list of ways their faith is visible. What could you change about yourself to make your list longer?

MYSELF   OTHERS

MEANT FOR EVERYONE

Focus Why does the Church want to reach everyone in the world?

GO TO THE SOURCE

Read **Acts 1:8–9** to discover how the Apostles would be able to carry out Jesus' command to be his witnesses.

LOOKING BACK

Saint Paul was a great missionary in the early Church who knew how to approach people whose beliefs were different.

In Acts 17, he visited Athens, Greece. The Greeks worshiped many gods. Paul showed respect for their beliefs, so he was able to use them as a starting point. He told the Athenians: "I even discovered an altar inscribed 'To an Unknown God.' What therefore you unknowingly worship, I proclaim to you."

Paul did not set himself above the Greeks. He said: "From one ancestor [God] made all nations to inhabit the whole earth, and he allotted the times of their existence and the boundaries of the places where they would live, so that they would search for God and perhaps grope for him and find him—though indeed he is not far from each one of us. For 'In him we live and move and have our being'; as even some of your own poets have said" (*Acts 17:26–28*).

The word *catholic* means "universal." When something is universal, it is for everyone. It is total and complete. The word fits the Catholic Church in two ways:

▶ The Church proclaims all the truths of the faith. In the Church we have the total message and everything we need for salvation with nothing left out.

▶ The Church is for everyone. She is sent out to all people everywhere in every time. When Jesus was ascending to his Father, he told his Apostles, "You will be my witnesses in Jerusalem, in all Judea and Samaria, and to the ends of the earth" (*Acts 1:8*).

This is why we say that one of the marks of the Church is that it is "catholic."

Universal Doesn't Mean Identical The Church has to reach out to everyone in the world in order to truly be herself. From the beginning, Jesus wanted the Church to be universal, welcoming of all people, and open to everyone. In order for this to happen, we, like the first disciples, have to spread the message.

Although the Church strives to be universal and reach everyone in the world, she does not have to look and act the same in every place she is established. The Church takes on different cultures, customs, and appearances in each part of the world where she puts down roots. The rich variety of liturgical traditions and cultural expressions of the faith are part of the Church's great glory.

❓ When have you been to a Catholic church different from your own parish and found some things to be exactly the same as your home parish and some things to be a bit different?

❓ What do you think is the same in all Catholic parishes, no matter where they are?

Everything Needed The Catholic Church has *every-thing* needed to be reconciled with God and to be made one with him. The Fathers of Vatican Council II listed all that is needed for salvation:

▶ correct and complete instruction in the faith

▶ full sacramental life of all seven sacraments

▶ ordained ministry that follows in direct succession from the Apostles

These things can only be found completely in the Catholic Church. People who are not members of the Church *can* be saved—but only because of the grace of God present in the Church.

ACTIVITY

CONNECT YOUR FAITH Write down some ways the Church is for everyone, welcoming all people, and going out to people everywhere. Then, show how your parish acts in the same way on a local level.

THE UNIVERSAL CHURCH

MY PARISH

MISSIONARY CHURCH

 Focus How does the Church carry out her missionary mandate?

God, in his great love, wants everyone to know and love him. Everyone who searches for the truth is on the way to salvation, but the whole truth has been given to the Church. So, the Church goes out to those seeking the truth, offering them salvation through faith in Christ.

The Church has been missionary from the very beginning and continues to be so today.

Missionary work requires patience; it doesn't succeed overnight! The Church acts like water on a seed—a whole tree doesn't grow instantaneously. It gradually leads people to Christ in these stages

▶ proclamation of the Gospel to nonbelievers

▶ establishment of Christian communities

▶ foundation of local churches

Missionaries enter into "respectful dialogue" with those who do not yet accept the Gospel. They respect other traditions and cultures and try to incorporate symbols and traditions of cultures into the way they teach about the Gospel.

Catholic missionaries have been among the greatest world explorers. Missionaries have found isolated tribes, explored unmapped lands, and gained new knowledge about cultures, languages, and even plant and animal life from distant places.

Missionaries help people needing food, shelter, medical care, education, and even protection from war and violence. Catholic missionaries are lay people, deacons, priests, bishops, or religious brothers and sisters. They work in every country in the world today, and are often in danger. There have been missionaries martyred in every land and time, including now.

Why is it important for missionaries to respect other religions and cultures?

Everyone Is Called You might be called to become a missionary someday. If not, you are *still* called to be part of the Church's missionary work—in fact, all Catholics are! One of the Patron Saints of Missionaries is Saint Therese of Lisieux, who never left her convent!

Where in the World

India	Saint Francis Xavier	1542
Canada/Northern United States	Saint Isaac Jogues	1640s
Ireland	Saint Patrick	circa 415
Colombia, South America	Saint Peter Claver	1610
Hawaii	Blessed Damian	1864
Eastern United States	Saint Frances Cabrini	1889
Southwest United States	Saint Katherine Drexel	1894

 If you could be a missionary in a distant land, where would you go? What kind of work would you do to help people? Find out about the life of one of the missionaries listed here.

Her prayers for the missions contributed so much that she has been recognized as a missionary herself. There are many opportunities to share in the missionary work of the Church with prayers and donations, and even projects in your local area.

 Visit **www.harcourtreligion.com** to learn more about missionary activities and for links to different missionary sites.

ACTIVITY

LIVE YOUR FAITH Design a poster showing the missionary activity of the Church. Write a prayer for missionaries and pray it with your family.

IN SUMMARY

CATHOLICS BELIEVE

As members of the Church, we are called to proclaim the Good News of Christ to the world.

▶ All Church members are called to be evangelists, to be bearers of the Good News.

▶ The Church is universal, going out to the whole world, welcoming people of all cultures and ages.

▶ Missionaries continue Christ's mission of healing and bring the message of salvation to people who have not yet come to know and believe in Jesus. Each of us is called to share in the missionary work of the Church.

PRAYER OF ACKNOWLEDGEMENT

Leader: God calls all of us, his disciples,
to be saints.
Let us listen well to the words of Jesus.

Reader 1: Be attentive to the wisdom of the Gospel according to Matthew.

Read Matthew 28:19–20.
(At the conclusion, pause for silent reflection; then continue with the following:)

Reader 2: Let us pray.
O God, give us the strength we need,
to take up the cause of those
who so willingly gave their
lives to serve others.

All: We will go out and tell the Good News.

Reader 3: God of light,
help us to see as you would
want us to see.

All: We will go out and tell the Good News.

Reader 4: God of all goodness and mercy,
open our hearts to be compassionate,
open our minds to understand the needs of others.

All: We will go out and tell the Good News.

Leader: God,
we know and believe
that you have chosen us
to be your servants,
your missionaries,
your saints.
Help us to respond to your call;
help us to receive this challenge
with confidence and trust
knowing you are with us.
We ask this through your Son,
who is Jesus Christ, our friend and brother.
Amen.

 "Go Out To All the World"
Derek Campbell, © 2002, GIA Publications, Inc.

REVIEW

A **Work with Words** Complete each sentence with the correct term.

1. Matthew, Mark, Luke, and John are called "the Four _____" because they were bearers of the Good News.

2. Jesus told the Apostles to make _____ of all nations.

3. Because salvation can only come through faith in Christ and his Church, the Church has a _____ to spread the Gospel.

4. The Church is _____ or "universal" because she is sent on a mission to the whole world.

5. Jesus told his Apostles, "You will be my _____ in Jerusalem, throughout Judea and Samaria, and to the ends of the earth."

B **Check Understanding** Indicate whether the following statements are true or false. Then rewrite false statements to make them true.

_____ 6. In the Catholic Church we find everything we need for salvation with nothing left out.

_____

_____ 7. Full sacramental life of all seven sacraments is present in the Catholic Church.

_____

_____ 8. The Church looks and acts the same in everyplace she exists.

_____

_____ 9. Christian communities and local churches play a critical role in leading people to Christ.

_____

_____ 10. Many great world explorers have been Catholic missionaries.

_____

C **Make Connections: Analyze** Write a one-paragraph response to the question.

God has called you to be an evangelist. Who do you know who needs to hear some Good News? Write about some specific ways you can share your faith with this person.

OUR CATHOLIC FAITH

WHAT NOW?

★ Study, know, and live your faith so that you can share it with others.

★ Pray for the grace to be a good example of a Catholic.

★ Reflect on how you live your faith and decide if there is anything you should change so you can be a better evangelist.

★ Decide how you can share in the missionary work of the Church right now. Choose a mission to pray for. Think of ways you can help that mission financially.

ACTIVITY

LIVE YOUR FAITH The universal nature of the Church represents our welcoming all. Who do you need to be more welcoming to?

▶ **Form groups of three and role-play talking about God. Pick any two or three of these phrases to get you started:**

The closest I have felt to _____ in the last six months was . . .

My favorite Catholic symbol is _____ because . . .

My favorite Catholic season is _____ because . . .

I sometimes wonder if God . . .

One thing I still don't understand about being Catholic is . . .

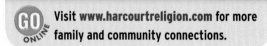 Visit www.harcourtreligion.com for more family and community connections.

 **PRAYER**

Jesus, be with me as I share your message.

PEOPLE OF FAITH

Saint Josefina (Josephine) Bakhita

When Josefina Bakhita was kidnapped and sold into slavery at a very young age, she couldn't have known then that it was part of God's plan for her. When she grew up, she realized it had been his plan, so that she could come to know him and spread the Good News about God and his Church.

Born in 1868 to a wealthy family in the Darfur region of Sudan, then under the control of Egypt, Josefina was kidnapped and sold into slavery when she was nine years old. Over the next six years, she would be sold and resold to many masters in the slave markets of Khartoum and El Obied. She endured beatings and other forms of abuse, including a painful process of tattooing that she later described in detail in her memoirs. This harsh life must not have seemed like a plan of God at first.

But the Lord helped her escape. In 1883 she was bought by the Italian consul, Callisto Legnani. He brought her to Italy to work as a nanny for a family he knew. Treated kindly, Josefina grew to love the country, and she converted to Christianity five years after her arrival. Within three years, knowing she was destined for a religious life, she was allowed to enter the Institute of Canossian Daughters of Charity in Venice.

For fifty years, she shared her faith generously with those who were less fortunate. Her gentle presence, her warm voice, and her willingness to help with any task comforted the poor and suffering people who came to the door of the Institute. After a biography about her was published in 1930, she became a sought-after speaker, raising funds to support missions.

Proclaiming the Good News of the Lord and eloquently verbalizing his praises, she said, "Seeing the sun, the moon, and the stars, I said to myself, 'Who could be the Master of these beautiful things?' I felt a great desire to see him, to know him, and to pay him homage."

She expressed her joy in the Good News of the Church. "O, Lord," she cried, "if I could fly to my people and tell them of Your Goodness at the top of my voice, oh, how many souls would be won!" A very forgiving woman, she once said that she would "kiss the hands" of those who sold her into slavery because it resulted in her becoming a Christian.

Sister Josefina, who later took the name Sister Moretta, died in 1947 in Italy. She was canonized by Pope John Paul II in 2000 and is considered the Patron Saint for believers in Sudan.

▲ Saint Josefina Bakhita, 1868–1947

GLOBAL DATA

Sudan

- At nearly one million square miles, Sudan is the largest nation in area on the African continent.

- Sudan is about 70 percent Muslim, 25 percent native beliefs, and roughly 5 percent Christian.

- Khartoum, the capital and largest city, is located at the junction of the Blue Nile and White Nile rivers.

- The Darfur region, where Josefina Bakhita was born, is one of the poorest and most disease-ridden areas in the world today.

The CHRISTIAN Faithful

PRAYER Be with all of those who serve the Church.

Is it all about going to Mass?
I didn't know my parish did so many things.
What is my place in the Catholic Church?

"**S**hoot, I left today's Church bulletin in the car. Would you go out and bring it in for me?" Jack's mom was at her desk, writing in her appointment book and on a calendar she always kept posted on the fridge.

"Sure," he said. "A new month, a new calendar, right?" Jack knew his mom and her schedules. Ever since he had been little, he had watched as she kept that calendar posted and filled with activities. He had learned about the days of the week and months of the year by watching her change it and talk about them.

"Yes and I'm coordinating all our schedules. I think your dad has a Knights of Columbus meeting that moved to Tuesday this week, and the choir has some extra practice times scheduled."

Jack scanned the bulletin as he stepped back into the house. It was like reading a small magazine! "Dad's meeting is on Tuesday, and so is my Altar Server meeting. We can spend some time together before and after. The religion classes for the twins and me are the same as always." He kept reading: training for visitors to the sick, RCIA, . . . a lot going on that he'd never heard of. "I bet our building has a big electric bill!" he joked.

"I didn't realize there was so much going on in the parish. It must take a lot of people to do all of these things."

ACTIVITY

LET'S BEGIN What can you tell about Jack's parish from this story? What does being Catholic mean to Jack and his family?

▶ **What organizations and ministries does your parish have? What do you know about them? How are you and your family involved in the life of your parish?**

_____

_____

_____

_____

PRIESTLY PEOPLE

Focus How are all Church members important to the Church?

Your parish is full of people who are involved in different ways. Your faith family offers many things for its members, for the local community, and probably around the world. With so many tasks, it takes a lot more than the parish priest to support such a thriving community.

The Apostles recognized that it was important to divide responsibilities in the early Church. As more and more members joined, there was more work to be done. We learn from the sixth chapter of the Acts of the Apostles that some new Christians were concerned that poor widows were being neglected. The Apostles realized they needed help.

Priests, Prophets, and Kings Every member of the Church has an important role to play in carrying out the Church's mission. We all share in the priestly, prophetic, and kingly offices of Christ; he wants *all* of us to be priests, prophets, and kings. Our roles differ depending on our state in life and our circumstances, but we are all called to help bring the Good News to the world. As diverse as the Church is, we are united by our mission.

Jesus gives us these roles; they are not honors we have earned. When Jesus showed us what a king should do, he showed us the job of a shepherd taking care of a flock of sheep. When he showed us how to be in charge, he got down on the floor and washed the feet of each Apostle and then told them to do the same. (See *John 13:3–15.*)

Common Priesthood When you were baptized you became part of the common priesthood of the faithful, sharing in the priesthood of Christ. As you pray and discover what God wants you to do with your life, you will be called to be part of the laity or the clergy.

❓ **What roles have you noticed people have in the Church? How are they all part of the same mission?**

CLERGY

Ordained and given sacred authority to serve the Church by
- ▶ teaching
- ▶ divine worship
- ▶ pastoral leadership

LAITY

Serve as priest/prophet/king in
- ▶ personal life
- ▶ family life
- ▶ social life and parish

clergy

laity

evangelical counsels

Consecrated religious life is a special vocation in the Church that draws members from both the clergy and the laity. Priests, lay men, and lay women answer the call to become members of one of the many religious communities in the Church. They make public vows of poverty, chastity, and obedience.

The Church's Hierarchy From that earliest division of Church leadership started by the Apostles, we have come to a more complex division of leaders called the "hierarchy." Each member of the Church's hierarchy has clearly defined roles and responsibilities. They are ordained to serve the Church.

▶ The pope has "supreme, full, immediate, and universal power in the care of souls."

▶ Bishops share with the pope concern for all the Churches, but they are the visible successors of the Apostles in their own dioceses. The bishops must authentically teach the faith, celebrate divine worship, and guide their Churches as true pastors.

▶ Priests—by their ordination into the ministerial priesthood—have sacred authority for the service of the faithful. They help their bishops by teaching, conducting worship, and governing in the name and the person of Christ in the community.

▶ Deacons are ordained not to the ministerial priesthood but to ministry of works of service to the community. They assist the bishops and priests in worship, especially in proclaiming the Gospel and preaching, in presiding at baptisms, marriages, and funerals, and in dedicating themselves to different works of charity and outreach to the parish and beyond.

ACTIVITY

SHARE YOUR FAITH Describe someone you have seen faithfully serving your parish. What role does this person play? What can you tell about this person based on what you have observed?

THE LAY FAITHFUL

Focus What is the role of the laity in the Catholic Church?

Without faithful Catholic lay men and women, there could be no Church. Everyone who is baptized is called to be holy. In both Baptism and Confirmation, all Catholics receive grace to help them lead holy lives. By cooperating with God's grace, all Christians can be faithful to Christ in all aspects of their lives—personal, family, social, and parish.

✝ SCRIPTURE

GO TO THE SOURCE
Read **Matthew 13:31–32** and compare its parable to the Parable of the Yeast in **Matthew 13:33.**

Leaven in the Heart of the World Community Lay people work in offices, factories, schools, farms, labs, stores, and any number of other busy places. Many do not spend their entire day focusing on religious matters, but they are called to bring their faith with them into all parts of their lives. The *Catechism of the Catholic Church* says lay people "are called to be witnesses to Christ in all circumstances and at the very heart of the community of mankind." Some lay people serve the Church in full- or part-time ministry. They are called "lay ecclesial ministers."

Jesus described those who serve the kingdom of heaven as *leaven*, which means to lighten or raise something, much like yeast makes bread rise. (See *Matthew 13:33*.) Lay people are called to be like "leaven in the world."

> ❓ Think about a finished loaf of bread. Can you take it apart and find the yeast in it? How can we know the yeast is there?

> ❓ What are some ways you have seen lay people bring Christ to someone or someplace?

The Laity at Worship The clergy lead the worship of the Church, but there are liturgical roles for the laity, too. Perhaps you are already performing some of them. Lay people can be altar servers, readers at Mass (lectors) and other sacraments, cantors and/or choir members, organists, or extraordinary ministers of the Holy Communion.

All of these roles help the assembly give praise and thanks to God during the Mass and other sacraments. Roles such as greeters and ushers, although not liturgical, help to bring people into the celebration.

Other Parish Ministries It is hard to imagine a parish today where the priests do all the work! It takes a whole community with many different gifts and talents to accomplish the mission of a parish. In addition to liturgical ministry roles, lay men and women volunteer their time and talents to serve the Church. They may have busy secular (nonreligious) jobs, but they can be found on weekends and at other times in the week helping at the parish.

Keep your eyes open to see how things get done at your parish. Who decorates the sanctuary? Who washes the altar linens? Who teaches religious education classes? Who ministers in Catholic schools? Who visits the sick and shut-ins? Who answers the phone, shovels snow, or counts money? Every time you see your parents or other lay people doing any of these things, you are seeing the laity helping accomplish the mission of the Church. Every time you help out in any way, you are part of the mission, too.

❓ What ministries have you and members of your family been part of in your parish liturgies?

❓ What roles would you like to try in the future?

CATHOLICS TODAY

Some lay women and men make Church ministry their life's work. Instead of working in the secular world, lay Church ministers work in parishes or dioceses.

▶ Lay people might be directors of religious education, teachers, or principals of Catholic schools, youth ministers, parish business managers, ministers to the elderly, ministers in Catholic social agencies, or directors of diocesan offices.

▶ In parishes without a priest, there are often lay pastoral administrators who manage the daily life of the parish while a visiting priest comes to celebrate the sacraments. Lay ministers receive special training. They serve the Church in vital ways, working in accord with the bishop and their pastor.

ACTIVITY

CONNECT YOUR FAITH Write a paragraph finishing this phrase:

By my Baptism, I was called to serve . . . _____

_____

_____

_____

_____

CONSECRATED LIFE

 Focus Why do some people decide to become religious priests, brothers, or sisters?

CHECK THIS OUT!

No matter what job you take or career you follow, you can live the life of a faithful Catholic. There are many ways to be faithful: some are called to priesthood, some are called to married life, some are called to be part of a religious congregation, others are called to live as a single person. As a young person, you should pay attention to God speaking to you in your heart to see what he is calling you to do.

To live our vocation is to be who we truly are. Ask the Holy Spirit to guide you to know what your vocation in life will be.

At Baptism, Jesus calls every disciple to follow him. Some Catholic men and women find Christ calling them to a different kind of dedication. They want to be more closely united with him, devoting their entire lives to God. These people choose some form of consecrated religious life so they can dedicate themselves "more intimately to God's service and to the good of the whole church."

People who live a consecrated religious life make a public vow or promise to follow the **evangelical counsels** of poverty, chastity, and obedience. They join a religious order or congregation, that is, a vowed community of people carrying out the Church's mission.

These three special gifts—poverty, chastity, and obedience—are not commands. The commandments tell us what we *must* do. The evangelical counsels tell us what *more* we can do beyond what is required. Consecrated religious men and women understand these gifts in a particular way and vow to live these three counsels. For consecrated religious, these vows have these meanings:

▶ Poverty: owning nothing in one's own name

▶ Chastity: giving oneself to God completely by living a celibate life for the sake of the Kingdom

▶ Obedience: promising to serve God and neighbor in one's religious community

In this way they are free to serve God wholeheartedly.

Think about your possessions. What do you own that might be keeping you from being close to Jesus?

Many Forms of Religious Life There are many forms of religious life. All through history, there have been men and women who felt a call to religious life in response to events and needs in the world around them. Some individuals felt led to gather other like-minded people around them to form religious communities.

The founders of religious orders established a way of life that others could follow. They generally set up a rule for all members to follow, selected the ministries to be done, and appealed to the bishop, or sometimes the pope, to recognize their group as an official religious community in the Church. Lay women religious are often called "sisters." Lay men religious are called "brothers." Priests who join religious orders are called "fathers," as all priests are.

Some members of these religious orders live a cloistered and contemplative life. They remain in one convent or monastery without traveling outside its walls, dedicating their lives to prayer for everyone in the world and to the study and preservation of Scripture and other religious texts. Often, cloistered women are called "nuns" and cloistered men are called "monks."

Other members live in active religious communities, where they go out to serve as missionaries, teachers, or hospital workers, and to do many other good works.

 What memories do you have of a faith-filled sister, brother, or priest?

ACTIVITY

LIVE YOUR FAITH List three things that would be appealing to you about living the consecrated religious life.

1. _____

2. _____

3. _____

▶ **Write a prayer for those who have accepted the call to live as a priest, sister, or brother.**

IN SUMMARY

CATHOLICS BELIEVE

All baptized Catholics are called to be priests, prophets, and kings to serve the mission of the Church, but there are different roles in serving.

▶ The pope and bishops belong to the Church's hierarchy, and lead the priests, deacons, religious communities, and the lay faithful. Priests serve in the ministerial priesthood and assist bishops in their

role of teaching, governing, and sanctifying. Deacons assist the bishop and priests in sacramental ministries and the ministry of service.

▶ The laity in the Church act as leaven, bringing the raising and lightening power of God's kingdom to the secular world where they live and work.

▶ Members of religious orders consecrate their lives as a sign of God's love and holiness and serve an important part of the Church's mission.

CELEBRATE

WISDOM PSALM

Leader: O Lord, open my lips.

All: That my mouth shall proclaim your praise.

Leader: Lord,
You have given each of us gifts and talents that can benefit others.
You call us to echo your word and your love in the world.
Help us to understand your wisdom and your teachings.

Amen.

Side 1:   How can young people keep their way pure?
By guarding it according to your word.
With my whole heart I seek you;
do not let me stray from your commandments.

Side 2:   The Lord is my portion;
I promise to keep your words.
I implore your favor with all my heart;
be gracious to me according to your promise.

All: Your word is a lamp to my feet
and a light to my path.

Side 1:   Your hands have made and fashioned me;
give me understanding that I may learn your commandments.
Those who fear you shall see me and rejoice,
because I have hoped in your word.

Side 2:   The Lord exists forever;
your word is firmly fixed in heaven.
Your faithfulness endures to all generations;
you have established the earth, and it stands fast.

All: Your word is a lamp to my feet
and a light to my path.

Psalm 119:9, 10, 57, 58, 73, 74, 89, 90, 105

♪ "Echo of Faith"
David Haas, © 2001, GIA Publications, Inc.

164

REVIEW

A **Work with Words** Circle the letter of the choice that best completes the sentence.

1. People who live a consecrated religious life make a public vow or promise to follow the
_____ of poverty, chastity, and obedience.

   a. Traditions   **b.** religious orders   **c.** evangelical orders   **d.** evangelical counsels

2. _____ are given sacred authority to serve the Church by teaching leadership in divine
worship and pastoral ministry.

   a. Laity   **b.** All ordained clergy   **c.** Nuns   **d.** Professors

3. Cloistered men and women are typically called _____.

   a. religious communities   **b.** clergy   **c.** monks and nuns   **d.** priests and nuns

4. _____ share with the pope concern for all the Churches and are the visible successors
of the Apostles in their own dioceses.

   a. Bishops   **b.** Priests   **c.** Deacons   **d.** Cardinals

5. The _____ serve(s) through their Baptism and Confirmation in personal life, family life,
social life, and parish life.

   a. laity   **b.** clergy   **c.** priest   **d.** monk

B **Check Understanding** Indicate whether the following statements are true or false. Then rewrite false
statements to make them true.

_____ **6.** We all share in the offices of Christ; he wants *all* of us to be priests, prophets, and kings.

_____

_____ **7.** Consecrated religious life is a special vocation in the Church.

_____

_____ **8.** Deacons are ordained to the ministerial priesthood and can preside at the Eucharist.

_____

_____ **9.** Men and women who feel a call to religious life gather with other like-minded people to form
religious communities.

_____

_____ **10.** Some Catholics are baptized into the common priesthood of the faithful.

_____

C **Make Connections: Cause and Effect** Write a one-paragraph response to the questions below.

Think of opportunities to serve in your parish. How have you served or how would you like to serve? What
effects do you think this ministry would have on you and on others?

OUR CATHOLIC FAITH

WHAT NOW?

★ Notice the ways members of your parish Church diaconate act as priests, prophets, and kings.

★ Learn more about the priesthood, the diaconate, and consecrated religious life.

★ Pray for the clergy and religious, and pray for vocations to these committed lifestyles.

★ Ask Jesus how he wants you to live your vocation now.

★ Choose a liturgical ministry you can be part of, if you aren't already. Learn who to contact to volunteer for this ministry and what training you will need.

★ Find ways in your parish that you can be involved in ministries and leadership roles.

ACTIVITY

LIVE YOUR FAITH Think and pray about your own vocation in life. Begin by writing a couple of paragraphs that finish this sentence:

I think I may be called to . . . _____

_____

_____

_____

_____

_____

_____

▶ Visit www.harcourtreligion.com for a link to the *Vision: Catholic Vocation Guide*, a great source of information about different kinds of religious communities. It also includes some neat ways to help you see what things you would do well in the service of the Church.

 Visit www.harcourtreligion.com for more family and community connections.

PRAYER

Lord, help me do right, love goodness, and walk humbly with you.

Blessed Edmund Ignatius Rice

Sometimes ordinary men are called by God to do extraordinary things. The Church, being catholic (universal) in its mission, has many roles for its followers to undertake. Education of the underprivileged is one of those many roles, and that was where Edmund Rice found his calling.

Born into a large family in Kilkenny, Ireland, in 1762, Edmund went to work for his uncle in a large import-export business in Waterford at the age of seventeen. After his uncle died, Edmund inherited the business. By all accounts, he was generous, charitable to the city's poor, and pious in his devotion to Our Lord. Married at the age of twenty-five, he lost his wife only two years later and spent much time caring for their infant daughter alone.

Edmund knew he had a calling to do more for God. He thought about becoming a monk, but a sister of the local bishop chided him for his desire to isolate himself from the world. She pointed to a group of ragged young boys passing by and reportedly said to him, "What! Would you bury yourself in a cell on the continent rather than devote your wealth and your life to the spiritual and material interest of these poor youths?" Inspired by her words, Edmund talked with the local bishop. The bishop advised Rice to take on the mission because he felt God was calling Rice to it. Rice settled his worldly affairs, arranged for the care of his daughter, and around 1800 he began his work of founding Catholic schools for troubled youth.

Edmund took the name "Ignatius," and he founded the Institute of the Brothers of the Christian Schools, better known as "Irish Christian Brothers." His first school, Mt. Sion, opened within two years, and by 1806 he had founded three others. In 1820, Pope Pius VII gave his blessing to the work and confirmed Edmund's group as the first congregation of religious men in Ireland. Brother Rice was unanimously elected superior general by the members. The confirmation of the new institute attracted attention, even outside of Ireland, and many men came and joined him to teach and help. Later he came up with the idea of establishing a "Catholic Model School" to show the universality of the Church.

Before his retirement a few years before his death in 1844, he had founded eleven schools in Ireland, eleven in England, and one in Sydney, Australia. He was beatified by Pope John Paul II in 1996.

▲ **Blessed Edmund Ignatius Rice, 1762–1844**

GLOBAL DATA

Ireland

- Ireland is a 26,600 square mile island to the west of Great Britain.

- Of Ireland's nearly four million people, 93 percent are Roman Catholic.

- Ireland was a center of learning in the early Middle Ages, after the fall of the Roman Empire, and was Christianized by Saint Patrick in the fifth century A.D.

- Ireland was granted its independence from Great Britain in 1922, after many years of often bloody warfare.

Faith in Action!

CATHOLIC SOCIAL TEACHING

DISCOVER

Catholic Social Teaching:
Dignity of Work and the Rights of Workers

IN THIS UNIT you learned about being a priest, prophet, and king; that God, through the prophet Micah, tells us to act justly, love tenderly, and walk humbly with God. This certainly applies to work.

Rights of the Worker

When eighth graders and their parents are thinking about what high school they are going to go to, one of their first concerns often is whether it will help them get into a good college, help them get a good job, and help them make a good salary. Although economic security is an important concern, it's not the bottom line. For Jesus and his Church, the bottom line is participating in God's ongoing work of creation and service to others. Advancing in your education should be about increasing your ability to carry out the reason God created you (your vocation). Work is much more than a job and money. As God's partners in the work of creation, workers have a special dignity that is so much more than the work they do.

But some employers don't treat their workers fairly. That's why the Church has always supported the right of workers to form unions. Every worker has a right to a fair wage and safe working conditions. Some Church leaders have said that a fair wage is a "living wage"—what it takes for a family to have the basic necessities of life. Farm workers in the United States are among those who continue to need the support of individual Christians and our Church institutions. But as Catholics, our concern is universal. Workers all over the world, especially children who are forced to work, need our support.

When you and your family talk about your future, what are you most concerned about?

GOD CALLS US TO ACT when we are confronted with injustice. Let's look at how two young lives made a difference.

FREE THE CHILDREN
"SWEATSHOP FOR A DAY"

In 1987 in Pakistan, four-year-old Iqbal Masih was sold into forced labor at a carpet factory. Iqbal worked fourteen hours a day, six days a week. One day when he was ten years old, Iqbal sneaked out of the factory and went to a rally where he was so inspired that he gave a speech about his hard life. He refused to go back to the factory and started speaking out against child labor. Iqbal's efforts helped to free thousands of other child slaves, which led to his murder in 1995 at the age of twelve.

In Toronto, Ontario, twelve-year-old Craig Kielburger saw a newspaper article entitled "Boy, 12, who spoke out, murdered." Craig started reading about child labor and talked with his classmates. Twenty of them formed a group called Free the Children (FTC). They sent petitions on child labor to government and business leaders, set up public displays, gave speeches, and raised money through car washes and walk-a-thons.

By 2002, FTC had over one hundred thousand members in thirty-five countries, mostly in small local groups. In the St. Cloud (Minnesota) FTC group, youth from Cathedral High School/John XXIII Middle School helped to create a "Sweatshop for a Day" event. For thirteen hours, they sewed and filled hundreds of bags with school supplies donated by their classmates. They sent these to the FTC headquarters in Toronto, where they were sent on to schools in poor countries. One participant said he couldn't believe what child laborers have to go through. "It's been hard to make even one bag." And Free the Children continues to inspire other young people to join in this struggle.

- **What do you think of what Iqbal and Craig did?**

- **Could you see yourself doing something like the students in St. Cloud did?**

- **Would you be willing to start or be part of a Free the Children group in your school? Why or why not?**

▼ Free the Children has begun a global campaign to build primary schools for children in Kenya, Sierra Leone, China, Sri Lanka, and other countries in need of schools.

SERVE Your Community

SERVING OTHERS WITH YOUR TALENTS

Make a list of a dozen jobs that involve serving others and how they serve.

Put a "Y" for "YES" after those professions that appeal to you.

Make a list of your own talents and interests and match them with your list of professions.

Talk your lists over with an adult you respect and ask for comments.

Pray every morning that you will find a way that day to serve someone. If you keep a journal, write about your experience.

SERVING PROFESSIONS	TALENTS/INTERESTS

INJUSTICE IN THE WORKPLACE

Make a list with your classmates of groups of workers in your community, country, and in other parts of the world who are treated unfairly. Have each person research one group and how the class might be able to help them. Be sure that one person finds out if there is a "Free the Children" group in your community. Choose one of these groups and create a plan for helping.

Project Planning Sheet

Others who should be asked to help

_____

_____

Ways to publicize your project

_____

_____

Other specific tasks

_____

_____

Your specific task(s)

_____

_____

Calendar for completing the project

_____

_____

When you think about your future and what you might want to do in life, what are the most important goals? Where does money fit in? Where does serving others fit in? What is most important to you and why?

_____

_____

_____

Did you follow through on the suggestion to find some way to serve others each day?

_____

_____

_____

Why or why not?

_____

_____

_____

What did you learn about yourself in doing the talents activity?

_____

_____

_____

What did you learn about the dignity of work and workers in doing the project?

_____

_____

_____

What did you learn about yourself in doing the project on workers who are treated unfairly?

_____

_____

_____

What did you learn about Jesus and about your faith in doing both projects?

_____

_____

_____

List one thing that might be different about you after doing this project.

_____

_____

_____

REVIEW

A **Work with Words** Match the words on the left with the correct definitions or descriptions on the right.

_____ **1.** apostolic succession

_____ **2.** magisterium

_____ **3.** infallible

_____ **4.** diocese

_____ **5.** presbyters

_____ **6.** catholic

_____ **7.** the clergy

_____ **8.** the laity

_____ **9.** evangelical counsels

_____ **10.** bishops

A. belong to the second degree of Holy Orders

B. those ordained and given sacred authority to serve the Church

C. universal

D. the living, teaching authority of the Church

E. vows of poverty, chastity, and obedience

F. meaning free from error

G. the authority of the pope and bishops traced back to Jesus, Saint Peter, and the other Apostles

H. the visible successors of the Apostles in their dioceses

I. Catholics who serve through Baptism and Confirmation in personal, family, social, and parish life

J. particular Church led by a bishop

B **Check Understanding** Circle the letter of the best answer to complete the following statements.

11. The pope, as the successor to Saint Peter and the leader of the entire universal Church, is called the

_____.

a. Presbyter
b. Deacon of Christ

c. Vicar of Christ
d. Archbishop

12. The _____ are the authentic teachers who pass on the faith to the People of God.

a. College of Bishops
b. pope

c. cardinals
d. both a and b

13. From the beginning of the Church, believers have professed their faith using summaries called

_____.

a. canons
b. creeds

c. doctrines
d. encyclicals

14. Matthew, Mark, Luke, and John are called "the Four _____" because they were bearers of the Good News.

    a. Evangelists   **c.** Heralds

    b. Messengers   **d.** Horsemen

15. In the _____, we can find everything we need for salvation with nothing left out.

    a. Word   **c.** Eucharist

    b. Catholic Church   **d.** Apostles

16. Because salvation can only come through faith in Christ and his Church, the Church has a _____ to spread the Gospel.

    a. missionary mandate   **c.** covenant

    b. missionary creed   **d.** none of the above

17. We all share in the offices of Christ; he wants all of us to be priests, _____, and kings.

    a. disciples   **c.** monks

    b. bishops   **d.** prophets

18. _____ are ordained to tasks of service in the Church.

    a. laity   **c.** priests

    b. bishops   **d.** deacons

. . . .

C Make Connections Write a short answer to these questions.

19. Evaluate. Is the unity of the Catholic Church or the diversity within the Church more important to your personal faith? Explain your answer.

_____

_____

_____

20. Synthesize. What are some of the common elements of the major creeds of the Church? Using these creeds as a model, write a summary of the ways you express and show the faith of the Church.

_____

_____

_____

_____

13 HONORING God

PRAYER Lord, help me to live for you.

*Sometimes I get my priorities messed up.
What's most important in life?
God is really important to me, but how
am I supposed to show it?*

Watching people was one of Jessie's favorite pastimes at school, at the mall, or at baseball games. In her own mind, Jessie put that activity in capital letters—she gave it so much importance. After all, someday she intended to be a reporter. How else would she get there except by "Watching People"?

Jessie got fairly good grades in school. She enjoyed most of her classes and looked forward to school each day. She was glad there was so much variety in the students in her school. Tall, short, big, little, active, quiet—all sorts of ethnic backgrounds and ages—Jessie took note.

Today was no different. She watched as students hustled from one class to the next and the halls flooded with talking, laughing students. *Oh boy*, thought Jessie, *here comes Gloria!* Jessie had realized awhile ago that Gloria always seemed to be in someone's face, creating a stir. It was as if Gloria was constantly upset, taking it out on others, whatever *it* was. So who, she wondered, will be the object of her scorn today?

Gloria was decked out in a loud red blouse. Her fingers held lots of shiny rings, and bracelets jangled on her wrists. The jeweled cross she wore was really big. It was set off even more by the blouse. Gloria attached herself to a small group of students hanging out in front of the cafeteria. Jessie overheard as Gloria dominated the conversation and shared some really nasty gossip about a classmate. The others enjoyed it, laughing. Gloria smirked.

Then someone said, "Cool cross."

ACTIVITY

LET'S BEGIN What's the irony or contradiction here? Is it just as bad to listen and accept gossip as it is to engage in it?

▶ **What percentage of people who wear crosses do you think do so as a real statement of faith?**

▶ **What are some examples of things people your age do that contradict faith in God?**

I AM THE LORD, YOUR GOD

Focus What do we owe God?

Does wearing a cross prove that someone is a Christian? If we say God is our number one priority in life, how do we live so that we aren't the only ones who know it? Do you have to wear a religious item to show that faith is important to you? Do you have to use religious language?

If God is really important to you, how can you show it?

If we really try, we can live like Jesus did, connecting what we say and how we act with what we believe. When we do that, we honor God, who is the source of all that is good.

His Covenant with Us God chose a people for himself long ago—the Israelites—and made a covenant with them. A covenant is a sacred promise. He declared, "I am the LORD your God, who brought you out of the land of Egypt, out of the house of slavery; you shall have no other gods before me" (*Exodus 20:2–3*).

God made an investment in the Israelites and their descendents, who became known as the Jewish people. God honored his covenant and then made a new covenant in Jesus Christ. He promises to take care of us, to give us new life, and he calls us together as his People, the Body of Christ. Our part of the covenant relationship requires that we show that we are God's People. Followers of Christ honor God for the life he gives us and follow the law and Jesus' teachings. An important way we do that is living a life that shows gratitude to God—we owe him everything!

The Ten Commandments are the laws of the covenant God established with the Israelites, and they still hold true to all of us today. Jesus taught about the commandments a lot, but he put them all into perspective with the Great Commandments to love God above all else and to love your neighbor as yourself. "On these two commandments hang all the law and the prophets" (*Matthew 22:40*).

▲ Moses and the Ten Commandments

✝ SCRIPTURE

GO TO THE SOURCE
Read **Matthew 22:34–40** to see how Jesus connects love of God with love of neighbor.

The first three commandments focus on our relationship with God, with loving God with all our heart, soul, and mind. This seems like a mighty task, but Jesus gives us many examples of how to do this.

Life: Making Connections by Faith
The first of the Ten Commandments is "I am the LORD your God . . . you shall have no other gods before me." This commandment calls us to live our faith and have a relationship with God; to believe in God, hope in him and love him above all else. Our lives are connected to God; all the other connections in our life flow from this main connection. This number one priority gives shape and meaning to everything else we do.

The word *religion* comes from the same Latin root word for "ligament." The purpose of religious practice is the same as the ligaments in our body: to hold us together.

There are several ways we can follow the First Commandment and give God the honor and importance he deserves. We show that God is our number one priority by

▶ adoring God, admitting that he is God and Creator, the source of all things, praising him as we realize that we need him to have life

▶ praying to him

▶ worshiping him

▶ fulfilling the vows and promises we make to him.

CHECK THIS OUT!

The three theological virtues of faith, hope, and charity (love) give us the foundation for living by the first commandment. They are called theological virtues because

1. their source is God himself

2. those who live in faith, hope, and love are pointed back to God

These virtues help us keep on track, believing all that God has revealed to us, putting all our trust in his care for us, and returning to him, on a much smaller scale, the love that he gives us.

ACTIVITY

SHARE YOUR FAITH How do you practice the first commandment and "Honor the Lord Your God"? Explain your answer to another.

WE CAN'T REPLACE GOD

 Focus What are some ways people fail to give God the honor he deserves?

Your parents may put limits in your way that you don't agree with. You may disagree on things or argue. But your relationship with your parents is more than temporary disruptions. A lifelong relationship is irreplaceable.

Putting Others in God's Place Our heavenly Father is irreplaceable, too. God is the only God there is. There is no other. No one and no thing can occupy his place in our lives. When we try to put other people or things in God's place, it will only disappoint us, dishonor God, and be unfair to those people or things.

The name we give to putting other people or things in God's place is **idolatry**. Idols are empty, powerless false gods. When we confuse what's important in our lives, we can elevate these idols—such as power, prestige, money, pleasure—to the place of God, making them the number one priority in life. It's like we worship them because we give them all our time and attention. When we practice idolatry, our lives eventually fall apart. The idols that we are worshiping cannot satisfy us and will keep us from experiencing true faith, hope, and love.

? **What are two types of false gods or idols that we, as a society, try and put in God's place?**

? **Is there any particular false god or idol with which people your age struggle?**

Leading Away from God When you get your driver's license, you will notice a lot more street signs warning drivers in advance that particular roads are "Dead Ends" or "Wrong Ways." You will be challenged to pay more attention to where you are heading.

Likewise, there are a number of attitudes and practices that take you down a "Dead End" or "Wrong Way" in your relationship with God. They challenge you to pay attention to where you are heading with your spiritual life.

First Commandment Issues

tempting God — testing God's goodness or power by word or deed, such as "if you give me an A on this test I will go to church every weeknight"

sacrilege — treating holy people, places, and things in an unworthy way, such as not consuming the Eucharist, the Body of Christ, or defacing a crucifix or statue

simony — buying or selling spiritual things, such as paying for the Sacraments of Baptism or a wedding Mass (donations can and should be made, but a price is never set on sacraments because their source is God and we receive them from the Lord as a grace, a freely given gift)

atheism — rejecting or denying the existence of God, such as "we human beings are in total control of our lives, we are the makers of our world"

superstition — identifying certain objects or practices with a religious power, such as "if I walk under this ladder, I will have bad luck," or "if I stick pins in this doll that looks like the principal, I will give pain to him"

Because these actions are all dead ends or take you the wrong way along the path of discipleship, they are considered sinful. They are contrary to the First Commandment.

ACTIVITY

CONNECT YOUR FAITH In the space below, write your own prayer to God by finishing the three sentences.

Dear Lord, you are God.

I have faith in you because . . .

_____

I hope in you because . . .

_____

I love you because . . .

_____

WHAT'S IN A NAME?

When we hold someone in tremendous respect, we speak of that person with an almost hushed voice. The Second Commandment—You shall not take the name of the Lord your God in vain—reminds us that the way we use the Lord's name must always show great respect for him. God is awesome. He is holy. So, his name is holy.

We can defame the name of God in a variety of ways. **Blasphemy** is showing contempt or lack of reverence for God and his name. It includes

▶ speaking words of hate or defiance against the Lord: for example, damning God

▶ speaking ill of God: for example, attributing evil to God

▶ misusing God's name: for example, using "God" itself as an expletive

The commandment not to use God's name in an offensive way also extends to respecting the names of Jesus—the Son of God, the Virgin Mary, and the saints. In Matthew 5:34–35, Jesus tells us ". . . Do not swear at all, either by heaven, for it is the throne of God, or by the earth, for it is his footstool, or by Jerusalem, for it is the city of the great King."

❓ When has your name—or the name of someone you care about—been "dragged through the mud"?

❓ What happened and what did it feel like?

LOOKING BACK

Our forebears in faith, the people of Israel, had such respect for the name of God that they never spoke or wrote of it directly. Instead, they indirectly referred to God as "Lord" or "the Almighty." In the Old Testament, the name "God" was not used. Instead, a series of unpronounceable letters was written: YHWH. It could only be uttered as a breath, an exhalation of air—because they felt the name of God was otherwise simply too awesome and holy for them to write or speak. From these letters we get *Yahweh*, another name used in praise and worship of God.

The Truth in God God is holy, awesome, and totally good. That would be reason enough to treat his name with respect.

But, God is also the measure by which all truth is calculated, for in the Lord there is no falsehood or lie. This means that the second commandment also forbids us from making false oaths. We cannot call on God, in whom all truth resides, to be a witness to a lie on our part.

Perjury is when we make a promise to tell the truth under oath and do not intend to keep it. The Lord is always faithful to his promises. Every promise that we make under oath involves a reference to God who is the Speaker of all truth. God's truthfulness and his own reliable promises must be respected in the oaths we ourselves take.

ACTIVITY

LIVE YOUR FAITH List three promises you could make to yourself, to others, and to God.

I PROMISE MYSELF TO . . .

I PROMISE OTHERS TO . . .

I PROMISE GOD TO . . .

IN SUMMARY

CATHOLICS BELIEVE

God calls us into relationship. We honor him when we love and respect him and his name, connecting what we believe with how we live.

▶ The first commandment calls us to put God first in our lives, to give him the praise and honor he deserves as the Creator of everything.

▶ We need to avoid putting so much importance on things or other people that they take God's place in our lives.

▶ God's name is holy, and we must always refer to his name with respect and reverence.

CELEBRATE

PRAYER OF PETITION

Side 1: God,
when we are really honest with ourselves,
we do not honor you as we should.
When we look ourselves squarely in the mirror,
we know that we do not make you
enough of a priority in our lives.

Side 2: When we sit quietly here for a moment,
and look at how we treat our friends and others sometimes,
we see that when we treat others badly,
we are doing the same to you . . .

Side 1: God,
deep down you know that we love you.
Deep down we know that you keep loving us
even when we forget to honor you
through our words,
our attitudes,
and our actions.

Side 2: Come now,
and shake us up!
Come now,
and move our hearts to change,
to see your presence in all creation,
to see your presence in our friends and others,
to see your presence in our families,
to see your presence in ourselves.

Side 1: When we see good in others,
we see you.
When we treat others with the respect
they deserve,
we truly honor you.
When we love others,
we are showing our love for you.

Side 2: Keep us true Lord,
keep constant watch and help us to love,
honor, and respect
all your people.
Then we will be close to you,
and close to your heart. Amen.

 "Give the Lord Your Heart"
Mike Mahler, © 2003, GIA Publications, Inc.

REVIEW

A Work with Words Complete each sentence with the correct term from the word bank at right.

1. The name we give to putting other people or things in God's place is

    _____.

2. Identifying certain objects or practices with religious power is called

    _____.

3. Faith, hope, and charity (love) are _____ because they come from God and point us back to him.

4. _____ is showing contempt or lack of reverence for God and his name.

5. When we lie under oath we are committing _____.

Word Bank

- superstition
- theological virtues
- idolatry
- sacrilege
- blasphemy
- simony
- perjury
- atheism

B Check Understanding Circle the letter of the choice that best completes the sentence.

6. Jesus taught that the _____ is/are to love God above all else and to love your neighbor as yourself.
    a. Ten Commandments
    b. Golden Rule
    c. Great Commandment
    d. First Commandment

7. The purpose of _____ can be compared to the ligaments in our body: to hold us together.
    a. religion
    b. commandments
    c. simony
    d. virtue

8. _____ is buying or selling spiritual things, such as having to pay for the Sacrament of Baptism.
    a. Sacrilege
    b. Simony
    c. Superstition
    d. Atheism

9. The _____ calls us to put God first in our lives, to give him the praise and honor he deserves as the Creator of everything.
    a. First Commandment
    b. Second Commandment
    c. Fifth Commandment
    d. old covenant

10. _____ is rejecting or denying the existence of God.
    a. Blasphemy
    b. Idolatry
    c. Atheism
    d. Tempting God

C Make Connections: Evaluate Write a one-paragraph response to the question.

What effect do "Dead End" attitudes and practices have on your relationship with God? Pick one specific attitude or practice, and consider how you can apply the theological virtues to head back toward God.

183

OUR CATHOLIC FAITH

WHAT NOW?

★ Think about your priorities. Where does God fall?

★ Find ways to make God more important in your life by including him in your thoughts and decisions.

★ Be honest with yourself: Do you focus too much on what you wear, the things you own, or who talks to you in the hallway?

★ Rely on God when you are unsure of something or need a friend.

★ Watch what you say and how you say it.

ACTIVITY

LIVE YOUR FAITH

▶ List three "idols" that you often make a bigger priority than your relationship with God (even if you aren't aware of it).

1. _____

2. _____

3. _____

▶ Now list two things you can do to intentionally strengthen the amount of attention you are giving to your relationship with God.

1. _____

_____

2. _____

_____

 **GO ONLINE** Visit www.harcourtreligion.com for more family and community connections.

PRAYER

I pray you are first, Lord, in all that I think, say, and do. Amen.

Blessed Damien De Veuster

As Joseph De Veuster was growing up in his native Belgium in the mid-1800s, his father was grooming him to take over the family's farming and mercantile business. Joseph's oldest brother became a priest in the Congregation of the Sacred Heart and his father wanted Joseph to stay and keep the business in the family. However, Joseph, the future Father Damien, had his mind set on a higher calling just as his older brother did. He wanted to serve and honor God by showing his love for others.

In 1859, Joseph entered the seminary at Louvain, Belgium, along with his brother. There he took the name of "Damien." Four years later, as his brother was preparing to leave on a mission to Hawaii, he became ill. Damien obtained permission from the Superior General to take his brother's place. He sought to demonstrate his love for God by ministering to the lepers in Hawaii, whom everyone else had shunned. In so doing, he sacrificed his health and, ultimately, his life.

He arrived in Honolulu on March 19, 1864, where he was ordained to the priesthood. At this time, leprosy was widespread throughout the island kingdom. Fearful of having it spread even further, the Hawaiian government decided to force those with the disease to a remote peninsula on the island of Molokai. No one who was uninfected wanted to have anything to do with them. However, Father Damien and three brothers in his order volunteered to go to Molokai and minister to the lepers.

Originally, the brothers agreed to take turns visiting and assisting the lepers in their distress, but Father Damien ended up spending the rest of his life in the colony. He arrived on May 10, 1873. Later, at his own request, he was allowed to remain on Molokai devoting his efforts to comforting and ministering to the lepers until his own death of leprosy sixteen years later.

Father Damien brought hope to the forsaken colony. He became a source of consolation and encouragement for the lepers, giving them a sense of dignity in spite of their condition. He also became their pastor, and the doctor of their souls and of their bodies. He helped build a community of faith, hope, and love. He gave people new reasons for living.

After being diagnosed with the disease in 1885, Father Damien drew his strength from the Eucharist. He believed that he was "the happiest missionary in the world," a servant of God and of humanity.

He was beatified by Pope John Paul II in 1995.

▲ **Blessed Damien De Veuster, 1840–1889**

GLOBAL DATA

Belgium

- Belgium is located in Western Europe, bordering the North Sea, between France and the Netherlands.

- Belgium became independent from the Netherlands in 1830 and was occupied by Germany during World Wars I and II.

- Belgium has about 10.4 million people, 75 percent of whom are Catholic.

- Belgium's capital, Brussels, is an important commercial and diplomatic center, and its second largest city, Antwerp, is one of Europe's leading ports.

14 HONORING Family Members

INVITE

PRAYER God, help me love my family like you do.

My parents and I used to get along great. It's harder now. Stress . . . expectations . . . conflict!!

Dad was still at work. Mom wasn't due home for another thirty minutes. Sure, school was over with for the day and the weather was California perfect for spring—even though they lived in the Midwest. But Jordan couldn't leave the house until all his homework was finished. Mom would definitely ask if he'd done it all when she got home. But all Jordan wanted to do was to spend some time with his buddies, Max and Danny, skateboarding.

First: homework. Jordan reached into his backpack and took out his algebra textbook. He could be done in a half hour if he concentrated. He'd only gotten done with three equations when a blonde tornado, otherwise known as his younger sister, Josie, blew into his room and launched herself into his side.

Between her snuffles and tears, she told Jordan in her halting four-year-old voice that Carl had torn apart her favorite stuffed teddy bear, Bud, because Josie had broken off a wing on his model airplane. Josie knew she wasn't supposed to play with his models. But even more so, Carl should know better. He was four years older than Josie.

Jordan needed to get his homework done and get on his skateboard. But Josie always came to him with her problems. That's what sixteen-year-old brothers were for, as far as Josie was concerned—complaints and reaching her favorite ice cream bars in the freezer. Jordan couldn't deny her.

So, they trudged up the stairs to see their eight-year-old brother, Carl. With Jordan as go-between, his little brother and sister both apologized and made up. Jordan helped re-glue the wing to the body of the model airplane. He got mom's sewing kit down and, as best he could, performed emergency surgery on Bud. Josie was only too pleased to be his nurse assistant.

Josie showed her appreciation by squeezing Jordan in a huge bear hug. Then she ran off with the repaired teddy bear. He could hear her laughing all the way down the hallway. He sighed. Homework wouldn't be finished before supper now. Max and Danny would have to wait till tomorrow.

ACTIVITY

LET'S BEGIN What's this story about? Who do you think functions as a positive role model for Jordan?

▶ **What different sorts of expectations are placed on you by your family? How do you respond? Why is family so important?**

BEING A FAMILY

 Focus What responsibilities do family members have to one another?

When we need our families, we expect them to be there for us. When other family members need us, they want us to be there for them, too. Every family is different, and each family member has a different role. No family is perfect and no human being is perfect. Sometimes it's hard to respect what others in the family need or have to do when we're focused on what we need or want. But respect in a family is very important, especially during challenging or difficult times.

Because we are not born as adults, we need our families to teach us a lot about life. During childhood we grow physically and mentally, mature socially, and learn from our parents and teachers. We rely on our parents and family members to take care of us, love us, laugh with us, and show us things by example.

The Fourth Commandment tells us we need to honor our parents and guardians by giving them

▶ obedience

▶ respect

▶ gratitude

▶ assistance

This fourfold response that children have toward their parents is called **filial respect**. Obeying, respecting, and helping our parents and guardians, and being genuinely grateful for all they do, helps children and families grow and interact in positive ways.

 **What is one way you have shown filial respect today?**

CATHOLICS TODAY

We celebrate the Feast of the Holy Family on the first Sunday after Christmas. This day celebrates the special family relationship between Mary, Joseph, and Jesus. The Holy Family is a role model for us, showing us that we don't have to be perfect to create the *domestic Church* where family members learn and live out their faith. Because all human beings are called to holiness, we can find it in the daily routines and minor details of family life. Mary, Joseph, and Jesus spent 90 percent of their time living out the demands of family: cooking, cleaning, earning a living, and doing household chores. Holiness can also be doing ordinary things with heartfelt compassion, kindness, humility, gentleness, and patience.

The Holy Family We know that Jesus obeys his heavenly Father. At the same time, Jesus was born into a family—as we all are. His mother is Mary. His foster father is Joseph. Sometimes it's hard to think of Jesus as a six-year-old, learning how to play a game, or as a teenager having fun with friends. But Jesus truly was a child, growing up in a real family.

✝ **SCRIPTURE** You may be familiar with the story of Jesus in the Temple. Mary and Joseph are on their way home from Jerusalem. They attach themselves to a busy caravan, where it is entirely possible for each to think the other is watching the child Jesus. When they realize their mistake, they search for him until he is found in the Temple. Jesus asks Mary and Joseph, "Why were you searching for me? Did you not know that I must be in my Father's house?" But they did not understand. Jesus left with them "and was obedient to them. His mother treasured all these things in her heart. And Jesus increased in wisdom and in years, and in divine and human favor" (*Luke 2:49–52*).

❓ **What is Mary's ultimate response to Jesus in this episode and why is this important for us?**

Jesus had, in effect, two homes, one in Nazareth and one in the Temple. His foster father, Joseph, headed the home in Nazareth. But his heavenly Father's home is symbolized by the Temple.

Mary and Joseph did not always understand Jesus, just as our own parents can be confused by the things we say or do.

✝ **SCRIPTURE**

GO TO THE SOURCE
Read **Luke 2:41–52** to find out what Jesus was doing in the Temple and why it was so surprising to Mary and Joseph.

▲ *Adoration of the Shepherds*, by Giuseppe Passeri (1654–1714)

ACTIVITY

SHARE YOUR FAITH Look back at the four attitudes that make up filial respect. Which of the four is easiest for you to practice? Which is hardest? Discuss with another.

EASIEST

HARDEST

FAMILIES AND RELATIONSHIPS

 Focus How do families help us have friendships and relationships with others?

The Holy Family of Jesus, Mary, and Joseph is certainly unique. There is no other family quite like it. No other family has a child who is the Son of God. Nevertheless, the Holy Family provides a model for all families.

What is the purpose of a family? What lessons can we learn from the Holy Family?

▶ Parents and guardians should nurture and support their children so that they can grow up in a safe, loving environment.

▶ A family ought to be where we learn about our faith and where all family members learn about and relate to God.

▶ Families should pray together.

▶ Families should seek to promote living by the virtues.

Parents are the prime movers in a family. As adults, they are responsible for the physical and spiritual needs of their children so that younger members can grow. Families draw out the best in all the members—adults and children—when they grow and work together.

What role models or sources do members of your family use for advice about living together the way God intends?

WHAT MAKES A HEALTHY, STRONG RELATIONSHIP?

TIME: We need to make time for a person to be a significant part of our lives. Giving time does not just mean being in the same room or the same town.

LOYALTY: Every good relationship demands that the people involved in it be true to each other, trust each other, be there for each other, and depend on each other's support.

TRUTH: A relationship built on lies will not go far. Only upfront, honest communication grows a healthy, strong relationship.

FLEXIBILITY: Not everything can be planned in a relationship; if so, one of the people involved is exercising too much control. Sometimes spontaneous things are the most surprising and life-giving.

JOY: The bonds between people cannot be formed solely by grief or by mutually confronting a dangerous or difficult situation; every relationship requires some laughter, fun, and finding joy.

Families come in all shapes, sizes, and each has its own flavor, with its own way of communication, its own emphasis on what's important, and its own favorite activities and food. The most important ingredient in a family is the adults providing a safe, loving environment for the children. When this happens, then the family itself can become a school of faith, with all its members learning from one another to live as God intends.

The purpose of a family will be helped or hurt by the quality of the relationships among all the members. To relate to another person means that we are connected in some way or that we are important to each other.

ACTIVITY

CONNECT YOUR FAITH Think about your relationship with a member of your family. What steps can you take to increase one or two of these elements in that relationship?

I can strengthen my _____ with _____ by

_____

_____

A PLACE TO GROW

Focus What are some things we can learn in our families?

We begin life within a family and from there we move into the larger world. We first form our core values within a family. Personal character is developed within a family first because it's there we first form a sense of who we are and what we are capable of. We learn what's important, how to act and treat others, and what it means to be in a relationship.

▶ It is within family that we first learn to take responsibility for our own actions.

▶ We get a sense of what's acceptable and appropriate.

▶ Our **conscience**—the ability to know right from wrong, good from evil—begins to be formed and built up by the example of our parents, other adults, and siblings.

▶ We learn how to make decisions based upon what we judge to be right or wrong, on discussing with people we trust, on the example of Jesus, and on prayer.

Name three things you've learned from your family that are important to the way you act outside of the home.

It Takes Work All families struggle to build strong relationships among their members. Why? Because relationships take work—they don't just happen. It takes a lot of time and energy to keep a relationship going. With all the demands placed on you by school and friends, sometimes you forget to take care of those with whom you should be the closest!

There is life inside and outside the family—and sometimes there is a mix and blending of the two. The key is working for a balance and giving *all* your relationships the attention they deserve.

What is easiest for you in forming and maintaining relationships with family members?

What do you need to work on?

Family contributes immensely to who we are later in life. This does not mean that when a family does not function well or when its members have hurt each other, members cannot ever get beyond their painful experiences or harmful memories.

Sometimes a family is so hurt it can't help itself. That is why it is important for your family to be part of a bigger family—the Church. Is there something deeply damaging occurring to you within your family, something you can barely acknowledge to yourself much less to someone else? The first step is the hardest but also the most important. Talk to a trusted teacher, guidance counselor, or a parish priest or other minister for help.

LOOKING BACK

Saint Margaret of Hungary was the daughter of the king. The king promised God that if their country was spared from an enemy attack, Margaret would be dedicated to the religious life. His prayers answered, Margaret was given into the care of the Dominican Sisters, with whom she took vows as a nun. Extraordinarily beautiful, Margaret was sought as a bride by the King of Bohemia. At first, her father encouraged her to leave the convent. With Margaret's prompting, his conscience led him to support her remaining a nun.

ACTIVITY

LIVE YOUR FAITH What does your family need most in order to improve the relationships among your family members? Compose a prayer asking God to help you and your family grow.

IN SUMMARY

CATHOLICS BELIEVE

Families are called to be schools of faith in which we learn how to love, act, and treat others.

▶ The obedience, love, and respect found in the Holy Family stands as a model for our own families.

▶ The relationships within a family demand as much care, concern, and energy on our part as with any of our other relationships.

▶ Within the family, we develop personal character, grow in our understanding of right and wrong, and learn what's truly important.

CELEBRATION OF THE WORD

Leader: Glory to the Father, and the Son, and the Holy Spirit:

All: as it was in the beginning, is now, and will be forever. Amen.

Leader: Let us quietly reflect on our families and how we can better be signs of God's love to one another.

Silence.

Reader: A reading from the letter of Paul to the Colossians.

Read Colossians 3:12–17.

The word of the Lord.

All: Thanks be to God.

Leader: We each belong to some type of family, and no matter how different the family, we are called to be loving, respecting, caring, and responsible for one another. Let us thank God for those who love and care for us, and ask him to bless our families today and always.

Silently offer your prayers for your family.

Loving Father,
You know the love of a parent for a child.
We ask you to strengthen our families so that we model that love.
We ask you to bless us with patience, courage, and hope.
So that we can become the people you call us to be.
We ask this through your Son, Jesus.

All: Amen.

 "Ubi Caritas Deus Ibi Est"

Joseph Gelineau © 1996 Ateliers et Presses de Taizé, Published and distributed in North America by GIA Publications, Inc.

REVIEW

A Work with Words Circle the letter of the choice that best completes the sentence.

1. Children need to give parents and guardians obedience, respect, gratitude, and _____.

    a. love   **b.** assistance   **c.** loyalty   **d.** a, b, and c

2. The fourfold response children have toward their parents that is addressed in the Fourth Commandment is called _____.

    a. adoration   **b.** filial respect   **c.** conscience   **d.** compassion

3. Every good relationship demands _____.

    a. b, c, and d   **b.** respect   **c.** loyalty   **d.** love

4. Our _____ enables us to distinguish between right from wrong and good from evil.

    a. free will   **b.** conscience   **c.** obedience   **d.** none of the above

5. The obedience, love, and respect found in the _____ stands as a model for our own families.

    a. Holy Fathers   **b.** Holy Family   **c.** Apostles   **d.** Church

B Check Understanding Indicate whether the following statements are true or false. Then rewrite false statements to make them true.

_____ **6.** Only the Church ought to be where we first learn about our faith and where all members learn about and relate to God.

_____

_____ **7.** Family bonds must be formed based on a range of emotions and experiences, including grief, joy, and fun.

_____

_____ **8.** Communication and faith are essential parts of healthy family relationships.

_____

_____ **9.** If a person acts out of fear, or ignorance, or because of pressure put on him or her by someone, the person's moral responsibility for the action could be lessened or removed.

_____

_____ **10.** The purpose of the religious life is to nurture and support children so that they can grow up in a safe, loving environment.

_____

C Make Connections: Explain Write a one-paragraph response to the following.

Write your prescription for a healthy family that models the Holy Family.

OUR CATHOLIC FAITH

WHAT NOW?

★ Make a commitment to spend time with your family.

★ Take an interest in family members' lives; know what's going on.

★ Work to repair broken relationships you have with members of your family.

★ Apologize to a family member that you have recently hurt.

★ Invite a friend over to share in the life of your family.

It is so easy for us to take for granted the great gift we have in our family. Sometimes when friends come over to relax, join us for supper, or some other activity, we see our family in new ways through our friends' eyes and their comments.

ACTIVITY

LIVE YOUR FAITH Because none of us is perfect, even though that is what we are striving for, we have a lot of work in front of us. You cannot change other members of your family. You can only control your own actions, words, and attitude. Take time now to make a plan to improve yourself as a member of your family. You may have to repair damage done to a relationship within the family. You may have to spend more time right now on one particular relationship because it is weaker than the others. Be specific as you make yourself a plan. Three things I can do this week . . .

 Visit www.harcourtreligion.com for more family and community connections.

 **PRAYER**

Lord, may I always be a person of love in my family.

Saints Felicity and Perpetua

Perpetua, a young noblewoman, lived in Carthage (present-day Tunisia) in the second century A.D. Carthage was part of the Roman Empire. The Roman emperors at that time were called "pagans," meaning they believed in many gods. They tried to force these beliefs on their subjects. Everywhere in the Empire, Christians were persecuted—even martyred—for their faith in Christ. Despite the persecution, many people came to the faith. Perpetua and her servant Felicity were among those who became Christians.

In A.D. 203, Perpetua and Felicity were arrested and imprisoned as a warning to the other Christians in Carthage. All they had to do to be set free was to renounce, or give up, their faith in Christ. Perpetua's father begged her to renounce her faith. She was respectful to him, but she couldn't agree to give up what she had become. She asked her father, "See that pot lying there? Can you call it by any other name than what it is?" Her father responded that he could not. She then explained, "Neither can I call myself by any other name than what I am—a Christian."

Her father did not understand her response. Instead he attacked her. She welcomed imprisonment because it protected her from his attacks. He seemed to hope that the darkness and heat of the dungeon would frighten her and convince her to give up her faith. Instead, God sent Perpetua wonderful visions that drove away her fears and filled her with the Holy Spirit. She was at peace, and she said the prison became like a palace to her. Her visions showed her what life would be like after death.

At the time of her arrest, Perpetua was twenty-two years old and the mother of a baby girl. Felicity was expecting her first child. It was illegal to execute a pregnant woman, and Felicity longed to give birth before the day set for the execution. Her devotion to Christ and to Perpetua was so great that she did not want to be left behind. Two days before the execution she gave birth. The child was adopted and raised by a Christian woman.

Perpetua, Felicity, and three others bravely faced the jeers of the crowd at their execution. They stood side-by-side as their throats were cut. Perpetua's last words to her brother, who had also become a Christian, were "Stand fast in the faith and love one another."

The story of Saint Perpetua and Saint Felicity was told by Perpetua in her diary. She recorded everything that happened to them until the day they died. A friend finished the story from the point at which Perpetua was forced to leave it. It is one of the great stories of faith and honor between members of an extended family.

▲ Saints Felicity and Perpetua

GLOBAL DATA

Carthage

■ Carthage was founded by Phoenician seamen on the southern shore of the Mediterranean Sea, opposite Italy in present-day Tunisia, around 814 B.C.

■ Carthage was a major commercial trade center of the Mediterranean region, as well as a center of learning and culture.

■ Carthage fought Rome in a series of three Punic Wars between 264 B.C. and 146 B.C., after which it was defeated and destroyed. Hannibal, who invaded the Roman Empire during the Second Punic War, came from Carthage.

■ Carthage was later rebuilt and was home to Saint Augustine of Hippo.

15 EVERYONE'S Dignity

 **PRAYER** Remind us that you are in every one of us.

We're supposed to take care of each other, right? Then how come people are starving and neglected? What can I, what can we, do?

Funding. Father Tom hated that word.

In Father Tom's experience, when the word "funding" came up, somebody's job was on the line or a great program was about to get axed. This time it was a great program.

Father Tom knew everything going on in the parish. Italian immigrants had settled near the waterfront, giving the area the name of Little Italy. People from all over the city flocked to this neighborhood for the superb Italian food. Father Tom had called it home for twenty years.

Father Tom had seen a growing trend during his time there. Grown children of the parishioners were not finding homes in the parish and were settling in the suburbs. This broke the pattern of grandchildren growing up in the same house as their grandparents. Other things were breaking as well.

The older people, cut off from their families, seemed adrift. The grandmothers, so used to cooking for large families, had difficulty cooking for just two or just themselves.

Then, a group of three Italian grandmothers found that they were better off together than they were apart, so they moved into one house. They shared everything—the cooking, cleaning, and watching each other's grandkids. They thrived. Tom watched it all happen and had a brainstorm. He invited the women to coffee and pitched them the idea of spreading the love to other aging people in the parish. He invited them to run what he called "Helping Hands." They said "Yes!" and never looked back.

Helping Hands had spread into many things, including getting free orthopedic fittings, arranging Meals on Wheels visits, starting a phone tag buddy system for people who are home-bound—even getting the batteries in smoke alarms replaced. The youth group and parishioners helped with minor home repairs. Helping Hands had become the glue that was holding the parish community together.

But now, Father Tom had been told to prepare for a 65 percent reduction in funding for Helping Hands. The thought of losing Helping Hands made him want to put his head in his hands and cry.

ACTIVITY

LET'S BEGIN Imagine that Father Tom shares this story with you and your family. How would your family respond? Imagine that he shared this story with God in prayer that night. What do you think God would say?

_____

_____

_____

_____

THE COMMON GOOD

Focus What is the common good and how is it achieved?

Kindergarten teaches children a basic lesson: the need to share. One child cannot hoard all the toys. Everyone shares. They have to "play nice" or chaos erupts.

Humans are social beings. Each individual must take others into account. We live *with* others. As Catholics, however, we know this is more than just a matter of cooperation. It is more than just the notion of "you work with me and I'll work with you."

Society functions best when each person respects everyone else as "another self," as real people like himself or herself, with real needs, hopes, and dreams: In other words, not seeing others as a means to get something for oneself, but as a person with the same basic rights that need to be respected and met.

The Basis of a Just Society The right kind of society is one that remains at service to people on every level. Societies that are organized in this way promote the **common good**, which means that all people, either in groups or as individuals, are given the opportunities to reach their fulfillment more fully and easily.

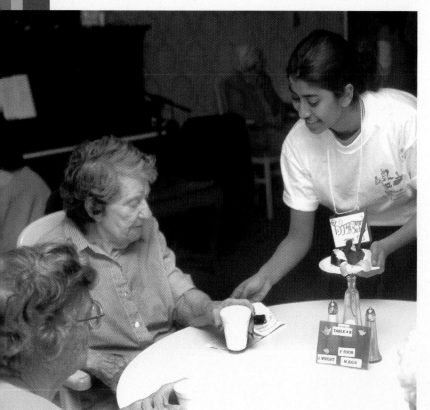

The common good is made possible by three essential elements:

▶ respect for the person and promotion of the fundamental rights that flow from human dignity

▶ social well-being and prosperity for everyone

▶ security and order as well as global peace

Not one single part of society is exempt from the common good. Society itself owes to every group, organization, and association the conditions that promote their own effectiveness and liveliness according to the common good. When society does this, it promotes social justice.

But it's a two-way street. Every group, organization, and association must try to improve human life and the common good. Likewise, those in political authority cannot exercise leadership beyond the boundaries of these three essential elements that define the common good.

common good

New Commandment

social sin

UNDERSTANDING THE COMMON GOOD

In his papal writing and in a 1979 speech to the General Assembly of the United Nations, John Paul II specified what is meant by the common good.

What are the fundamental rights of persons?
- the right to life (from conception to natural death)
- the right to live in a united family
- the right to develop oneself in a moral environment
- the right to develop one's intelligence
- the right to seek and know the truth
- the right to share in work that wisely uses earth's resources
- the right to support one's family
- the right to establish a family
- the right to religious freedom

What does prosperity mean?
- general development of spiritual goods so all may benefit
- general development of physical goods so all may benefit

How can peace and security be achieved?
- the absence of war, *along with*
- effective and fruitful justice between individuals and nations *and*
- the practice of love between individuals and nations

ACTIVITY

SHARE YOUR FAITH In small groups, choose three basic rights and discuss how they are being met. Name some ways that people your age could promote the rights.

RIGHT	FAMILY	SCHOOL	LOCAL COMMUNITY
1.			
2.			
3.			

LIVING AS A CATHOLIC IN TODAY'S WORLD

 Focus Why does the Church comment on political authority and structures?

The Church is concerned with the way in which society is organized and the way in which it functions because everyone and everything in this world is oriented—or should be oriented—toward God.

The Church speaks out about social and economic matters, because sometimes groups or individuals undermine our human rights. The Church takes action to help society function properly.

In striving for the common good, the Church teaches about family and marriage as the basic "unit" of society, the value of human work and workers' rights, economic institutions in service to people, political authority, the international community, safeguarding the environment, and promoting peace.

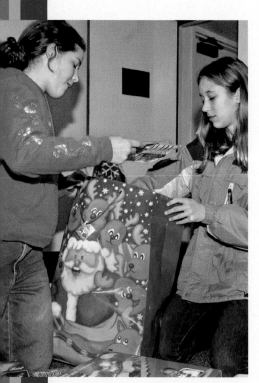

Each of us has a responsibility to respect the rights of others and to make sure our actions do not make it difficult for people to have their needs met. We are called to accept Gospel values and the Church that teaches them. We say "yes" to everything that makes the common good possible. We work within society to promote virtue in all aspects of life.

This means that sometimes we will have to say "no" to those practices in society that do not correspond to the common good, that go against the Gospel and Church teaching. The standard by which we judge our "yes" or "no" is the human person. What truly helps people in their physical needs by giving them access to food, shelter, and basic human rights? What helps people become closer to one another and God? What deprives people of their human rights and dignity? What brings them down as persons and prevents them from becoming closer to God?

What are some things that you can say "yes" to in society?

What are some things that you should say "no" to in society because they do not promote the dignity of the person?

Society Step by step, in large and small ways, the structure and character of society should be geared toward love. Jesus is clear, "This is my commandment, that you love one another as I have loved you" (*John 15:12*). His **New Commandment** is not meant solely for individuals in their relationships, but is meant to be followed by groups and organizations, even by nations in how they deal with their citizens and with other nations.

Political authority and governments are not higher than God. Their authority is legitimate when they are committed to the common good of society and use morally acceptable actions to lead and govern. It is therefore the responsibility of citizens to work with the proper authorities to build up a society based on truth, justice, freedom, and solidarity. Society and its members have the right to information (such as news) based on the values of truth, justice, and freedom. All of us have to be careful in the ways we use the media to communicate.

Solidarity means that we stand with and are related to people who are deprived of their human rights. We don't merely help from afar those who are poor or oppressed; we get to know them and their situations. We identify with their experiences and join with them in community. Sometimes, citizens must disobey the immoral directives of civil authorities and follow their consciences to uphold truth, justice, solidarity, and freedom.

The highest compliment we could pay to society is the same compliment that we would pay to an individual: love. Each of us can take the appropriate action to build society according to the command of Jesus.

CHECK THIS OUT!

Global peace and security is one of the three elements of the common good. So the Church teaches that everything possible must be done to avoid war. There are too many evils associated with war to enter into armed conflict lightly. The impact and result of war is devastating for the entire human race, and especially harms the poor, because it diverts precious resources that could be used to make their lives better. Entering into war as a last resort does not relieve a country or its armed forces from following national laws and the moral law. For example, targeting innocent civilians or harming an enemy soldier who has ceased aggression and surrendered are actions against the moral law.

ACTIVITY

CONNECT YOUR FAITH What are some ways that the national government does or does not promote the common good through laws, programs and organizations, and policies? Record three ways here, and then explain how each does or does not reflect Jesus' command to love one another as he has loved us.

THE SIGNIFICANCE OF *ONE*

 Focus How do the actions of some affect the whole group?

We don't underestimate the power of *one*. Building a just, loving world—contributing to the common good— starts with a single person, Jesus Christ. Like a stone that creates ever outward ripples in a pond, Jesus, through the continuing action of the Church, creates ripples in world society.

Justice, love, and peace are furthered by the specific, concrete actions of each individual. One small step within our own homes and in our neighborhoods, towns, and counties can have a real effect the world. If every person waited for someone else to contribute to the common good, nothing good would happen. The good from each person's action to promote justice, peace, and love is combined to have a greater and greater influence on the world.

The same is true when we turn from God. Our sins do not damage just ourselves and our relationship with God. Sins wound our human nature—who we are and how we relate beyond ourselves—and therefore they injure human solidarity.

A personal act of discrimination against someone who is of a different skin color ends up wounding the common good. An individual act of bullying by a classmate against another will end up wounding the common good of the whole school.

Why? All sins are social, even thoughts or actions that go no further than one's self—because we are social in nature. The same is true of our virtues, because what strengthens or makes each of us personally, individually better does not remain isolated. By our human nature we are social. Therefore, **social sin**, the sum of personal sins that then become part of society—like discrimination and prejudice—can only be combated by an accumulation of virtue, that is, many just, peaceful, and loving actions by many individuals.

 In your family or among your friends, who would you say is the most just and loving person? Why do you think that?

LOOKING BACK

In times past, some people in the Church accepted slavery. It was viewed as regrettable, but also as the way things were in society. In modern times, the Church has spoken out forcefully against this terribly unjust practice. In 1965, the Second Vatican Council condemned all forms of social and cultural discrimination as incompatible with God's design. Each person is created in the image of God and is gifted with dignity equal to all other humans. That equality—guaranteed by the Creator—requires our heartfelt efforts to reduce sinful social and economic inequalities.

ACTIVITY

LIVE YOUR FAITH How often do you hear or make the statement, "It's not my problem!"?

▶ **Name two social sins that might change if we stopped saying "It's not my problem."**

_____

_____

_____

_____

IN SUMMARY

CATHOLICS BELIEVE

Because God created us with equal human dignity, we are required to work for the common good so that all people have what they need and can reach their fulfillment more fully and easily.

▶ The common good comes about in a society when the fundamental rights of the person are met, social well-being of all people is the goal, and there is security and peace.

▶ The Church works to make sure that public and political authority acts within the truth, justice, freedom, and solidarity. Each and every member of the Church can do this by making wise decisions based upon the human dignity of the person.

▶ Our individual actions to promote global social justice, peace, and love begin close to home. We can make a difference.

PRAYER OF COMMITMENT

Reader 1: We are all God's people,
we are all created in his wonderful image!
If we believe this,
than we cannot stand by and do nothing,
when others are hurting
when others are treated
in ways we would never want to be treated.

Reader 2: If we believe in God's law,
if we believe in the teachings of Jesus,
if we want to follow and walk as brothers and sisters in Christ,
then we are called to act with justice.

All: We are called to act with justice!

Reader 3: When we see people treated with cruelty,
we are called to love tenderly.

All: We are called to love tenderly!

Reader 4: When we see people near us who are in need in any way,
we are called to serve!

All: We are called to serve!

Reader 5: So, let us respond to our commitment in prayer.

(pause)

God, of all that is loving and just,
challenge us,
humble us,
to have our hearts opened
when we see injustice.

Reader 6: Help us to do more than
just talk about doing good,
let us truly act
as your Son Jesus did,
and as you still do.

All readers: We ask this in Jesus' name.

All: Amen.

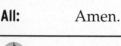 "We Are Called"
David Haas, © 1988, GIA Publications, Inc.

REVIEW

A Work with Words Circle the letter of the choice that best completes the sentence.

1. Societies organized to promote the _____ give opportunities to all people to reach their fulfillment more fully and easily.
   - **a.** common good
   - **b.** justice system
   - **c.** theological virtues
   - **d.** global peace

2. The _____ of people include(s) the right to life, to a moral environment, to a united family, and to religious freedom.
   - **a.** theological virtues
   - **b.** fundamental rights
   - **c.** common good
   - **d.** fundamental values

3. The standard by which the Church judges "yes" or "no" to social practices is the _____.
   - **a.** liturgy
   - **b.** Traditions
   - **c.** human person
   - **d.** social sin

4. _____ mean(s) that we stand with and are related to people who are deprived of their human rights.
   - **a.** Common good
   - **b.** Justice
   - **c.** Solidarity
   - **d.** Fortitude

5. _____ is the effect of personal sins over a period of time that affect society.
   - **a.** Social sin
   - **b.** Common sin
   - **c.** Discrimination
   - **d.** Prejudice

B Check Understanding Indicate whether the following statements are true or false. Then rewrite false statements to make them true.

_____ **6.** Human dignity and global peace are essential to the common good.

_____ **7.** John Paul II founded many of his writings in the area of human rights.

_____ **8.** Three essential elements to promote the common good are respect for fundamental rights, prosperity, and security for some.

_____ **9.** Citizens must obey the directives of civil authorities unless the directives are immoral.

_____ **10.** Sins wound our human nature and therefore they injure human solidarity.

C Make Connections: Interpret Write a one-paragraph response to the questions.

"Justice, love, and peace are furthered by the specific, concrete actions of each individual."
What does this statement mean to you? What specific, concrete actions can you take to promote the common good in your family, school, neighborhood, or community?

OUR CATHOLIC FAITH

WHAT NOW?

★ Get to know people outside your immediate circle of family and friends.

★ Find out about local and global political issues and needs.

★ Become interested in global trends that effect everyone's standard of living.

★ Come to the aid of others in your neighborhood, school, or town.

★ Set aside part of your money from allowance or jobs and donate to people in need.

★ Clean out your closet and give away unnecessary clothes.

ACTIVITY

LIVE YOUR FAITH Do Your Homework!

▶ Go online or visit the public library to investigate charitable outreach or United Nations organizations that help people in poorer countries with better living conditions or more healthful diets. After investigating their activities, you may want to persuade your family members, friends, or classmates to contribute to these outreach efforts or become involved in some other way.

▶ Visit www.harcourtreligion.com for info on Catholic organizations and links:

- **Catholic Relief Services**
- **Catholic Fund for Overseas Development**
- **Catholic Near East Welfare Association**

▶ Or you can check out these Christian nonprofit organizations:

- **Feed the Children**
- **Food for the Hungry**
- **The Christian Foundation for Children and Aging**

▶ Be ready to explain which one you like most.

 Visit www.harcourtreligion.com for more family and community connections.

 **PRAYER**

Jesus, give me the ability to reach out to others as you did.

Pere Jacques Marquette

Pere Marquette was born in Laon, France, in 1637. He began his great adventures when he entered the Society of Jesus at the age of seventeen and was ordained a priest in 1666. He sailed for Canada the same year, landing at Quebec. He wanted to bring the Catholic faith to the Native Americans. By learning the Algonquin and Huron tribal languages, he was able to teach and minister to the people. They honored him by giving him a calumet, a pipe that symbolized peace.

In 1668, Marquette traveled to the Great Lakes region and founded the mission of Sault Sainte Marie on the waterway between lakes Superior and Huron. After building a church and converting a large number of Native Americans, he traveled widely throughout the territory, preaching the Gospel and making converts among various tribes.

Five years later, he joined Joliet on his voyage of discovery. With five Frenchmen in two canoes, they paddled down the Fox and Wisconsin rivers and into the Mississippi. They were searching for a route to the Pacific Ocean that did not cross into Spanish territory. The journey downstream took them more than a thousand miles, reaching the mouth of what is now the Arkansas River. There they turned around, fearing to enter Spanish territory, but they learned that the Mississippi flowed into the Gulf of Mexico, thus paving the way for LaSalle's journey to the river's mouth nine years later.

Though he did not reach the end of the Mississippi, he did work for the good of the native populations by serving faithfully as a minister of God to the Native American populations along the Mississippi River. He also ministered to those who accompanied him and fellow French explorer Louis Joliet on their voyage.

In addition to converting Native Americans along the river, Pere Marquette drew maps and kept a detailed journal of the voyage. His journal became all the more valuable when Joliet's journals were lost in a boating accident. Marquette died of dysentery in 1675 at the age of thirty-nine. The results of his expedition opened vast fields for other missionaries, spreading Catholicism into the new territory that was later to become the midwestern United States.

▲ Pere Jacques Marquette, 1637–1675

GLOBAL DATA

Canada

- Canada is the world's third largest nation in area, following Russia and China.

- Canada shares the longest unfortified border in the world with the United States, more than 3,000 miles.

- Canada has a population of about 32 million, 45 percent of whom are Roman Catholic, most of whom live in the French-speaking Province of Quebec.

- Canada was first explored by the French under Jacques Cartier in 1534. The first city, Quebec, was founded in 1608.

Faith in Action!

DISCOVER

Catholic Social Teaching:
Solidarity of the Human Family

IN THIS UNIT you learned about the common good, the need to stick up for others, and that peacemaking starts with building and nuturing relationships.

Solidarity

We are in "solidarity" with the whole human family because we are all brothers and sisters made in God's image. Our solidarity with the whole human family means we must be willing to sacrifice for the common good of everyone. Individuals must be willing to sacrifice some of their time, talents, and possessions for others. Nations must be willing to sacrifice some of their people, wealth, and power for the sake of the well-being of other peoples and nations. Selfishness by individuals and nations is a sin against human solidarity and the tenth commandment.

The common good of the whole human family requires some organization of society on the international level. The "right" of a nation to make war against another nation has been limited by international law and the United Nations as well as by Church teaching. War must be a matter of self-defense and a last resort, and the way a nation wages war must also be in accord with international law. In the words of Pope John Paul II right before the U.S. war against Iraq in 2003, "People of the earth and their leaders must sometimes have the courage to say, 'No! . . . No to war!' War is not always inevitable. It is always a defeat for humanity. International law, honest dialogue, solidarity between States, the noble exercise of diplomacy—these are methods worthy of nations and individuals in resolving their differences . . ."

International peacemaking is a big part of solidarity, but peacemaking involves many things. It starts with building and rebuilding peaceful relationships with those around you. It means promoting a caring relationship with creation. And it means challenging the violence around you, from kids picking on other kids to war itself.

 What do you think Pope John Paul II meant when he said "war is always a defeat for humanity"? Do you agree with him?

BEING IN SOLIDARITY with others means building relationships and maintaining them in harmony. Let's look at how one group practices solidarity.

"TEENS ACTING FOR PEACE"

MAKING PEACE TOGETHER

Teens Acting for Peace (TAP) is a program created by the Institute for Peace and Justice. It trains high school and eighth-grade youth to be peacemakers by living and teaching the "Pledge of Nonviolence" in elementary schools. Since 2002, teams of eighth graders at St. Roch Catholic School in St. Louis, Missouri, have been doing monthly presentations in the other eight grades at their school. Each month the focus is on a different part of the Pledge—"Respect for Self & Others," "Communicate Better," and "Listen," "Forgive," "Respect Nature," "Play Creatively," and "Be Courageous" in the face of violence in all its forms.

Tim Cummins, the eighth-grade teacher, loves to share this anecdote about the TAP program's effectiveness. "One afternoon, two sixth-grade boys were arguing outside of my classroom. I went to investigate the matter, and noticed that three eighth-grade students, Megan, Wendy, and Lindsay, were now standing with the two boys. I walked over to the group to investigate further, and Megan turned to me and said, 'Don't worry about this argument. We can help these guys work this out. After all, we're their TAP leaders.'

"I was impressed by their attitude and watched as they handled the situation. They had both boys remain calm and tell them what had happened. They spoke to them about the meaning of respect and asked how they could have handled the situation better. Both boys apologized to each other and to their TAP leaders. The group finally broke up and the girls went away smiling, proud of their achievement."

Over the years, these TAP leaders and their students have created valentine's cards for men in prison, led prayer services at school, and organized a school cleanup each Earth Day. Once a year, near the birthday of Martin Luther King, Jr., in mid-January, the whole school renews its commitment to peacemaking and the Pledge of Nonviolence.

How can you be a peacemaker every day?

▼ **St. Roch Catholic School presents a certificate to recognize participants in its Teens Acting for Peace program.**

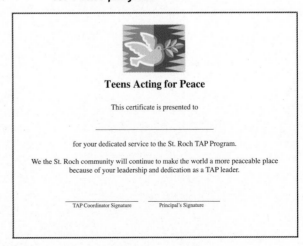

Teens Acting for Peace

This certificate is presented to

_____

for your dedicated service to the St. Roch TAP Program.

We the St. Roch community will continue to make the world a more peaceable place because of your leadership and dedication as a TAP leader.

_____ _____
TAP Coordinator Signature   Principal's Signature

INDIVIDUAL PEACEMAKING

Write down at least one way you have already been a peacemaker

1 at your school

2 at home

3 in your neighborhood

Choose one situation you are part of or know about where you could be a better peacemaker. Write down how you will try to do it and when.

Ask your teacher for a copy of the Youth Pledge of Nonviolence or go online at www.harcourtreligion.com to link to the Institute for Peace and Justice's Web site. Consider taking the pledge.

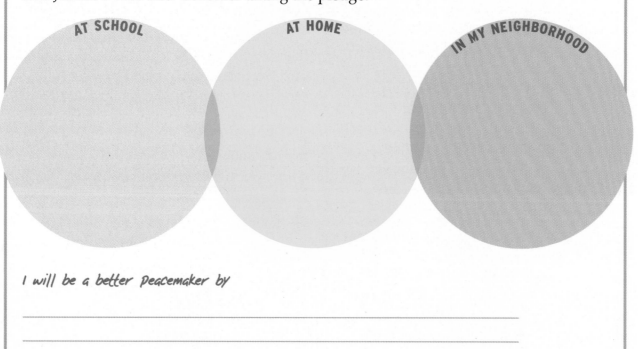

AT SCHOOL

AT HOME

IN MY NEIGHBORHOOD

I will be a better peacemaker by

_____

_____

GLOBAL PEACEMAKING

Identify with your classmates different nations or parts of the world where wars are going on and discuss alternative ways to reach the same goals without a war.

REFLECT On Your Experience

What does it take to be a peacemaker?

Why is it hard to challenge others who are hurting those around you?

What did you learn about war and its effects on the lives of others? Who are the main victims in war?

What happened when you invited others to join you in this project?

What did you learn about yourself in doing this project?

What did you learn about Jesus and about your faith?

List one thing that might be different about you after doing this project. How will your life be different because of these actions?

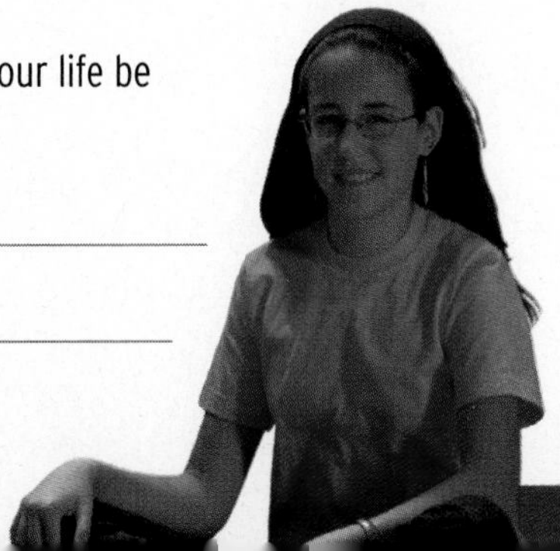

A **Work with Words** Use the clues below to complete the crossword puzzle.

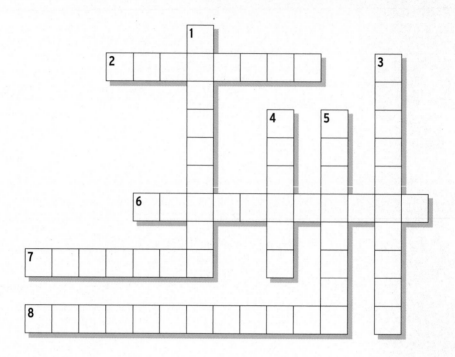

Across

2 Putting other people or things in God's place

6 These virtues include faith, hope, and charity (love)

7 Lying under oath

8 Identifying certain objects or practices with religious power

Down

1 Showing contempt or lack of reverence for God and his name

3 Standing with and relating to people who are deprived of their human rights

4 Buying or selling spiritual things

5 The purpose of this can be compared to the ligaments of the body: to hold us together

· ·

B **Check Understanding** Indicate whether the following statements are true or false. Then rewrite false statements to make them true.

_____ **9.** Jesus taught that the First Commandment is to love God above all else and to love your neighbor as yourself.

_____

_____ **10.** Atheism is testing God's goodness or power by word or deed.

_____

_____ **11.** The fourfold response children have toward their parents that is addressed in the Fourth Commandment is called filial respect.

_____ **12.** Our free will enables us to know right from wrong and good from evil.

_____ **13.** Children need to give parents and guardians obedience, respect, loyalty, gratitude, and assistance.

_____ **14.** Societies organized to promote the common good give opportunities to all people to reach their fulfillment more fully and easily.

_____ **15.** The fundamental rights of people consist of the right to life, liberty, freedom of religion, and the pursuit of happiness.

_____ **16.** The standard by which the Church judges "yes" or "no" to social practices is the human person.

_____ **17.** Common sin is the effect of sin over a period of time that affect society.

_____ **18.** Every good relationship demands loyalty—that the people are true to each other, trust one another, and depend on each other's support.

C **Make Connections** Write a short answer to these questions.

19. Evaluate. Why do you think the First Commandment is first? How do you follow this commandment in your life?

20. Cause and Effect. Name one thing you see in society today that does not promote the dignity of the person. How does this practice devalue people? What effect does this practice have on society?

INVITE

PRAYER God, I rely on you.

Traditions can be comforting when life gets a little crazy. Sometimes what I believe is different from what I end up doing. Why do my parents take going to Mass on Sunday so seriously?

"**U**gh." Abby let out a long, slow groan. She was in the middle of a great dream when a loud and obnoxious ringing interrupted her. It was the alarm clock. She slammed her hand down on it to shut it off.

Abby squinted out of her right eye and glanced at the alarm clock. "No!" She knew she only had half an hour to get ready. She also knew it was useless to ask her parents to let her sleep in. She was really going to have a hard time getting back into the early morning routine.

Abby's parents had warned her about staying up too late at night and not eating well at camp, but she had ignored that advice. Her cabin leaders turned off the cabin lights every night at 10:00 P.M., but they didn't stick around after that. Abby and her cabinmates were up almost all night.

The freedom to do as she pleased thrilled Abby. Her parents weren't super strict, but they were firm about certain routines, especially family dinners and bedtimes. They had dinner at 6:30 P.M. every night, and she had to have lights out and music off by 10:00 P.M. "But my parents aren't here," Abby had smiled to herself.

Abby's family routines disappeared the very first night when she and her three cabinmates stayed up until 1:00 A.M., eating junk food and telling ghost stories. They did the same thing the next night, not only adding new friends to crowd into Abby's cabin, but also bringing new bags of popcorn, chocolate, and candy.

Abby knew she was eating badly—glass after glass of chocolate milk, gooey syrup on pancakes, french fries, and soda.

The week of not enough sleep and poor eating caught up with her by Saturday when her parents came to pick her up. She had a terrible headache and slept most of the way home.

So when the alarm went off Sunday morning, waking her up from the first decent sleep she'd had in a week, she wanted to throw it out the window. She felt sick to her stomach and exhausted, and she didn't want to get up!

ACTIVITY

LET'S BEGIN What are two routines that Abby's family follows? What does Abby learn about the power of good routines?

▶ **Think about the routines in your life. Which routines are helpful to you? Which routines are not? Have you ever abandoned your routines? What was that like? How do you think having routines helps you?**

LOOKING BACK

In 1962, Blessed John XXIII convened more than twenty-five hundred bishops in the Second Vatican Council, or Vatican II. They proposed, examined, and approved changes to the liturgy "to adapt more suitably to the needs of our own times those institutions which are subject to change" (*Introduction, Constitution on Sacred Liturgy*).

Some of the changes were very noticeable and included changing the language of the Mass, and other sacraments, from Latin to the language of the people. The altar was turned so that the priest now faces the people as he celebrates Mass. Although formal Gregorian chant could be used with the Latin Mass, local musical traditions can also be incorporated, a change that was particularly welcome in mission churches. And though the Gospel is to be proclaimed by the priest or a deacon, a lector can now proclaim the other Scripture readings.

THE CHURCH WORSHIPS

Focus What are liturgy and sacraments?

Every day you go through the same steps in many things you do: the way you get ready for school, certain streets you take to get to a friend's house, specific times of day you go online or watch TV. Patterns can be comforting and familiar, but they can also keep our bodies—and our minds—healthy. When you don't have to think about *how* you do something, you can enjoy doing it and you can start thinking about *why* you do it.

Symbols and Rituals We have patterns for keeping our souls healthy, too. The Church uses patterned actions called rituals in its **liturgy**, the official public worship of the Church. The word *liturgy* originally meant a "public work," or an action in the name of or for the people. In Christian meaning, the term describes the participation of all the faithful, in the work of God. When we worship, we give thanks and praise to God.

Rituals make use of actions and symbols. Symbols have several layers of meaning. When you peel an onion, you always get onion from outer layer to inner core. With symbols, you always get the same material object (ring, candle, bread, water) but many additional meanings besides the obvious "outer layer."

A symbol is a sign of something else that is not physical, but is abstract or spiritual, like justice or country. Symbols use real elements to get across a deeper meaning.

Because rituals remain pretty much the same and use symbols and gestures that are repeated, they free us to go beyond the actions that make them up, and to go beyond ourselves, too. In ritual, we are free to enter more deeply into our religious mystery and discover the spiritual meaning "layer by layer."

What deeper religious thoughts do you get when you participate in the Mass?

Effective Signs We all participate in celebrating the liturgy. The priest, deacon, and others may lead us, but we all take part in our prayers, singing, silences, and gestures. It isn't just human action at Mass. Jesus is present with us, acting in and through the priest, Scripture readings, and most especially the Eucharist. He is present through the rituals and symbols in all of the sacraments.

The liturgy is truly a work of the whole Body of Christ, Jesus the Head, and all of its members. The liturgy includes the celebration of the sacraments and the Liturgy of the Hours (public prayers that the priest and the people say together). The **sacraments** are signs of God's grace, given to us through the Church by Christ. The visible symbols and rituals of the sacraments illustrate the graces and effects that are received.

The Church celebrates seven sacraments, which come from the life and teaching of Jesus: the Sacraments of Initiation (Baptism, Confirmation, and Eucharist), Sacraments of Healing (Penance and Reconciliation and Anointing of the Sick), and the Sacraments at the Service of Communion (Holy Orders and Matrimony).

liturgy
sacraments
sanctifying grace
actual grace
precepts of the Church

ACTIVITY

SHARE YOUR FAITH Choose any three symbols used in the Church's worship listed below. Write what the average person might know about the object. Write the meanings you associate with that symbol when worshiping. When finished, compare your answers with those of others, and place any different meanings in the last row.

| water | ashes | vestments | oil | bread | bells | candle |
| wine | incense | palm branches | table | color | music | |

	SYMBOL	SYMBOL	SYMBOL
	_____	_____	_____
TO OTHERS:			
TO ME:			
NEW MEANING:			

VISIBLE AND INVISIBLE REALTIES

Focus What is the connection between worship and moral living?

Perhaps the most famous line in *The Little Prince*, by Antoine de Saint-Exupery, is this: "It is only with the heart that one can see rightly; what is essential is invisible to the eye." God's gift of grace is the desire and ability to know and love God as his adopted sons and daughters. Grace is an invisible but essential part of our lives.

God takes the first step with us, loving us, and offering us his life. Because we are made in his image and have free will, we are free to respond to his grace. His grace makes it possible for us to respond, but we still make the choice on whether to do so or not. Grace connects to what makes us truly human, to our desire to be with God and to be like him, to be free and to be in union with him.

Our Response How do we respond to God's grace? And what does our response look like? One important way is to live a holy (God-like) life by participating in the sacraments and following Jesus' example. Our spiritual life includes our prayers, celebration of the liturgy, and participation in the sacraments. It strengthens our moral life—how we live by Jesus' example and Church teachings. The reverse is also true. The challenges and temptations of everyday life tell us that we need God's help. We can find his help through prayer and the sacraments. We need the spiritual life to have a moral life.

It is vital that we pray and prayer is always possible. As Saint Paul reminds us, "Pray in the Spirit at all times in every prayer and supplication" (*Ephesians 6:18*). Prayer and the Christian life are inseparable. You can pray invisibly when watching a track meet, emptying the dishwasher, or waiting for a ride home.

We can give thanks and praise to God by leading moral lives. Although worship in a church building is visible, we can worship in an invisible or spiritual way every minute of the day by leading moral lives. God makes it possible to follow his commands by his grace. Grace strengthens our moral life, which will only be complete and perfect when we are together with God in heaven.

We obey the Ten Commandments, live out the Beatitudes, pray, and follow the precepts of the Church. The **precepts of the Church** are Church laws that name specific actions that all Catholics must carry out to help them grow in love of God and neighbor.

PRECEPTS OF THE CHURCH

1. Attend Mass on Sundays and avoid unnecessary work.

2. Celebrate the Sacrament of Reconciliation at least once a year if there is serious sin.

3. Receive Holy Communion at least once in the Easter season.

4. Fast and abstain on days of penance.

5. Give your time, gifts, and money to support the Church.

The Church also teaches that we have the responsibility to help provide for the material needs of the Church, based upon our ability.

 How can each of these precepts help you grow in your relationship with God?

ACTIVITY

CONNECT YOUR FAITH Which of the precepts of the Church are easiest for you to follow? Which are the most difficult? Give yourself a rating from 1 to 5 on each one, with 5 being excellent. Make up three additional "Personal Precepts" for your continued spiritual exercise and growth.

SUNDAY

Focus How can we make Sunday a day for worship and rest?

From the earliest times of Christianity, Sunday has been celebrated as the Lord's Day: the first day, the eighth day, the day beyond time, the day of Jesus' Resurrection and the day of post-Resurrection appearances, the day of Eucharist. Sunday is a symbolic day for all that Christianity is!

Sunday is the major celebration of the Eucharist, because it is the day of the Resurrection. It is the day we gather together as a Christian family, and a day of joy and rest. Sunday is at the center of the entire liturgical year.

The Third Commandment The third commandment required the people of the Old Law to observe the Sabbath; we observe Sunday. The Sabbath represented God's rest at the end of the first creation, as told in Genesis. Christians celebrate it on Sunday because that was the day of the new creation begun by the Resurrection of Christ. Because Sunday is the most important holy day of obligation, we are required to participate in the Mass on Sunday or Saturday evening. It is highly recommended that we receive Holy Communion every time we celebrate the Eucharist. Christ longs to give himself to us and be close to us; partaking of his Body and Blood is our response saying, "Yes, I want to become like you."

REMEMBER TO KEEP HOLY THE LORD'S DAY

▶ Participate in Mass.

▶ Avoid work that would prevent us from attending Mass.

▶ Avoid unnecessary work that would take away from the needed relaxation of mind and body.

▶ Perform "good works" that strengthen family bonds and friendships. Contact the lonely or sick or attend parish gatherings.

▶ Set apart some leisure time—broaden your interests at museums (even virtual tours), walk outdoors, read, play music, and do restful activities.

▶ Don't place demanding athletic practices or long hours of work on others that could prevent them from observing the Lord's Day.

ACTIVITY

LIVE YOUR FAITH At one time, "keeping the Sabbath" meant that people could not work or play on Sunday. It's come to mean the spiritual practices you engage in that help you care for your soul. In addition to taking part in Mass, what are other ways for you to take time on Sundays to remember who you are and whose you are? All of us can practice keeping Sabbath in our own ways. Outline your own "Keeping Sabbath" plan below.

KEEPING SABBATH

IN SUMMARY

CATHOLICS BELIEVE

The way we worship and pray has an impact on the choices we make and the ways we live our daily lives.

▶ The liturgy of the Church is the work of the whole Body of Christ. The liturgy uses symbols and rituals to form us in prayer and communicate God's gift of life; symbols and rituals show us the deeper meanings of the mystery.

▶ Our spiritual life—God's grace in us, the celebration of the liturgy, and our participation in the sacraments—strengthens our moral life—how we live by Jesus' example and his teachings and follow the precepts of the Church.

▶ Sunday is a very special day. As the Lord's Day, Sunday observance includes required attendance at Mass, the omission of unnecessary work that would distract from the day's purpose, and attention to living a good life.

CELEBRATION OF THE WORD

Leader: In faith and in hope we gather here this day,
to hear the word of God.

Reader: Let us listen to the Gospel of Luke.
Read Luke 18:1–8.

The Gospel of the Lord.

All: Praise to you, Lord Jesus Christ.

(If time allows, invite students to share their Gospel reflections.)

Leader: O God,
we are your newest generation,
who long to know the stories of our faith;
to grow in our understanding of the message your word has for us,
and to share this "good news" with all your people.

All: Teach us Lord, we pray.

Leader: O God,
We are your people,
who long to grow in the practices of our faith;
to share fully in the celebrations, rituals, songs and prayers;
to be active participants in the Body of Christ.

All: Teach us Lord, we pray.

Leader: O God,
We are your people, your newest generation,
we long to serve all your poor ones,
with the gifts you freely gave us,
and with the love and compassion of your Son, Jesus.

All: Teach us Lord, we pray.

Leader: O God,
Like the widow who persisted,
we dare ask for more . . .
We long to be people of prayer,
who turn to you in times of trouble and fear,
who talk with you in our loneliness and doubt,
who cry out to you in our pain and sorrow,
who reach toward you with our questions
and searching,
and who share with you our joys and our praise.
We ask this through your Son, Jesus. Amen.

 "Enséñame/Teach Us, Lord"
Donna Peña, © 2002, GIA Publications, Inc.

REVIEW

A **Work with Words** Complete each sentence with the correct term from the word bank at right.

Word Bank

- ritual
- Mass
- Church canon
- sanctifying grace
- liturgy
- actual grace
- sacraments
- precepts of the Church

1. Catholics must follow the _____—Church laws that help them grow in love of God and neighbor.

2. _____ is the official public worship of the Church.

3. God gives us _____—help in our particular needs, or to do a particular good act or to avoid evil.

4. God's divine life within us that makes us his friends and adopted children is called _____.

5. _____ are effective signs of God's grace given to the Church by Christ.

B **Check Understanding** Circle the letter of the choice that best completes the sentence.

6. _____ is present through the rituals and symbols of all the sacraments.
   - **a.** Virtue
   - **b.** Signs
   - **c.** Jesus
   - **d.** Mystery

7. The liturgy includes the celebration of the sacraments, most importantly the Eucharist, and the _____.
   - **a.** prayers of the People
   - **b.** Liturgy of the Hours
   - **c.** liturgy of the Saints
   - **d.** precepts of the Church

8. The Sacraments of Initiation are Baptism, _____, and Eucharist.
   - **a.** Anointing the Sick
   - **b.** Reconciliation
   - **c.** Holy Orders
   - **d.** Confirmation

9. The Third Commandment requires us to keep holy the _____.
   - **a.** Lord's Day
   - **b.** precepts of the Church
   - **c.** law of God
   - **d.** a and c

10. _____ (called *charisms*) are intended for the good of all the Church.
    - **a.** Special graces
    - **b.** Sacramental grace
    - **c.** Sanctifying grace
    - **d.** Actual grace

C **Make Connections: Cause and Effect** Write a one-paragraph response to the question below.

What can you do to keep the Sabbath day holy? What difference do you think this might make in your life?

OUR CATHOLIC FAITH

WHAT NOW?

★ Look for connections between the way you pray and the way you act toward God, others, and yourself.

★ Honor the Lord on Sunday by participating in the Mass with your family and avoiding unnecessary work.

★ Despite your busy schedule you can always carve out part of Sunday to remember "who you are and whose you are."

★ Participate in the liturgy. Your voice is needed to respond to the prayers; your mind is needed to listen to the readings; your presence is needed to show the People of God.

★ Hold on to your favorite Catholic symbols and seasons. Allow them to lead you to a deeper understanding of spiritual truths.

ACTIVITY

LIVE YOUR FAITH There are many cycles in life. Write in some activities or rituals you always do within the times of each cycle.

Sunday

Monday

Tuesday

Wednesday

Thursday

Friday

Saturday

Morning

Afternoon

Night

Spring

Summer

Autumn

Winter

▶ Reflect on which times give you the best opportunity to pray. When are you most likely to feel God's presence? Make a sign to remind yourself to pray and listen at these times. Hang it in a place where you are most likely to see it.

 Visit www.harcourtreligion.com for more family and community connections.

 **PRAYER**

Holy Spirit, share your gifts with me.

Saint Maria del Transito de Jesus Sacramentado

Saint Maria del Transito de Jesus Sacramentado had to wait for her own dreams to come true. She lived her life for others and set aside her personal goals to care for her family. When she became ill, she had to put her dreams aside again. But as she waited, she chose to trust the plans of God. She prayed all the time and her faith grew. In the end, God fulfilled her dreams in surprising ways.

Maria del Transito Eugenia de los Dolores Cabanillas was born August 15, 1821, in Argentina. She was the third of eleven children. Her father did well in business, and the family was wealthy. Maria's father also had a deep Christian faith. The children grew up in a godly home. One of Maria's brothers became a priest. Three sisters became nuns.

Maria was taught at home as a child. When she was older, she was sent to the famous school at Cordoba. She studied there and cared for her younger brother as he prepared for the priesthood. When Maria's father died in 1850, the rest of the family moved to Cordoba. Maria stayed at home to help her mother care for the children. Maria's mother, brother, sisters, and five orphan cousins lived in the small house. Maria was devoted to God in prayer and to the Mass. She also visited the poor and sick of Cordoba.

Maria's mother died in 1858. With her family grown or gone, Maria found herself free then to pursue her calling. She entered the Franciscan order at the age of thirty-seven. She gave more and more of her day to prayer. In 1872, Maria moved to Buenos Aires to enter a Carmelite monastery. Health problems forced Maria to leave in 1874. Later in the year she entered a new convent, but again she had to leave because of health problems.

During this time of sickness and loss, Maria turned to God. She had time to think and to pray more about an idea. All her life she had wanted to teach and help poor children. With encouragement and help from two friends, Maria started the Congregation of the Franciscan Tertiary Missionaries of Argentina. The Congregation helped the poor and orphans.

The new Congregation had great success. Three colleges were founded during Maria's life. But Maria's health was still poor. Daily work and sacrifice led to her death in August 1885. Through the trials of her life, she was an example of a servant. She trusted God's plan for her, prayed faithfully, and gave her life for others.

▲ Saint Maria del Transito de Jesus Sacramentado, 1821–1885

GLOBAL DATA

Argentina

■ Argentina is the second-largest country in South America, after Brazil.

■ Argentina is as long as the United States is wide.

■ Over 90 percent of the people are Roman Catholic.

■ Argentina is the place where scientists found one of the world's oldest dinosaur fossils.

■ Argentina became independent from Spain in 1816.

■ Argentina was the home of political leader Eva Peron, known as "Evita."

FAITHFUL Living

**PRAYER** Help me keep my promises.

Sometimes it's easy to keep a promise . . .
but sometimes it's really hard!
Maybe I should avoid making promises for the rest of my life!

Mike ground his teeth till his jaw hurt. His head hurt, too. He was tired of arguing with Joey, his younger brother. Plus, he knew his mom was upset with him, though she didn't come out and say it. He sighed deeply. He wished he could go back in time and take back his promise to Joey.

While Mike was wolfing down his cereal that morning, Joey had bounded into the kitchen grinning from ear to ear. "So what time do we leave?" Joey blurted out excitedly. Mike glanced up. "To go where?" he asked.

"Paradise Park, of course!" Joey replied. "What are you talking about?" Mike got up to rinse his bowl. "You promised to use your Buddy Pass to take me to Paradise Park today, remember?"

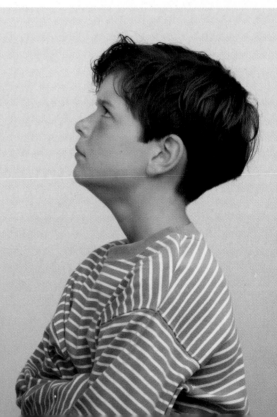

"No, I . . ." Mike started to reply but the words got stuck in his throat. Then he did remember. A panicky feeling suddenly gripped his stomach.

When Mike had bought a Paradise Park Gold Pass, he was excited. It gave the holder special privileges, like no-wait lines, staying on the ride to go again, and four Buddy Pass days—special days when he could bring a friend for free. Mike had been showing off his Gold Pass to his family when Joey asked if Mike would take him on the second Buddy Pass day. Mike was feeling so good at that moment that he said yes. Then he promptly forgot about it.

Mike never considered that the second Buddy Pass day would be the perfect midsummer day to hang out at Paradise Park with his best friend, David, and their other friends. He hadn't known there would be a special evening concert and fireworks show at 11:00 P.M. Worst of all, Mike didn't know that David wouldn't be able to afford a pass and would want Mike to get him in on his Buddy Pass.

Now Mike felt trapped. Joey almost started crying when he told him he had promised David the Buddy Pass. "But you promised me first!" Joey yelled.

Mike found his mom checking her e-mail in the den. He explained his dilemma and then asked, "Mom, what do I do?" She thought for a few minutes before answering. Then she said, "I can't tell you what to do. But I think you already know what the right thing to do is. You've got a little while before you leave. Why don't you think about it?"

"Just tell me what you want me to do!" Mike grumbled as he trudged to his room. But he had already made up his mind.

LET'S BEGIN What do you think Mike will do? How can he find peace in either decision?

▶ **When have you wanted to break a promise because something different (or better) came along? How did you decide what to do? Suppose you never made another promise to anyone. How would that hurt your relationships?**

MARRIAGE AS A SIGN OF CHRIST'S LOVE

Focus What does a couple promise in marriage?

When you make a promise to do something with or for someone, that person plans on you keeping your promise. He or she may change other plans because of what you said you would do. Keeping your promises strengthens your relationships by showing that you are true to your word and can be trusted. So making a promise enriches your life, but it sometimes makes life a little more complicated.

It's the same thing with your relationship with God. Making and keeping promises with God deepens your friendship with God. It also brings challenges.

Together God is Trinity. His very being is community. Because we are made in God's image and likeness, God did not create humans to be alone. From the beginning, men and women have been partners. We find our true selves in relationship with others. In other words, we know ourselves better when our ties with family, friends, and others are strong. We become our best selves when we strengthen those ties by keeping our promises to others, whether the promise is small like helping around the house or large like committing our lives permanently to another person in marriage.

The sacraments give us grace to be faithful to our commitments and relationships. By his presence at the Wedding of Cana, and by performing his first miracle there (See *John 2:1–11*.), Jesus showed the goodness and importance of marriage. Christian marriage is a sacrament, an effective sign of Christ's presence.

The Promises of Marriage In Catholic marriages, a man and woman freely pledge to be faithful and true to each other forever. The Sacrament of **Matrimony** is a symbol of the union of Christ and his Church. God gives spouses special graces to make their love more perfect, strengthen their unity, and make them holy in their love for each other.

As a sign of Christ's love for his people, married couples have an awesome responsibility. They freely choose to make a permanent covenant of faithful love with each other. This covenant was founded by God the Creator and given special laws. The couple must be to each other and to all they meet what Christ is to the Church—totally loving and sacrificing, giving themselves in service, faithfully working to keep their marriage unbreakable.

In a public celebration within the liturgy, before a priest or deacon, witnesses, and family, the couple pledges to love each other as God loves us. Sometimes it's hard to believe that God is always with us, forgives us, cares about us, and loves us beyond our understanding. When in doubt, we can look to happily married couples and say, "OK, that gives me a glimpse of God's love. If Mort and Mattie are *that* forgiving, *that* compassionate, *that* caring, how much greater must God's love be!"

> **What does a loving and faithful marriage teach us about God's love?**

> **How can your loyal commitment to someone or something show God's love to someone else?**

Words of Faith

Matrimony

Holy Orders

CATHOLICS TODAY

Some of the Eastern Catholic Churches use crowns at their marriage rite. In fact, the sacrament is referred to as "holy crowning." The priest prays prayers of blessing and places the crowns on the heads of the bride and groom. The crowns symbolize that the couple are the king and queen of their home, that they should give themselves to each other, and that they are part of the kingdom of God.

ACTIVITY

SHARE YOUR FAITH Wedding vows are promises you make to the person you marry. What kinds of values and ways of behaving do you think are important in a successful marriage? Write some of the promises you would like to make when you get married.

I _____, promise to _____

_____

_____

_____

THE ORDAINED PRIESTHOOD

Focus How is Holy Orders a sacrament of service?

Matrimony is not the only sacrament that involves making a promise or being at the service of Communion. The other is the Sacrament of **Holy Orders**, in which men promise to dedicate their lives to God and the Church and are ordained as deacons, priests, or bishops.

Like Matrimony, Holy Orders involves making promises that deepen relationships to God and others through service and giving witness to faith in daily life. Although all followers of Christ must serve, bishops, priests, and deacons assume the service of authority for the Kingdom through teaching, worship, and pastoral governance.

All the people in the Church are part of the priesthood of Christ. This is called the "common priesthood of the faithful." Based on the common priesthood, another way to participate in the mission of Christ is to take up the ministry through the Sacrament of Holy Orders, where the task is to serve in the name and in the person of Christ the Head in the midst of the community. In the ministerial priesthood the priest receives a sacred power for the service of the faithful.

How does a man know he is called to serve as a deacon or a priest? Here are some starters:

▶ The man discerns through prayer, careful thought, and many conversations with others, God's call to live out his baptismal promises in Holy Orders. He is invited by and receives this calling from a bishop (deacon and priest) or the Pope (Bishop).

▶ The community can help the candidate discern his calling, which he must receive from a bishop or the Pope.

▶ The man has a solid spiritual life and the personal gifts needed by the Church. He must have certain talents and abilities that would help the church family. The Sacrament of Holy Orders grants a special role of leadership on the priest. He has a distinctive relationship with Christ and the Church.

What is the main difference between the common priesthood of the faithful and the ministerial priesthood?

The Celebration of the Sacrament After years of discernment, studying theology, working in a parish, and performing different ministries, the candidate for the priesthood is ordained. The Sacrament of Holy Orders usually takes place in the diocesan cathedral, and the bishop is the minister. After the Litany of Saints, the bishop lays his hands on the candidates' heads, prays in silence, and then sings or recites a solemn prayer of consecration, asking the Holy Spirit to bless the man with the graces needed to fulfill his ministry.

Like Baptism and Confirmation, ordination prints an indelible character upon the one ordained. He enters into a permanent relationship with the Church, as he acts in the person of Christ as a leader in the Church community.

Why do you think all three of these sacraments mark the recipients?

Acting in Christ's Name Priests act *in persona Christi* (in the person of Christ) and *in persona ecclesiae* (in the person of the Church). Through their membership in the Body of Christ and the special graces of the Sacrament of Holy Orders, priests are special signs of Christ, the Head of the Body. A priest's leadership should inspire the faith of the community. This happens when a priest's ministry flows from a heart transformed by the Spirit and always open to God and his People. In choosing to live a celibate life in imitation of Jesus, the priest grows in deeper intimacy with God. In choosing obedience in imitation of Jesus who was perfectly obedient to his Father, the priest obeys the bishop and pope, knowing that Jesus works through them.

ACTIVITY

CONNECT YOUR FAITH Name three ways a parish priest can make a difference in the lives of his parishioners.

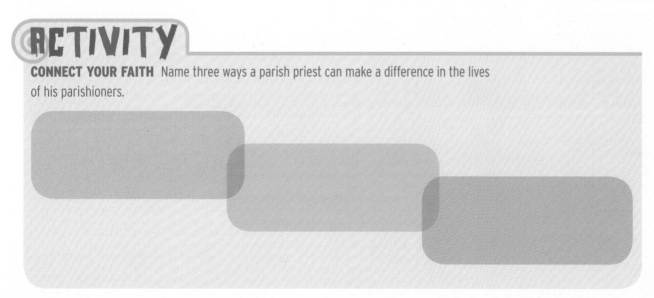

FAITHFUL LIVING

 Focus How can you live out the sixth and ninth commandments?

Faithful living in marriage means that you will be able to count on the goodness of your partner every day until old age. Being faithful in marriage involves many things. Most importantly the husband and wife

▶ commit to each other and only each other. This results in a unique unity between the couple. Polygamy—the practice of having more than one spouse at a time—opposes this unity.

▶ make a permanent and unbreakable commitment that is blessed by God. Divorce would separate what God has joined together; it goes against God's plan and his laws. Catholics who divorce and remarry remain in the Church, but they cannot receive Holy Communion.

▶ are open to having children if they are blessed with them. The unwillingness to have children turns marriage away from its greatest gift—a child.

The Sacrament of Matrimony gives the couple the grace to be faithful and true to their marital vocation. Living out the marriage covenant (agreement) requires the couple to follow the sixth commandment, "You shall not commit adultery," and the ninth commandment, "You shall not covet your neighbor's wife," Divorce, polygamy, cheating on one's spouse, and living together before marriage are all serious offenses that take away from the importance and meaning of marriage.

No matter how hard some couples try, however, their marriage promise may be too difficult to keep. And no matter how much we try, there is no way to soften the painful experience of divorce. Making promises makes life richer—and sometimes more complicated. Our faith tells us that playing the "blame game" and making a spouse, parent, or stepparent "the enemy" only makes the pain worse. The Church recognizes that those in pain need our prayers and support.

Commandments for All of Us The virtue of chastity helps you maintain the right balance of body and spirit in human sexuality. Your sexuality is part of who you are; it's more than whether you are biologically a male or female. It includes the way you think and feel about things, the way you pray, the way you are inclined to act, and the interests you have.

Chastity helps you express your sexuality in the right way. It helps you remain pure in the ways you act and think. It helps you show love in the appropriate ways. Some thoughts and actions harm a person's dignity and go against the virtue of chastity to such a degree that they are sins: masturbation, sexual intercourse outside of marriage, pornography, and homosexual actions.

The ninth commandment reminds us that the proper attitudes toward sexuality involve the ways people think, too. Desiring to act in improper ways can lead people to do the thing they desire, causing disrespect to their own bodies or those of others. Working to focus your heart on what is good and practicing temperance are important. The virtue of modesty is all about decency. It's about being discreet in the way you dress, and the things you say (or choose not to say).

The more you practice the virtues, like modesty and chastity, the more you'll be able to rely on them. Participating in weekly Eucharist and the frequent celebration of the Sacrament of Reconciliation can give you the strength to practice self-control and make good judgments.

ACTIVITY

LIVE YOUR FAITH Complete the following statements with a partner:

"Where there is modesty, there is . . ."

"Where there is chastity, there is . . ."

IN SUMMARY

CATHOLICS BELIEVE

The sacraments strengthen us to be faithful to our commitments and our relationships.

▶ The Sacrament of Matrimony strengthens the couple to live out their promises to be true and faithful, to be open to the gift of children, and to be models of the love Christ has for his people.

▶ All baptized persons share in the priesthood of Christ. Some men are ordained for special participation in the mission of Jesus. Through the Sacrament of Holy Orders, they receive the grace to act in the name of Jesus to lead and serve the Church community.

▶ Practicing and living by the virtues of modesty and chastity can help all people, no matter what their state in life.

PRAYER

PRAYER OF PETITION

Sing: *Jesus, give us strength.*

Reader 1: A reading from the holy Gospel according to Mark
             Read Mark 12:28–33.

             The Gospel of the Lord.

All: Praise to you, Lord Jesus Christ.

Leader: Loving God,
             Be with us now as we call out to your greatest gift, Jesus,
             and ask for strength and guidance.

             Our response is . . . Jesus, give us strength.

Reader 2: To keep the promise of faithfulness:
             in times of question and doubt.
             For this we pray . . .

All: Jesus, give us strength.

Reader 3: To keep the promise of love:
             of our God, of self, and others.
             For this we pray . . .

All: Jesus, give us strength.

Reader 4: To keep the promise of friendship:
             with those we walk with each day,
             with those we find hard to love.
             For this we pray . . .

All: Jesus, give us strength.

Reader 5: To keep the promise of service,
             in times of indifference,
             when we are busy, self involved, or distracted.
             For this we pray . . .

All: Jesus, give us strength.

Leader: Lord, Jesus,
             Give us strength today and always,
             to serve you in all we do,
             and to faithfully follow wherever you lead.

All: Amen.

 "Jesus, Give Us Strength"
Tony Alonso, © 2002 GIA Publications, Inc.

REVIEW

A Work with Words Circle the letter of the choice that best completes the sentence.

1. Christian _____ is an effective sign of Christ's presence joining a man and a woman in a holy union.
   a. marriage
   b. priesthood
   c. Confirmation
   d. fellowship

2. The Sacrament of _____ is a symbol of the union of Christ and his Church.
   a. Confirmation
   b. Eucharist
   c. Matrimony
   d. Baptism

3. Married couples freely choose to make a permanent _____ of faithful love with each other.
   a. covenant
   b. character
   c. confirmation
   d. none of the above

4. The virtue of _____ helps you maintain the right balance of body and spirit in human sexuality.
   a. hope
   b. modesty
   c. chastity
   d. faith

B Check Understanding Complete each sentence with the correct terms from the word bank at right.

5. From the beginning, men and women have been _____.

6. Jesus performed his first _____ at the Wedding of Cana.

7. Bishops, priests, and _____ assume the service of authority at their ordination for the Kingdom through teaching, worship, and pastoral governance.

8. Through the Sacrament of _____, ordained men serve in the name of and in the person of Christ the Head in the midst of the community.

9. Like Baptism and Confirmation, ordination prints an indelible _____ upon the one ordained.

10. The virtue of _____ helps you be discreet in the ways you dress, act, and talk.

Word Bank

modesty
marriage
healing
deacons
ministers
partners
miracle
Holy Orders
character
chastity

C Make Connections: Compare and Contrast Write a one-paragraph response to the question below.

Compare and contrast the way marriage is presented in two current movies or books. How are the principles of Christian marriage being lived out in both?

OUR CATHOLIC FAITH

ACTIVITY

LIVE YOUR FAITH Think about the promises you are living with now. Use the chart below to explore how you make and keep your promises. Think about the following:

▶ **What promises have you made?**

▶ **What responsibilities come with them?**

▶ **How are you doing in keeping them?**

Promises	Responsibilities	Results

▶ Write a new song about a good and faithful marriage, using the phrases below and some of your own. Don't forget to give your song a title.

Faithful love

Keeping our vows

A promise is

God's in my heart, I hope you can see.

The bumpy road is built on rock

"I do"

Promise me

Tell me when . . .

 Visit www.harcourtreligion.com for more family and community connections.

 PRAYER

Jesus, I promise to be your faithful follower.

Eusebius Kino

Many people make promises to God when times are hard—when they are sick or need help. But many people also forget to keep those promises when the pressure is off. At the age of eighteen, Eusebius Chinus was very sick. In fact, he almost died. While he was sick, he made a vow that, if he lived, he would enter the priesthood and become a missionary. Eusebius recovered and he didn't forget his promise. He became an explorer and missionary. He baptized more than forty-five hundred Pima Indians in Arizona before his death.

Eusebius Chinus was born in northern Italy in August 1645. After he recovered from his illness, he studied for twelve years for the Jesuit order in Austria and Germany. Eusebius was good at math and astronomy, and he thought his knowledge of math would be helpful in China. Math was highly respected there. But instead in 1680 the young Jesuit was sent to New Spain—Mexico.

In Mexico, Chinus changed his name to Kino and Kino founded the mission of Lower California. Father Kino crossed the Rio Colorado and became the first to explore Baja California. There he found a land route to California. Father Kino provided the first reports and sketches of this almost unknown land. Over time, he would explore more than twenty thousand miles. Kino explored the Southwest, mapping it as he went. His map was the standard for one hundred years.

Father Kino did mission work in Mexico and southern Arizona. He founded over twenty churches and many chapels among the Pima Indians. God gave him a special ability to reach their hearts and minds. Father Kino also introduced cattle to the Indians. He taught them to raise sheep, goats, and mules, and he trained them in carpentry, blacksmithing, and baking. Kino also introduced crops from Italy, including apricots, citrus, figs, peaches, pears, and wheat. All of these are still important to the economy of the region.

Father Kino was shot by hostile Indians on March 15, 1711. He died faithful to the promise he made as a teenager, and he remains one of the greatest missionaries of this country.

▲ Eusebius Kino, 1645–1711

GLOBAL DATA

Southwestern United States

- Southwestern United States was home to the Anasazi, from roughly A.D. 1 to A.D. 1300, who lived in pueblos such as those found in Chaco Canyon.

- Descendents of the Anasazi such as the Hopi, the Acoma, and the Zuni peoples, were joined by Apaches and Navajos in the 1500s.

- Southwestern United States was explored by Spanish conquistadors in search of gold, silver, and precious gems, beginning with Cabez de Vaca in 1528.

- Spanish missionaries developed a network of missions throughout the region, converting thousands of Native Americans to Catholicism.

- San Xavier del Bac, a mission started by Father Kino in 1700, still stands today outside of Tucson, Arizona.

18 THE CHURCH Year

INVITE

PRAYER — God, help me know how to live.

*What's next for me?
A new beginning to see things differently?
About time. But I wish some things would stay the same.*

Tayshan burst through the doors of the classroom and into the hallway for the last time. The final bell of the year had just rung. "SEE YA! I'm out of here!" He had spent the last three months thinking about this day—his last day at Nativity—and now it had come. "I'm in high school now," he thought.

That thought made him stop suddenly in his tracks. He pictured St. Xavier High School, the giant, old, city-wide high school across from the university. Tayshan felt his stomach tighten a bit at the thought of walking up the wide marble steps and through the dark wood doors at St. X.

What would that be like? Something like his first day at the junior high two years ago? He hadn't talked to anyone the whole day. He'd carried all his books around in his backpack because he didn't want to look like he didn't know how to work the combination on his locker.

When he finally tried the combination the next day, he bumped into a boy who was fumbling with his locker. "You know how to open this thing?" The boy turned to Tayshan. "No," Tayshan had answered, and for some reason that made both of them laugh out loud. Jason—everyone called him JayRay—soon became his best friend. At least that wasn't changing, they'd still be together at high school.

Tayshan went to his good old locker for the last time. As he cleaned out his pictures, notes from friends, and sports stuff, he thought about JayRay and him walking into the auditorium at St. X together for the first time. He had heard about freshman orientation, how the freshmen were given twenty minutes to learn the school song and then perform it on the stage while the upper classmen laughed and yelled, trying to break their concentration. JayRay already had plans about how he was going to have fun with *that*. "We'll be okay," Tayshan thought to himself.

He also thought about what his brother had told him about St. X. There were so many after-school clubs to be in, you just had to make sure you didn't join too many. His brother knew which teachers were the best, most fun, or scariest. He'd told Tayshan about the awesome football games and how cool it was to meet kids from around the city, not just their own neighborhood. The class trip over spring break would be the best part.

"Yeah, I'm ready to leave for high school." Tayshan closed his empty locker and walked through the door at the end of the quad for the last time. "I just hope St. X is ready for me!"

ACTIVITY

LET'S BEGIN What are some of the changes that Tayshan is looking forward to? What does he hope remains the same? What exactly is he celebrating?

▶ How do you celebrate new beginnings in your life? How do you deal with a new situation that you're looking forward to, but feel a little nervous about as well?

THE LITURGICAL YEAR

 Focus What does the Church celebrate through the year?

So many things in our lives change with each new year. Did you ever look back at last year and realize how different you are today than you were a year ago? Things you worried about then may look easy now that you've been through them. It's like winning the big basketball game or passing final exams. You get ready for them by practicing or studying and when the time comes you take what you've learned and use it to win a victory. When you've finished what you started, you celebrate— you might hang your final exam on the fridge or save a team photo in your album. You want to hold on to something that helps you remember how it all happened.

Remembering and Celebrating The Church does the same thing. We want to remember special events in the story of Jesus' life and our own story. We celebrate the Paschal mystery through a yearly cycle of seasons and feasts called the **liturgical year**.

One reason we call it the liturgical year is because the Scripture readings, prayers, and songs of the liturgy reflect what season or feast we are in. In the cycle of 365 days, the Church remembers the whole life of Jesus from his Incarnation and nativity to his death, Resurrection, and Ascension. We remember his continued presence with us through the sending of the Holy Spirit at Pentecost and the expectation of his coming again at the end of time.

As Catholics, you might say that we have our own calendar. Instead of celebrating President's Day, Valentine's Day, or the first day of spring, we celebrate different events from the life of Christ: his birth, miracles, prayer, preaching, suffering, death, and Resurrection. On Passion (Palm) Sunday we emphasize his death; on Easter we celebrate in a special way his Resurrection; and on other Sundays we may listen to the stories of Jesus' miracles and teaching.

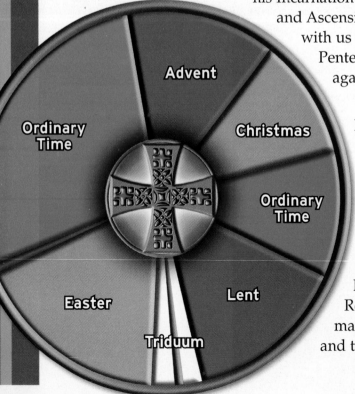

The Whole Every day really celebrates everything that Jesus accomplished for us through his Passion, death, Resurrection, and Ascension. Whether Christmas or Ash Wednesday or the feast of a saint, we celebrate only one thing: the Paschal mystery. Sunday after Sunday we celebrate the Risen Lord and what he has done for us.

The liturgical year begins in Advent, typically falling in late November or early December, moves to the Christmas season, then to the first, shorter part of Ordinary Time, on to Lent, the Triduum, and the Easter Season, then to the longer part of Ordinary Time that lasts many weeks. We end the year with the Feast of Christ the King.

Look at each of the seasons of the liturgical year, and you'll discover that even though each one may emphasize one part of Jesus' life, ministry, or saving work, each also celebrates the whole of it. The anticipation of the Messiah during Advent and the joyous news of his birth would not be worth celebrating if Jesus had not preached, healed, and forgiven people, and ultimately given us new life by dying and rising. In every season and feast, the Scripture passages we proclaim, prayers we pray, and songs we sing all come back to the great mystery we celebrate each and every Sunday of the year.

What's your favorite Church season or feast day and why?

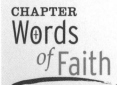

What's Extraordinary About Ordinary Time?

► It's the longest season of the year, either thirty-three or thirty-four weeks depending upon the year.

► It happens two times during the liturgical year, once between Christmas and Lent and again after Easter.

► It gets its name from the way the Sundays of the season are counted. The word *ordinary* comes from the Latin word *ordinis*, which means "number." There are so many Sundays of Ordinary Time that we need to keep track of them, so they are counted consecutively.

ACTIVITY

SHARE YOUR FAITH Work with a partner to describe what you already know about the Church's seasons.

	FOCUS	SYMBOLS/COLORS	PARISH AND FAMILY PRACTICES
ADVENT			
CHRISTMAS			
ORDINARY TIME			
LENT			
TRIDUUM			
EASTER			

A TIME FOR EVERYTHING

Focus How is the celebration of the liturgical year the same but different?

Whether you're shopping or playing baseball or reading this page, you are part of the Body of Christ. The liturgical year helps you pattern your life on Jesus' life. It helps you live the life of Christ a little more deeply year after year. You don't just come around full circle every 365 days, arriving at the same place you were the year before.

Every year your experiences, needs, and dreams change. So do your relationships with your family and friends. Your relationship with God changes, too. Some years you find yourself really relating to Christmas; another year, you find yourself really paying attention to Lent, or All Saints Day, or simply "going to communion."

Past, Present, Future So what you hear, feel, think about, and experience during liturgical worship and family rituals surrounding a season will change as you change, but you will continue to celebrate the same important seasons and feasts. Everyone needs that continuity in their lives. It's comforting to know that "For everything there is a season, and a time for every matter under heaven" (*Ecclesiastes 3:1*).

The Church celebrates those special times no matter what else is going on in our lives or in the world. While we are busy experiencing different things in our lives, she helps us join those experiences with the experience of Christ and the Church. The community of the Church and its traditions keep us connected—to ourselves and to each other.

✝ SCRIPTURE

GO TO THE SOURCE
Read **Ecclesiastes 3:1–8**. How many contrasting "seasons" are there in these verses? Can you think of any others? What does "under the heavens" mean to you?

The Trinity in the Liturgy

The Church's liturgy is far more than human actions. The Trinity is present and active in our worship, bringing about the mysteries of faith we celebrate throughout the liturgical year.

FATHER

In creating the world, God the Father gave us all the gifts the Church uses in the sacraments: wheat, wine, oil, water, beeswax, and much more. More importantly, he gave us the gift of his Son, whose saving work is the source of all the grace flowing from the sacraments. In each and every liturgy, we bless and praise God the Father for all these great gifts. We acknowledge that he gave us the blessing of creation and most importantly the gift of salvation through his Son, Jesus. The Father has shared the Holy Spirit with us so that we might share in the new life his Son has made possible.

SON

Jesus is the origin of our sacraments. He is also the principal priest in every sacrament. Bishops, priests, and deacons serve as his ministers. When the Church baptizes, Christ baptizes. When the Church confers Holy Orders, Christ ordains the priests. In each and every liturgy, Jesus Christ is present as is his mystery of salvation through the work of the Holy Spirit and his own Body, the Church, that is a sign of hope, a means of grace, and a way to meet God.

When we participate in the Mass and sacraments, we are participating in Jesus' offering of himself to his Father. Christ is the priest of the new covenant. He established the Eucharist at the Last Supper and offers it through the work of the priest who leads the celebration. Only ordained priests can preside at Mass and consecrate the bread and wine, changing them into Christ's Body and Blood.

HOLY SPIRIT

The Holy Spirit prepares the assembly gathered to meet Christ at every Mass. The Holy Spirit's mission in the liturgy is to show Christ to us, making him and his mystery of salvation present by his power, and to work in the Church so that the gifts of Holy Communion can bear fruit.

ACTIVITY

CONNECT YOUR FAITH What season are you in these days? When you think of your faith relationship with God and the Church, would you say that you are in summer, spring, fall, or winter? Explain your answer to others.

TO LIVE THE LIFE OF CHRIST

Focus Why is participation in the Eucharist and regular prayer important?

We are always "a work in progress." We are always becoming what the Church already tells us we are: children of God, witnesses of our faith, forgiven people.

As we celebrate Eucharist week after week, we grow deeper in understanding the Mass. We know it's a memorial of all he has done for us: Christ's Passover, his work of salvation finished through his death on the cross and Resurrection, and made present in the liturgy. The Eucharist is at the very center of the liturgical year and all of the Church's life; everything we do leads to and flows from the celebration of the Mass. In it Christ connects all of us to the sacrifice he made on the cross and gives us new life.

The liturgical year commemorates the saving work of Christ. This memorial means more than remembering Jesus' deeds recorded in the Gospels. It means we feel, act, think, and love in such a way that others can see what Christ's actions and character are like when they observe our actions. That is the whole point of a memorial: to be transformed by remembering what Christ is like, to become like him.

Throughout the Church year we celebrate the lives of the saints who help us model Christ: Mary the Mother of God, the Apostles, the martyrs. These days show that the Church on earth is joined to the liturgy of heaven. Our deceased relatives and friends can also help us see the connection between heaven and earth. They, too, help us.

The Church Invites Us to Regular Prayer Exercise programs and healthful diets have something in common: They are regular patterns or routines that are good for your physical health. The Church, too, has its regimen of regular prayer that helps keep Catholics in good spiritual health. Participation in the Sunday Eucharist, the Sacrament of Reconciliation, and the feasts of the Church year can help us grow spiritually healthy and be strengthened to live as Christ did. Daily prayer and the Liturgy of the Hours are two more ways we can enter into a conversation with God and open our minds and hearts to him.

The **Liturgy of the Hours** is the Church's public prayer to make each day holy. This prayer is offered at set times during the day and night. In some monasteries and convents, monks and nuns gather throughout the day to praise God in the Liturgy of the Hours for his gifts and to mark the holiness of the day. Although women and men religious pray these prayers, the Liturgy of the Hours is also the prayer of the whole People of God. All are encouraged to pray the principle hours, Morning Prayer, and Evening Prayer. Some parishes gather together to do so. You may like to use a special book called the *Office* containing the official prayers of the Church's Liturgy of the Hours.

However, any prayers of praise, thanks, and petition are great daily or weekly prayer routines. Your own personal daily prayers keep you in touch with God. You may have some favorite prayers like the Our Father and Hail Mary. Perhaps you've created your own prayers and memorized them as you've used them. As you mature, the Church encourages you to taste a variety of prayer experiences to add to your "prayer diet."

ACTIVITY

LIVE YOUR FAITH What new beginnings do you want to pray over? What new beginnings do you want to celebrate or give thanks for? Write a prayer naming what you need as you continue your journey.

MY PRAYER

IN SUMMARY

CATHOLICS BELIEVE

We grow in our understanding of Jesus and in our relationship with him as we celebrate the different seasons of the liturgical year, which helps us pattern our lives on the life of Christ.

▶ The seasons and feasts of the liturgical year emphasize different aspects of the one Paschal mystery of Christ, connecting us more closely to the Passion, death, Resurrection, and Ascension of Jesus.

▶ Because we are different each year, we enter into the Church's seasons and feasts with different needs, hopes, and relationships with God and others.

▶ The Eucharist is at the very heart of what it means to be Catholic. Participation in Sunday Mass and our own regular personal prayer help us live the life of Christ.

PRAYER OF PRAISE

Leader: God of all creation,
from the wind of winter,
to the blazing heat of summer,
from the smell of spring blossoms,
to the sound of rustling fall leaves,
in the changing of every season,
You are there.

Side 1: When we laugh and enjoy the company of friends,
when we cry and are lonely and need someone to listen,

Side 2: When we lash out in anger and break a trust,
when we build up a relationship with kind words and actions,

All: God is near, in all things, always guiding the way.

Side 1: When we care for this planet, when we recycle and reuse,
when we are careless and carefree with the fruits of the earth,

Side 2: When we score the winning goal and our team wins,
when we lose with dignity, knowing how you play is key,

All: God is near, in all things, always guiding the way.

Side 1: When we sit in silence, indifference, or avoidance,
when we speak out in truth for justice and what is right in our world,

Side 2: When we surround ourselves with objects, material possessions
and wealth,
when we share all we have, knowing God is enough,

All: O God,
teach us,
shape us,
and hold us close
until we meet face to face,
and rest in your gentle love. Amen.

♪ "May the Road Rise to Meet You"
Lori True, © 2001, GIA Publications, Inc.

REVIEW

A Work with Words Complete each sentence with the correct term from the word bank at right.

1. We celebrate the Paschal mystery through a cycle of seasons and feasts called the _____.

2. The liturgical year begins with the season of _____.

3. The _____ is present and active in the liturgy of the Church, bringing about the mysteries of faith we celebrate.

4. In each and every liturgy, we bless and praise God the _____ for the blessing of creation and most importantly the gift of salvation.

5. The _____ is the Church's public prayer to make each day holy.

B Check Understanding Indicate whether the following statements are true or false. Then rewrite false statements to make them true.

_____ 6. In the cycle of 365 days, the Church remembers the earthly life of Jesus from his Incarnation and birth to his death.

_____

_____ 7. Jesus is the origin of our sacraments and the principal priest who celebrates them.

_____

_____ 8. The Holy Spirit's mission in the liturgy is to show Christ to us, making him and his mystery of salvation present by his power.

_____

_____ 9. In the Liturgy of the Hours, the sacrifice that Christ made on the cross is renewed and gives all of his Church new life.

_____

_____ 10. The Assumption, All Saints Day, and Ash Wednesday are holy days of obligation.

_____

C Make Connections: Evaluating Write a one-paragraph response to the question below.

What part of the liturgical year is most meaningful to you now and why? How has your experience of that particular season or celebration changed over time?

OUR CATHOLIC FAITH

WHAT NOW?

Start a "spiritual workout" program:

* Participate in the Mass on Sunday and the holy days of obligation.

* Find time every day to pray.

* Explore the prayers of the Liturgy of the Hours.

* Investigate other forms of prayer that may be new to you.

* Consider actions you can take within each season that would bring you closer to Christ.

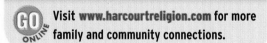

ACTIVITY

LIVE YOUR FAITH The Paschal mystery is all about the natural way we experience hope, loss, and rebirth. It is a spiritual view of life that celebrates the good things in life, the "deaths," and the new beginnings. It is the mystery that Jesus taught us to accept.

▶ What joys have you had in life so far?

▶ What kinds of losses, failures, or "deaths" have you gone through?

▶ What new beginnings, second chances, or "comebacks" have you experienced?

▶ What pieces of your faith do you think must remain the same in order for you to make your way through the Paschal mystery of your life?

▶ What pieces of your faith do you need to develop more fully in order to keep on making your way through the Paschal mystery of your life?

▶ How can you celebrate the life God has given you so far?

GO ONLINE Visit www.harcourtreligion.com for more family and community connections.

PRAYER

God, I know you are with me in every season of my life.

Saint Benedict the Black

Benedict's parents became Christians after they were brought from Africa to Sicily as slaves. Benedict was a slave until he was eighteen years old. Because of his origin and the color of his skin, Benedict was mocked by others. It was a hard way to begin life, but Benedict made a choice that he would make repeatedly throughout his life. He did not respond out of anger. He chose to respond in the spirit of love. He chose to follow God.

Benedict was given his freedom at age eighteen, but he still worked in the fields for his former master. A hermit named Lanzi saw Benedict's response to the people who mocked him. He told those who spoke unkind words that they would hear great things of Benedict. Lanzi invited Benedict to join the group of hermits. Benedict decided to sell what little he had and give the money to the poor. Then he joined the group. Later Benedict joined a friary and was given the role of cook.

The mid-sixteenth century was a time of great change in the Church. Benedict's convent wanted to make changes to follow the Franciscan ideal more closely. Benedict was chosen as the one to oversee the reforms. Benedict was not happy with this new role. He could not read or write and was not even a priest, but he chose to obey. Benedict led wisely. He was known for his holiness and did much to help the poor.

Benedict always referred to possessions as "ours," never as "mine." In the end, Benedict wanted only to return to the kitchen. He spent the rest of his days cooking for his brothers and sharing the love of Christ. Many people came to the kitchen to meet with Benedict. The holy man listened and responded to the poor and the sick. Benedict died at the friary. Upon his death, King Philip III of Spain paid for a special tomb for the simple friar. Known as Saint Benedict the Black, he is the patron of African Americans in the United States.

▲ Saint Benedict the Black, 1526–1589

GLOBAL DATA

Sicily

- Sicily is the island at the tip of Italy's boot and is the largest island in the Mediterranean Sea.

- Sicily has a population of 5 million people.

- Sicily celebrates the Table of Saint Joseph with a feast to honor the father of Jesus. The tradition goes back to the Middle Ages.

- Sicily has an active volcano, Mt. Etna.

- Sicily has more vineyards than any other Italian region.

Faith in Action!

CATHOLIC SOCIAL TEACHING

DISCOVER Catholic Social Teaching:
Call to Family, Community, and Participation

IN THIS UNIT you learned about the importance of family rituals and how the sacraments of Matrimony, the Eucharist, and Reconciliation help to build community in our families, parishes, and neighborhoods.

Call to Community

Family is where it all starts. It's the first community we are part of. It's the first "school" where we learn virtues and how to care for others. Sometimes it's even called the "domestic church" because it's where we first worship God and learn what it means to follow Jesus.

But no family is perfect. All families have to work hard at building a sense of community and rebuilding community when they make mistakes and hurt one another. Learning to say we're sorry and mean it when we have hurt others is essential. So is forgiving those who have hurt us. Some families ritualize this by writing down the hurts they've done to others and then burning these in the fireplace or burying them.

When everyone participates in taking responsibility for what needs to be done—chores, prayer, family fun, consoling or encouraging one another, family service, and family decision making—then that family is truly becoming "family."

Every family has a "mission" to extend its love beyond family members to include others in need around them. This idea of "family service" should be something that all family members participate in, not only in doing what is decided, but also in deciding what to do. Our Church is clear about this. In every community or group you are part of, the Church says that you are the "subject," not the object. You have the right and the duty to participate both in family decisions and in family service. And this can work at school as well.

? **What do you need to apologize for and make amends for in your family?**

? **Who is a family member or friend that you need to forgive?**

252

AS THE "DOMESTIC CHURCH," families are where we first learn about our faith. Let's look at how one school reinterprets the idea of "family" to create a community.

FAITH FAMILIES
NOURISHING COMMUNITY

The School of the Madeleine in Berkeley, California, is a typical Catholic elementary school with one classroom per grade, thirty-five students per grade, kindergarten through eighth grade. What's different is that the school is divided into eighteen "Faith Families" made up of two students per grade. The eighth graders are the "heads of the family" and meet ahead of time with their religion teacher to plan activities. Their responsibility is to ensure that each younger student is actively engaged in the activity. Each Faith Family has one faculty or staff member serving as a moderator.

Each month, the Faith Families meet to participate in service activities that benefit the school, the parish, or the larger community. The moderators' role is to provide support if things start to fall apart, but they are not in charge. Examples of the activities include preparing Thanksgiving dinners for needy families, writing letters to shut-ins, preparing decorations for the parish-sponsored dinners for the homeless, wrapping toys at Christmas time, preparing Easter baskets for children in hospitals, sending cards to graduating eighth graders, and so on.

Normally, students attend liturgies and prayer services in Faith Families. The older students are expected to model appropriate behavior for the younger ones. This eliminates the traditional groupings with eighth graders fooling around in the back of the church. According to Michel Calegari, the principal, "We have amazing opportunities to establish and nourish community and appropriate service activities. We are told by the various high schools that our students gravitate to community service with energy and enthusiasm. This is who we are." And this is who you can be too!

What do you like best about this approach?

▼ Faith Families at the School of the Madeleine include two students from each grade.

BUILDING COMMUNITY AT HOME

Discuss with the rest of your family different ways of building a greater sense of "family" or "community" in your home. Make a list and decide which ones you all want to do at some time. Then choose the one you want to start with, make a plan for doing it, write or draw a picture of what you plan to do on a piece of paper, post the paper as a reminder, and then say a prayer that you will all have the love to follow through.

BUILDING COMMUNITY AT SCHOOL

Discuss with your classmates how you can help younger students at your school in these categories:

- feel more a part of the school community

- do better in their schoolwork, in sports, and in art and music

- participate in community service

- participate more fully in prayer and worship

Make a list under each of the categories above.

Decide which category you want to start with and create a plan for achieving your goal.

Project Planning Sheet

Specific tasks

_____

_____

Equipment needed

_____

_____

Others who should be contacted about this

_____

_____

Your specific task(s)

_____

_____

Calendar for completing the project

_____

_____

REFLECT On Your Experience

Were you able to persuade your family to do the first project? How did it turn out?

What was the hardest thing about this whole effort?

What was the most satisfying thing about it?

What did you learn about yourself by building community at home?

How did your school project go?

What did you learn about the importance of building community?

What did you learn about yourself in doing the project?

What did you learn about Jesus and about your faith in doing it?

List one thing that might be different about you after doing this project.

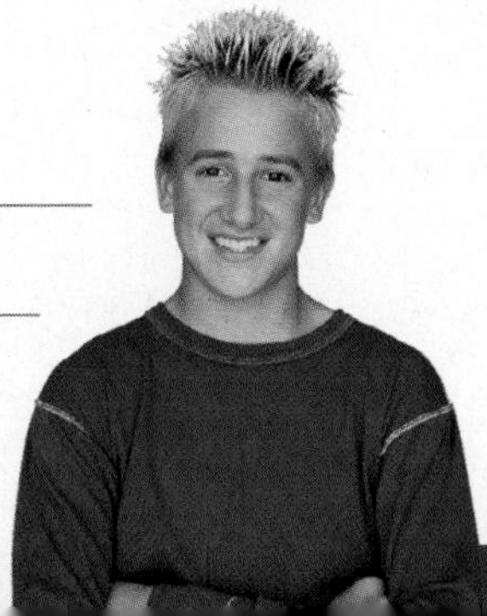

A **Work with Words** Use the clues below to complete the crossword puzzle.

Across

1 A Sacrament of Initiation

6 Effective signs of God's grace given to the Church by Christ

7 This virtue helps you be discreet in the ways you dress and the things you say

8 _____ grace is God's divine life within us, which makes us his friends and adopted children.

Down

2 Beginning of the liturgical year

3 The Liturgy of the _____ is the Church's public prayer to make each day holy.

4 Church laws that all Catholics must carry out to help them grow in their love of God and others

5 The official public worship of the Church

B Check Understanding Complete each sentence with the correct term from the word bank at right.

Word Bank

Eucharist
special graces
obligation
covenant
liturgical year
marriage
Jesus
Lord's Day
actual grace
rituals
oath
chastity
liturgy

9. _____ is present through the rituals and symbols of all the sacraments.

10. The Third Commandment requires us to keep holy the _____.

11. _____, called *charisms*, are intended for the good of all the Church.

12. Christian _____ is an effective sign of Christ's presence for the Church and the couple.

13. Married couples freely choose to make a permanent _____ of faithful love.

14. The viruté of _____ helps you maintain the right balance of body and spirit in human sexuality.

15. In the _____, the Church remembers the earthly life of Jesus from his Incarnation to his return.

16. The Holy Spirit's mission in the _____ is to show Christ to us, making him present by his power.

17. In the _____, the sacrifice Christ made on the cross is renewed and his Church is given new life.

18. The Assumption and All Saints Day are holy days of _____.

C Make Connections Write a short answer to the questions below.

19. Interpret. How do you experience God differently through the symbols or rituals of the Church? Give a specific example.

_____

_____

20. Analyze. Think about a marriage that you think is strong. In what ways does that marriage reflect the relationship of Christ and the Church?

_____

_____

CHAPTER 19 THE COMMUNION of Saints

When people die, do they ever completely leave us?
When some people die, it feels like they're still close by.
How come I can still remember some people as
clearly as I did when they were alive?

"**B**uenas noches, Mom," Esperanza said as she hung up the phone. Down the hall, she could hear her grandma talking.

"That's weird," Esperanza thought. "I just got off the phone. Who could she be talking to?"

She began to panic. Had someone broken in? Was her grandma in trouble? This was the first time Esperanza had stayed with her grandma since her grandpa died. Her adrenaline kicked in.

"Abuela!" she shouted. "I'm coming!"

"Buenas noches, mi querido," Esperanza heard her say as she dashed into the room. *"Goodnight, my dear?"* she thought. Her grandmother's back was turned away from Esperanza, and she seemed to be talking to someone.

"Abuela, are you okay?" Esperanza asked. She was surprised by her grandma's calm smile.

"I'm fine, Esperanza," she said. She hugged her with one arm. The other cradled an old wedding photo. "I was just talking with your abuelo."

"Grandpa?" Esperanza wondered. "But he's gone, Grandma."

"Not really, Esperanza," her grandmother sighed. "His memory lives in my heart. Talking to him makes me feel better. Sometimes it helps me decide things. Just now, we were saying our prayers together, just like we used to."

Esperanza looked at the picture. "I remember when I said my prayers with him, too. I miss how his eyes shined," she said, her own eyes becoming shiny with tears.

"I know you miss him," Grandma said as she hung the photo back on the wall and smiled. "I'm sure he prays for you."

Esperanza yawned. "Good night, Grandma," she said. "And buenos noches, Abuelo."

ACTIVITY

LET'S BEGIN What does Grandma's practice of speaking with her husband who passed away say about their relationship? Why did Esperanza's attitude change after their talk?

▶ **Who is someone that you wished you could talk to after they had died. How can people who have died support us through prayer?**

_____

_____

_____

_____

YOU ARE NOT ALONE

Focus What is the communion of saints?

You may have experienced a loss of a loved one, a friend, relative, or someone you've known through school. When people lose someone, they feel so many things. It can take a long time to see how the person who has died is still with them through their memories, the things they do that the person enjoyed, or their daily routines that reflect what they've learned from and shared with the person.

In the Catholic Church, we recognize this connection with those who have died in a special way.

Celebrating Life Living in New Orleans, Louisiana, is a unique experience. Funerals are often festive. Mourners march to the cemetery twirling colorful umbrellas, while a brass band plays "When the Saints Go Marching In."

This celebration draws a bridge between life and death, and shows how Catholics think differently when it comes to concepts like time and family. Spiritually, we live in the past, present, and future. We are connected to Jesus, to all the Church members who lived in the past, and those who live now.

We call this unity of Church members on earth, in purgatory, and in heaven the **communion of saints**. We all want to be included among the saints—God's holy people, living and dead. That begins now, through holy things and events such as the Eucharist, which brings us together with many believers to form one Body in Christ.

This vision of the community of saints goes back to the earliest days of our Church.

"They devoted themselves to the apostles' teaching and fellowship, to the breaking of bread and the prayers" (*Acts 2:42*). People would share their food and their faith, and the treasure of faith was made richer when it was shared. When we remember those special days, we have a kind of "communion" with those early Christians who are alive with God today!

CHECK THIS OUT!

In Mexico, Catholics celebrate, honor, and pray for their dead in a festive gathering known as *los Dias de los Muertos*, or Days of the Dead. The cemeteries and nearby streets are lined with flowers, paper skeletons and skulls, candy, and parades. People build special altars to their departed, filled with offerings of bread baked in the shape of a skull, candles, incense, yellow marigolds, and photos of their relatives. The Mexican people believe the souls of the departed visit their families on October 31 and leave on November 2. They celebrate with food, music, and dancing, often mocking the decorative skeletons with sayings such as "Death is so skinny and weak she cannot carry me." These festivities reflect the Mexican tradition of living with joy and happiness and laughter in the face of death.

SCRIPTURE

GO TO THE SOURCE
Read **Acts 2:42–47**. Discuss how the early Church is similar or different from your parish.

Being in Communion We call the Eucharist "communion" because it unites us with God and the communion of saints in a special way, just as all our sacraments do. We offer our prayers for those who have died not only at their funeral Mass, but every time we celebrate the Eucharist when we pray for those "who have gone before us marked with the sign of faith." We're also in communion with all the Church members—those with us and those who have gone before us—when we share our talents and treasures to support each other and the Church. When we

▶ hug a friend who's hurting

▶ sing in the church choir

▶ share our lunch with someone who's hungry

▶ share our allowance with the Church

We serve Jesus and live in solidarity and communion with all people—living, dead, and still to come.

We connect with them in many ways, such as the names of saints that we take at Baptism and Confirmation. But we especially remember them in our prayers. The saints in heaven are intercessors who pray *with* and *for* us to God. They are companions on the journey, just like a friend you might ask to pray for your mother if she's sick. We don't pray *to* saints, but we believe their holy friendship draws us closer to God.

We also pray for the souls being purified in Purgatory and ask them to pray for us. This communion in prayer brings us closer to each other and to God.

🔮 Have you ever asked a living friend or relative to pray for you?

🔮 How is this similar to asking a deceased grandparent or your patron saint to pray for you?

CHAPTER
Words *of* Faith

communion of saints

sacramentals

icons

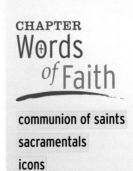

CATHOLICS TODAY

Halloween seems all about costumes and candy, but it takes its name from "All Hallows Eve"—the night before All Saints Day. On November 1, the Church remembers all the souls who are with God in Heaven. All Souls' Day is November 2, when we pray for the souls being purified in purgatory.

ACTIVITY

SHARE YOUR FAITH In groups of two or three discuss how a person you know (such as a family or parish member) makes the communion of saints a regular part of his or her spirituality.

HOLINESS IS ALL AROUND YOU

Focus How do sacramentals help us?

Step inside your church and you're surrounded by sacred things. You dip your hand in holy water and make the Sign of the Cross. Your eyes are drawn to the cross near the altar. Candles, bells, and incense awaken your senses. There's no doubt you're on holy ground.

Sacramentals are sacred symbols and objects that help us respond to the grace received in the seven sacraments. Although they aren't actual sacraments that bring us grace, they do bring us closer to God and strengthen the spiritual side of our everyday lives.

On many Sundays, you'll see special blessings. Catechists or lectors might be blessed for their ministries in the Church. Mothers often are blessed on Mother's Day, and teenagers might be blessed when they get their driver's licenses. Even certain things that help us in our lives—everything from medals to motorcycles—can be blessed. In some parts of the world, Catholic fishermen even have their boats blessed. These blessings always include a prayer and some special sign, like the Sign of the Cross or the sprinkling of holy water, which reminds us of Baptism.

What sights, smells, or sounds make your parish church feel sacred to you?

When have you been involved in a special blessing? What was the occasion, and how did it make you feel?

CATHOLICS TODAY

Parishes are busy on Ash Wednesday and Palm Sunday as people come for the blessing and distribution of ashes and palms. Many parishes make their ashes for Ash Wednesday by burning palms from Palm Sunday of the previous year. Many Catholics place their palm leaves near a crucifix in their home until their parish collects palms for burning.

▶ One of the most uniquely Catholic sacramentals is the **crucifix**—*a cross with the Body of Christ on it. This connects us with Jesus, the sacrifice he made for us, and the joy of his Resurrection.*

Stations of the Cross are often found on the walls of the church building. These show fourteen scenes that help us think and pray about Jesus' suffering, death, and burial. At each station we pray, "We adore you, O Christ, and we bless you, because by your holy cross you redeemed the world."

Incense is burned at special times, creating a fragrant scent and mystical smoke. It has been used for ages as a way to honor God. Remember that one of the Wise Men brought frankincense to Jesus. Today we use it to bless things like the altar and the Book of Gospels, as well as people.

The *Rosary* is both a sacramental and a prayer devotion to Mary. The blessed Rosary beads—which are made up of five sets of ten smaller beads, some larger beads, and a small crucifix—help us mark the Hail Marys prayed as the various mysteries of Mary and Jesus are reflected upon. The Mysteries of the Rosary include the Joyous, Sorrowful, Glorious, and Luminous Mysteries.

Candles also have a lot of meaning. The *Paschal Candle* is the first light that celebrates Jesus' rising at Easter. It symbolizes Resurrection at Baptisms and funerals. The *sanctuary candle* shines near the tabernacle to show that Jesus is always present in the Blessed Sacrament. Smaller candles, or *vigil lights*, often glow near statues. They represent people's prayers and hopes.

Of all sacramentals, blessings have a special place. *Blessings* include praising God for his great works and gifts and praying that someone will use God's gifts wisely, be protected, grow in holiness, and more.

ACTIVITY

CONNECT YOUR FAITH Think about the sacramentals you've seen or practices or prayers you've been involved in. Then, choosing one of the sacramentals listed below (or one that is not on the list), describe how you can use it to grow closer to God this week.

Crucifix   Stations of the Cross   Incense   Rosary   Candles   Blessings

This week I can use _____ to _____

_____

_____

IMAGES AND IMAGINATION

Focus How can art help you to pray?

No person has seen Jesus since his Ascension into heaven nearly two thousand years ago. But thousands of artists have glorified Jesus in their artwork. Early on, **icons**, or religious pictures in a certain style, showed Jesus; Mary, the Mother of God; and other holy people. It's said that Saint Luke drew some of the first icons of Jesus and Mary.

Not Idolatry Many beautiful paintings, mosaics, and statues were created in the early centuries of the Church. Unfortunately, during the early Middle Ages, some Eastern Tradition Christians in southern Europe and Asia treated these images as idols. Other folks believed that such idol worship violated the first commandment, which says we shouldn't worship false gods.

In the year A.D. 730, the emperor Leo III ordered that all crucifixes, statues, and paintings be destroyed. Iconoclasts, or image breakers, were sent out to destroy Church artwork. This continued until A.D. 787, when a Church council ruled that icons, if used properly, can help Christians worship God. Today, beautiful icons cover the walls of many Eastern Catholic churches.

When we venerate or honor an image, we honor the person that image portrays. It's a sign of respect for that person, but it doesn't replace the unique love and adoration we give to God. It doesn't violate the first commandment. (See *Exodus 20:2–5*.)

Most churches, for example, have a statue of Mary, the Mother of Jesus. You often will see people pray in front of this statue. They are honoring Mary for the great love she showed by bringing God's Son into our world. Likewise, God greatly loves Mary, so we ask her to pray for us. We *honor* Mary, but we *worship* God. We pray *with* Mary and pray *to* God.

▲ *Christ and the Angels*, by Alberoi Bazile (1920–)

✝ SCRIPTURE

GO TO THE SOURCE

Read **Exodus 20:2–5** (the first commandment). Discuss whether statues and other religious images distract or help you in worshiping God.

Two Great Images, One Great Artist There are many awesome pieces of religious art, but Michelangelo created two of the greatest around A.D. 1500. His marble sculpture *Pieta* shows Mary lovingly holding the body of Jesus after the crucifixion. It's in a chapel at St. Peter's Basilica in Rome. Michelangelo's best-known work is a mural on the ceiling of the Sistine Chapel in the Vatican. It shows many scenes from the Bible, including God creating the world. These two works are true labors of love.

Artistic License Back in the Middle Ages, artists often showed Jesus in fancy settings. Marble pillars and velvet curtains might surround him and he might wear clothes fit for royalty, perhaps holding a gold chalice. But, the Holy Family was a working-class family, likely living in a very simple house, in solidarity with the poor.

Many images show a light-skinned, well-groomed Jesus. Chances are, as a roaming preacher in long-ago Palestine, he had darker skin and a scruffier style, like many of the people he taught. Artists often draw Jesus to look like the people who will view their art, so their audience might relate to and respect Jesus.

🔲 **When you imagine Jesus, what does he look like in your mind's eye?**

🔲 **If you were to paint or sculpt an image of Jesus, what message do you hope people would see in your work?**

LOOKING BACK

Catholic churches are known for their stained-glass windows. Although these are beautiful, they can also be practical. In the Middle Ages, when very few people besides the clergy could read, great churches were designed to include stained-glass windows that showed stories from the Bible. These helped common people learn the stories of their faith even though they could not read words—they "read" the stories in the windows.

ACTIVITY

LIVE YOUR FAITH At home this week, using clay, paint, or whatever you'd like, create an image of Jesus or a favorite saint. Also write a prayer that helps describe what your creation means to you.

IN SUMMARY

CATHOLICS BELIEVE

Catholics are connected with each other across time through prayer, practices, and sacred objects and images.

▶ The communion of saints links people striving to do good on Earth with souls being purified in purgatory and the saints in heaven.

▶ Sacramentals are holy objects, prayers, and practices that help us respond to God's grace and bring us closer to him.

▶ Religious art, especially icons, helps us to honor the saints and glorify God.

MEDITATION ON THE SAINTS

Leader: Place yourselves in Jesus' presence.
Close your eyes and turn to that place deep within your heart,
where you and God are one.
Take a deep, relaxing breath, and enter into the meditation:

(Read the following, slowly and meditatively.)

Our God is a wonderful and loving God,
who has called forth
heroes in the faith who have shown us by their lives
the struggles and rewards of commitment
and of following the Lord every day. *(pause)*

We look to the saints
and ask them to pray for us,
to be with us as we walk the road of faith. *(pause)*

We take into our hearts
these holy men and women,
as people who can teach us
what it means to follow Jesus. *(pause)*

(Read slowly and reverently. After each, all respond "pray for us.")

Holy Mary, Mother of God,
Saint John the Baptist,
Saint Joseph,
Saint Peter and Saint Paul,
Saint Andrew and Saint Stephen,
Saint Francis and Saint Dominic,
Saint Mary Magdalene,

*(Other saints can be added; then conclude
with the following:)*

All holy men and women,
Those saints in your own families.

Prayer: Loving Father,
we thank you for those who have gone before us,
for those whose lives have taught us,
and who chose to embrace the life
of Jesus, your Son.

 "Christ is Alive"
Lori True, © 2004, GIA Publications, Inc.

REVIEW

A **Work with Words** Complete each sentence with the correct term.

1. Sacramentals are sacred _____ and _____ that help us respond to the grace received in the seven sacraments.

2. The _____ show(s) fourteen scenes that help us think and pray about Jesus' suffering, death, and burial.

3. _____ are religious paintings often done by Eastern Christians in a certain style that show Jesus, Mary, other holy people, and religious events.

4. The unity of Church members on earth, in purgatory, and in heaven, is the _____.

5. The emperor Leo III ordered that _____ destroy all crucifixes, statues, and paintings.

B **Check Understanding** Indicate whether the following statements are true or false. Then rewrite false statements to make them true.

_____ 6. When someone has died, Catholics offer prayers for them at their funeral Mass and in private prayer.

_____

_____ 7. Saints are our intercessors who pray *with* and *for* us to God.

_____

_____ 8. On All Saints Day, the Church prays for the souls being purified in purgatory.

_____

_____ 9. *Blessings* are special sacramentals that include praising God for his great works and gifts.

_____

_____ 10. Catholics believe that when we venerate or honor an image, we worship the person that image portrays.

_____

C **Make Connections: Interpret** Write a one-paragraph response to the question below.

When have you been impacted by a symbol or image that relates to Jesus? Write about the picture or symbol and its effect on you.

OUR CATHOLIC FAITH

ACTIVITY

LIVE YOUR FAITH Being Catholic means never being alone. Our faith is communal, which means we celebrate sacraments with all who believe. Our faith is universal—it builds bridges between nations and cultures. And it connects the living and the dead so that we can love and support each other.

Symbols and memories keep us in touch with loved ones who have died. Old letters and pictures— or even a holy card from their funeral—help us remember them and hold them in our prayers.

▶ Gather symbols and images—things you can actually see and hold—that remind you of a friend or relative who has died. Make a list of things that made this person special to you. What was it about your friendship that strengthened your love of God and the Church?

▶ Write a prayer or poem thanking God for the gift he or she was in your life, and asking your friend or relative to remember you while he or she is with God.

▶ Explore the Hispanic celebration of los Dias de los Muertos, the Days of the Dead, or research the way St. Francis looked at death as something to be embraced. Are these perspectives different from your outlook on death?

 Visit www.harcourtreligion.com for more family and community connections.

 **PRAYER**

Holy Spirit, help me remember to pray for my loved ones who are now in your care.

Venerable Louis Martin and Zelie Guerin

The Church is a communion of saints. We will feel part of those who have gone before us as if we were in communion with them when we look to their lives as models of how to live our lives. Two of the best models of Christian parents are Louis Martin and Zelie Guerin of France.

Both Louis and Zelie aspired toward religious lives in their youth but neither entered into an order. Instead they pursued secular careers, he as a watchmaker and she as a lace designer, but individually and together, they followed a path of devotion to the Church and its people.

They married soon after they met in 1858. Over the next fourteen years, they had nine children, four of whom died as infants or young children. Despite the losses of these children, Louis and Zelie remained devoted to their faith. They continued to go to church and teach the catechism to their five surviving daughters. Each of their surviving daughters eventually entered religious orders.

In their village of Lisieux, Louis and Zelie were charitable to those less fortunate than themselves. Although they weren't wealthy, they shared what they had with others. Zelie would give food to the poor who begged at their door, teaching her children by example to follow in the footsteps of Jesus. They even helped those who were oppressed to fight for their legal rights.

After Zelie's death from breast cancer in 1877 at age forty-six, Louis carried on the family tradition of love for the faith. His daughters Leonie, Celine, and Therese were educated at a Benedictine boarding school, while Pauline and Marie were educated at a Visitation convent in LeMans. Louis considered it an honor to give his daughters to God, and never opposed their vocations. Even when one of them dropped out of an order, he encouraged her to secure a place in another order, which she did.

In his later years, Louis' physical and mental health suffered. Yet despite this, his devotion to his faith never wavered. He was admitted to a sanatorium and died in 1892 after telling his children that he would meet them again in heaven.

Daughter Therese, by that time a devout Carmelite, eulogized her father and mother with the words, "God gave me a mother and a father more worthy of heaven than of earth." Pope John Paul II declared them "Venerable" in 1994 to extol their heroic virtues as Catholic parents.

▲ Louis Martin (above), 1823–1894; Zelie Guerin, 1831–1877

GLOBAL DATA

Lisieux, France

- Lisieux is located in the Normandy region in France.

- Lisieux has a population of just over 24,000 and is one of the oldest towns in Normandy.

- Lisieux was almost completely destroyed in World War II, but several old churches remained standing.

- The shrine of St. Therese "The Little Flower," located there is one of the most popular pilgrimage sites in Europe.

CHAPTER 20

SAINTS Examples for Living

 **PRAYER** Lord, help me follow your example.

It's hard to live up to the saints' example.
Who are the real heroes today? Who can I look up to?
What should I look for in a role model?

"**S**orry I'm late again, Coach!" Danny said as he hustled into the dugout.

Garrett slid down the bench to make room for Danny's gear bag. Danny unzipped it and pulled out a brand new bat.

"Sweet!" Garrett said. "Where'd you get it?"

"My dad bought it on his last trip," Danny shrugged. "Even had something cheesy engraved on it."

"Dan the Man, Future Hall of Famer!" Garrett said with a laugh. "Is he serious? Well, it is a sweet bat. You gonna use it?"

"I dunno. I like my old one. He's just trying to out-do Mom again," Danny said, pulling out another bat. "This is the one she gave me. You can use the new one if you want."

Garrett held Danny's bat in his hands. "So are your folks here *together* today?" he asked.

"Dad just dropped me off and went to the airport . . . business again," Danny said. "Mom figured Dad would be here, so she's not. I could call her to see if she can pick me up, but can I get a ride home with you instead?"

"No problem," Garrett said.

Trev waddled into the dugout, lugging a cooler.

"Make your dad haul those drinks!" Danny wisecracked.

"Yeah, right," Trev sighed. "He's at the casino. Said he's gonna win my college tuition."

Trev and Danny both singled to start the game. Then Garrett ripped a triple to drive them home.

"*You're* the future hall-of-famer" the coach said with a wink as Garrett dusted himself off at third.

"No, Dad," Garrett thought, "*you* are."

ACTIVITY

LET'S BEGIN What two or three messages do you get from this story?

▶ **Think about your priorities. Is one of them to help others? Think about someone who's made sacrifices for another. How have they helped or inspired you? Who's in your own "hall of fame"?**

_____

_____

_____

_____

_____

MARY HAS A SPECIAL PLACE IN GOD'S PLAN

Focus How would life be different if Mary had not said "Yes" to God?

Who are the everyday heroes in your life who inspire you? Who demonstrates a virtue that you want to also develop? As Catholics, we have always seen Mary as such a person. A person of authentic faith.

✝ SCRIPTURE The Angel Gabriel came to Mary, saying "Greetings, favored one! The Lord is with you." But Mary was greatly troubled at what the angel said and wondered what sort of greeting this might be.

"Do not be afraid, Mary, for you have found favor with God. And now, you will conceive in your womb and bear a son, and you will name him Jesus. He will be great, and will be called the Son of the Most High . . . of his kingdom there will be no end."

Gabriel continued, "The Holy Spirit will come upon you, and the power of the Most High will overshadow you; therefore the child to be born will be holy; he will be called the Son of God."

Mary said, "Here am I, the servant of the Lord; let it be with me according to your word." (See *Luke 1:26–38*.)

CHECK THIS OUT!

Gabriel's words begin the Hail Mary:

Hail Mary, full of grace, the Lord is with you.

Then we hear Mary's cousin, Elizabeth:

Blessed are you among women, and blessed is the fruit of your womb . . .

The Hail Mary prayer actually comes from Scripture, and it shows us that Gabriel and Elizabeth first knew how special Mary was. From the moment Mary's soul was created in her mother's womb, she was unique. God made her without original sin. All humans struggle to choose things that please God over things that simply please us. God created Mary free from the stain of original sin and she remained free from all personal sin throughout her life. This prepared the way for Jesus, who saves us all from sin. The expression **Immaculate Conception** refers to the Church's teaching that Mary was preserved free from original sin from the first moment of her conception.

▶ *The Annunciation*, by Lorenzo di Credi (1458–1537)

Humble, Yet Honored Who could blame Mary for being confused and worried? It's not every day that an angel shows up. This announcement must have puzzled her. But then Gabriel explained that it was by God's power that she was going to have a child. What could Mary think? This incredible honor could cause incredible scandal. Did she wonder how Joseph would react? But Mary took a leap of faith and said she would do his will.

The angel Gabriel's visit to Mary to announce she would be the mother of God is known as the Annunciation. After the angel's visit, Mary went to her cousin Elizabeth, who was also expecting a child. Elizabeth's reaction when she saw Mary is quite famous, "Blessed are you among women, and blessed is the fruit of your womb" (*Luke 1:42*). Mary was a virgin at Jesus' conception, and she remained a virgin throughout her life.

Mary's "yes" was the first of many sacrifices she made for God. She gave birth to Jesus in a stable in a strange city instead of in her home. She and Joseph spent the early days of Jesus' life protecting him from the wrath of an angry king.

Jesus' sacrifice on the cross hurt Mary greatly as well. Her son was dying in a brutal way—not at all like the greatness the angel predicted. But as she stood near the cross with John, she heard Jesus tell her, "Woman, here is your son." And to John, he said, "Here is your mother" (*John 19:26–27*). Mary would not only become mother to John, but to all who love and follow Christ.

Mary lived her life in total obedience to God; she was without sin. When she died, we believe that God took Mary's body and soul into the glory of Heaven. We call this the **Assumption**. It's different from Jesus' Ascension because Mary went up through God's power. She could not do this herself. She shares in the glory of Jesus' Resurrection, and this gives us hope that someday we, too, will rise to share life in heaven with Jesus and Mary.

How do you respond when God gives you a tough challenge? What are some things our Church does to honor Mary?

Words of Faith

Immaculate Conception

Assumption

saint

devotions

canonization

✝ SCRIPTURE
GO TO THE SOURCE
Read **Luke 1:39–45**. What helps Elizabeth recognize that Mary will be the Mother of God?

SHARE YOUR FAITH What is God asking you to say "Yes" to? Mary went to Elizabeth, her soul's friend. Who do you go to for soulful conversation or advice? Share your answers with another.

THE GREATEST OF SAINTS

Focus How does the Church honor Mary?

All four daughters of one Catholic family in St. Louis have some form of Mary in their name. One Catholic diocese has eighty-four parishes, and forty-five are named St. Mary's. In the Church's liturgical year, there are sixteen feast days marked to honor Mary in some way. And, people in different parts of the world consider May and October special months to honor Mary with popular devotions and practices.

No one who knew this humble Jewish girl from Palestine would have imagined so much honor would one day be given to her. She is the greatest **saint**, a person who led a holy life giving God glory and enjoys eternal life with God in heaven.

Mark Your Calendar People around the world celebrate on New Year's Day. It's an important day for the Church, too, as we celebrate the Solemnity of Mary, Mother of God. We honor Mary for bringing the Son of God to us.

This is one of three holy days of obligation devoted to Mary. Being so close to Christmas, it also reminds us that what we believe about Mary is based on what we believe about Jesus. Her life is a continuing inspiration to our faith. The more we learn about Mary, the stronger our faith in Jesus becomes.

The second of these most special days is August 15, when we celebrate the Feast of the Assumption and our belief that God took Mary—body and soul—into heaven. The third special day is December 8, the Feast of the Immaculate Conception, when we celebrate the special care God took by creating Mary free from original sin.

WHERE IT HAPPENED

IN 1917, three children experienced apparitions (special visions or appearances of Jesus, Mary, or other saints) in the town of Fatima, Portugal. Mary told them that God wanted people to seek forgiveness and live faithful lives. She told people to pray the rosary to help bring peace to our world. At least fifty thousand people from all over Europe—believers and nonbelievers alike—witnessed the final apparition of Mary, during which, they said, the sun danced in the sky.

In 1981, on the anniversary of the first apparition, Pope John Paul II was wounded in an assassination attempt. He credited Mary with saving his life. Two years later, on that same anniversary date, he went to Fatima to consecrate the world to the Immaculate Heart of Mary. In doing so, he fulfilled one of Our Lady's promises made there in 1917 to three little children.

Fatima, Portugal

Devotions **Devotions** are prayers and practices that honor Jesus, Mary, and the saints. One of the most popular devotions to Mary is the Rosary, which Catholics have prayed for eight hundred years. If you look at the Rosary as just a string of beads to hold as you pray lots of Hail Mary's, you're missing the point. The mysteries of the Rosary help us focus on events in the lives of Jesus and Mary and apply them to the challenges and good times in our lives. For example, you might pray the Joyful Mysteries of the Rosary, thinking first about the Annunciation. As you pray the Hail Marys, you might also ask God to come into your life in a special way.

May is a month many people dedicate to Mary. Many parishes have a devotion called "May Crowning." Children set fresh flowers around a statue of Mary, and a crown is placed on the statue. This honors Mary, who God chose as Mother of Jesus and Queen of Heaven.

How does our honoring and understanding Mary strengthen our relationship with Jesus?

ACTIVITY

CONNECT YOUR FAITH

▶ How does your family honor Mary? Your parish? Your school? Describe one of those ways here, then work with a small group to plan a special way for your class to honor Mary.

THE CHURCH OF SAINTS

Focus Why are the saints important to the Church?

Raymond Kolbe had a vision of Mary when he was twelve years old. She offered him two crowns and asked if he'd accept either. One crown was white, symbolizing that he should live a pure and holy life. The other was red, meaning that he should die for his faith. Raymond said that he'd take both.

Five years later, when he began studying for the priesthood, he took the name "Maximilian." He became a great priest who founded monasteries and magazines, first in his native Poland, and then in Japan and India. He was very devoted to Mary and worked to bring sinners back to Christ. Impressive as his life was, Maximilian is best known for how he died.

After the Nazis invaded Poland in World War II, Father Maximilian bravely protected refugees and published materials that criticized the Nazis. He was thrown into Auschwitz, the deadly Nazi prison camp. One day in 1941, a prisoner escaped. Camp rules required that ten men be killed to make up for the escape. When a married man who had young children was chosen to die, Maximilian volunteered to die in his place. He lived as Jesus commanded, so great was his love for his fellow man. "No one has greater love than this, to lay down one's life for one's friends" (*John 15:13*). After a holy life, he died a martyr's death. He had both crowns.

How do you think Maximilian found the courage to give up his life?

Role Models In 1971, Maximilian Kolbe was beatified, a big step on the way to becoming a saint. In the crowd at his ceremony was Francis Gajowniczek, the man for whom Maximilian gave his life.

When the church names saints, it lifts up holy people as heroes of our faith. When Maximilian Kolbe was canonized, named a saint, by Pope John Paul II in 1982, he became a hero not just to the Gajowniczek family, but to all of us.

▼ Maximilian Kolbe

We celebrate the Feast of Saint Maximilian Kolbe on August 14. He is with Mary not only in heaven, but also on the Church's calendar, as the Feast of Mary's Assumption is the next day, August 15. These feasts of Mary and other holy women and men spiritually unite the Church on earth with the Church in heaven. When we remember saints, we give glory to Jesus for using them to show us the way to his Father.

The saints not only intercede for us in prayer, but they also serve as role models. Their stories inspire us to live holy lives. They made great sacrifices for their faith, often dying to protect their virtues.

The Road to Sainthood All faithful members of the Church are called saints because Jesus has called us to be the holy people of God. In another sense, the term *saints* refers only to some deceased members of the Church who have led lives of heroic virtue, have been canonized by the Church, and are in heaven. **Canonization** is the process by which the Church declares someone a saint.

✝ **SCRIPTURE**

GO TO THE SOURCE

Read **John 15:12–13**. Maximilian Kolbe lived out this scripture. What kind of love does Jesus expect of us? What sacrifices can you make every day for people you love?

ACTIVITY

LIVE YOUR FAITH The Path to Sainthood

▶ Everything we do, we do in community. We believe together, worship together, study and have fun together. List some things your class can do together to put you all on your way to sainthood.

We can live a life of virtue by _____

_____

We can live a life for others by _____

_____

IN SUMMARY

CATHOLICS BELIEVE ✝

The Church honors Mary and all the saints with special feasts and devotions.

▶ Mary has a special role in God's plan, and by saying "Yes" to God, she became the mother of his Son and of all those who believe in him.

▶ The Church honors Mary as the greatest of saints and honors her with many feast days and devotions. Mary prays for us and asks God to work miracles through her intercession.

▶ All of us are called to be saints, holy men and women who accept God's friendship and live lives of service to others. The Church declares some people canonized saints for their lives of heroic vritue and holiness.

CELEBRATE

LITANY OF MARY

Leader: Mary, God chose you as the mother of his Son and called all nations and generations to bless the gift of grace he gave you. In the company of those who have gone before us, we call upon you in prayer. To each title, respond *pray for us.*

Holy Mary . . . *pray for us.*
Mother of God . . . *pray for us.*
Mother of our redemption . . . *pray for us.*
Mother of a lost child . . . *pray for us.*
Mother of comfort and understanding . . . *pray for us.*
Mother who shares our joys . . . *pray for us.*
Mother who endures our sorrows . . . *pray for us.*
Mother whose heart was pierced by a sword . . . *pray for us.*
Mother most merciful . . . *pray for us.*
Woman responsive to God's word . . . *pray for us.*
Woman willing to believe the impossible . . . *pray for us.*
Woman who rejoices in her lowliness . . . *pray for us.*
Woman with an undivided heart . . . *pray for us.*
Woman wrapped in mystery . . . *pray for us.*
Woman moved by the Spirit . . . *pray for us.*
Woman champion of the poor and lowly . . . *pray for us.*
Woman graced by a husband's love . . . *pray for us.*
Woman widowed by a husband's death . . . *pray for us.*
Woman at the cross . . . *pray for us.*
Woman patient and waiting . . . *pray for us.*
Woman clothed with the sun . . . *pray for us.*
Queen of the fullness of times . . . *pray for us.*
Queen of beauty unalloyed . . . *pray for us.*
Queen of integrity . . . *pray for us.*
Queen of painful meetings . . . *pray for us.*
Queen of all our heart's treasure . . . *pray for us.*
Queen of our destiny . . . *pray for us.*
Queen of peace . . . *pray for us.*

Almighty Father, in your wisdom and goodness you chose Mary to the mother of your Son, Jesus. Through her intercession, remember us and our needs. Protect us from all that keeps us from you and bring us the happiness that comes from trusting in you alone.

All: Amen

♪ "Magnificat"

David Haas, © 1997, GIA Publications, Inc.

REVIEW

A **Work with Words** Circle the letter of the choice that best completes the sentence.

1. The expression _____ refers to the Church's teaching that Mary was preserved free from original sin from the first instant of her conception.
   - **a.** Annunciation
   - **b.** Assumption
   - **c.** Immaculate Conception
   - **d.** Ascension

2. The angel Gabriel's visit to Mary to tell her she was chosen to become the Mother of God is called the _____.
   - **a.** Annunciation
   - **b.** Assumption
   - **c.** Immaculate Conception
   - **d.** Ascension

3. A(n) _____ is a person who led a holy life on earth giving God glory and enjoys eternal life with God in heaven.
   - **a.** disciple
   - **b.** priest
   - **c.** angel
   - **d.** saint

4. The _____ happened when God took Mary's body and soul into the glory of Heaven.
   - **a.** Annunciation
   - **b.** Assumption
   - **c.** Immaculate Conception
   - **d.** Ascension

5. _____ are prayers and practices that honor Jesus, Mary, and the saints.
   - **a.** Devotions
   - **b.** Obligations
   - **c.** Eucharistic prayers
   - **d.** Prayers of the Saints

B **Check Understanding** Complete each sentence with the correct term.

6. The Solemnity of Mary, Mother of God, is one of three holy days of _____ devoted to Mary.

7. The mysteries of the _____ help us focus on events in the life of Jesus and Mary and apply them to our lives.

8. Special visions or appearances of Jesus, Mary, or the saints are known as _____.

9. _____ is the process by which the Church declares someone a saint.

10. All faithful members of the Church are called _____ because Jesus has called us to be the holy people of God.

C **Make Connections: Synthesize** Write a one-paragraph response to the question below.

Think of someone you know who could be on the way to sainthood. What do you see in his or her life that inspires you? Write an encouraging note to that person telling him or her about how his or her life has impacted you.

OUR CATHOLIC FAITH

WHAT NOW?

★ Explore the everyday saints in your life.

★ Discover the stories of the Church's great saints.

★ Learn about the saints' qualities. Think of ways to imitate them.

★ Commit yourself to living out some of the virtues.

★ Make a few sacrifices for someone else once in awhile.

★ Pray for the strength to live your faith amid life's challenges.

ACTIVITY

LIVE YOUR FAITH We are surrounded by stories of people who have been or may one day be sainted—living or dead, flawed but holy. We're called to lift them up and learn from their lessons.

▶ On your own, or with your family or class group, explore the lives of holy people you've known. It could be a friend, coach, pastor, church leader, or scoutmaster—just about anybody you admire. Discuss those people's virtues and the good things they've done for you or others.

▶ Explore the Internet or other resources to find out more about canonized saints. Go to www.harcourtreligion.com for links to Web sites about the saints. Find out more about the saint you were named after. Discover the saint whose feast on the liturgical calendar falls on your birthday. Or find out about the patron saints of your favorite hobby or future career.

▶ Share with your classmates or family what makes these saints famous, plus any fun or quirky facts you find along the way. Write a prayer asking that saint to pray for you and your needs.

 Visit www.harcourtreligion.com for more family and community connections.

 **PRAYER**

Oh Lord, today I want to be aware of my favorite saint, _____.

PEOPLE OF FAITH

Mariam Thresia Chiramel Mankidiyan

Ever since the first saints were canonized by the Church, they have served as role models for many people, giving us examples of how to live. In many cases, saints and other blessed religious set their examples by helping the poor, the sick, and others less fortunate than themselves.

Mariam Thresia Chiramel Mankidiyan was inspired by the saints' examples. Born in India in 1876, her family had once been wealthy but lost their fortune. In accordance with custom, families of girls to be married had to give a dowry to the boy's family. With seven girls, Mariam's family became impoverished by this custom.

She grew up with a strong devotion to God, fasting four times a week and praying the Marian Rosary several times a day. When she was ten years old, she vowed to remain a virgin and to experience the sufferings of Christ. By the time she was fifteen, she began helping the poor, nursing the sick, and comforting the lonely people of her parish. In her village of Kerala, she tenderly gave medical and spiritual care to even those suffering the worst cases of smallpox and leprosy. If they died, she took care of their orphaned children.

Mariam placed her trust with the Holy Family of Jesus, Mary, and Joseph. She had frequent visions of them and received guidance from them, especially as she converted sinners. Finally, by the early 1900s, her true calling made itself known to her. With the blessings of the Vicar Apostolic of her province, she had a prayer house built and moved in with three companions. They led a life of prayer and austerity, but they continued to minister to the poor and sick.

At the time, Indian society was divided into castes, or classes. The lowest caste was the Untouchables. Defying custom, Mariam and her companions ministered to all in need, including Untouchables.

In 1914, under Mariam's guidance, the Congregation of the Holy Family, or CHF, came into existence. She was appointed its first Superior, and the order grew rapidly throughout India and the world. Over a period of twelve years, she opened three convents, two schools, two hostels, a study house, and an orphanage. She died in 1926, and many years later, her example would be followed by Mother Teresa of Calcutta. Mariam was declared Venerable in 1999, by which time the CHF had grown to one hundred seventy-six houses on three continents.

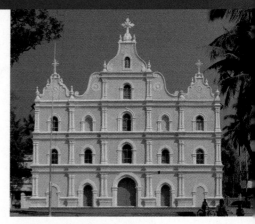

▲ **Saint Thomas Church in Kerala, India**

GLOBAL DATA

India

- India has an area of 1.1 million square miles in the middle southern region of Asia, bordered on two sides by the Indian Ocean and on the north by the Himalayan Mountains.

- India has an ancient history dating back about five thousand years to settlements in the Indus River valley, now within the borders of Pakistan.

- India is the world's second largest nation in population with more than a billion people, 94 percent of whom are Hindu and Muslim.

- Portuguese missionaries brought the Roman Catholic Tradition to India in the late fifteenth century.

CHAPTER 21 FROM Age to Age

PRAYER Lord, make me an instrument for peace in the world.

How have other people survived their problems?
What can I learn from other people's successes and mistakes?
Will my own problems help me give others advice someday?

Thanksgiving dinner was over and Sara felt stuck. Her cousins were at their other grandma's, so Sara was the only kid sitting around with the grown-ups. She knew she'd acted like a grouch through the whole meal and could feel the questions coming her way.

"Are you and your mom still arguing about that cell phone?" Sara's grandma asked.

"All my friends are getting them, Grandma," Sara jumped in. "Mom's so old-fashioned!"

Grandma rolled her eyes and smiled. "Remember how we handled the phone issue?" she asked Sara's mom.

"How could I forget?" Mom said. "If I wanted my own phone, I had to buy it and pay the bills. That's the same deal I've made with Sara."

"Oh, I get it," Sara said suspiciously, "now it's *your* turn to do it to *me*!"

Grandma sighed. "You mother was mad at *me* back then," she said, "but she started babysitting to try to earn enough money for a phone in her room."

Her mom nodded, "But I never did. While I was babysitting, I found I had a real love for working with little children. So I volunteered for a week at a summer camp for city kids. I decided to volunteer there for the rest of the summer. Those little kids deserved a better day than just sitting watching TV."

"But even without my own phone, I still managed to talk to my friends. I even convinced a couple of them to volunteer with me!"

"Oh," Sara paused and stared at her mom as if she were seeing her for the first time. She tried to imagine her mom as a fourteen-year-old girl.

Grandma took in the whole scene and then she said, "Sara, I hope you'll find your gifts and give back to the world as your mother tried to do. That's not old-fashioned, is it?"

ACTIVITY

LET'S BEGIN Discuss whether you think Sara's grandmother's ideas are old-fashioned.

▶ **What lessons have you learned from older people that make sense in your life today? Think of an event in the past that you don't want to see happen again. Is there an experienced person you could ask about how to handle the problem?**

THE EARLY CHURCH

Focus How did the Church become connected to political structures?

Sometimes you discover yourself when you reach out to help someone else. Then, maybe what becomes most important to you isn't what all your friends are into. But following your heart and stepping out to give of yourself when no one else is interested can be a lonely place, even a scary place sometimes. From age to age, brave Christians have struggled to witness to their faith.

Christians in Hiding It wasn't easy being Christian in the early years. Although Christian communities were small and scattered, the Roman Empire saw them as a threat. Christians ignored Roman gods, who were seen as the source of the emperors' power. For over two hundred years, emperors persecuted people who didn't worship their gods, torturing and killing thousands of Christians whom we honor as **martyrs**, people who lose their lives in witnessing about Christ. Still, many people were inspired to become Christians because of the martyrs' courage and the Church's vision and charity. Most Christians feared being arrested because of their faith. So they worshiped in hiding, often in one another's homes.

GO ONLINE Visit www.harcourtreligion.com for a time line of the eras and key events in the history of the Church.

Free to Worship Things changed when Constantine, an emperor who worshiped the sun, dreamed that he would conquer his enemies through a special sign of Christ. His soldiers marked their helmets with a cross. They won, and Constantine issued the Edict of Milan in A.D. 313, giving Christians the freedom to worship. Constantine supported the Church and eventually tried to run it. In 381, Christianity became the religion of the Roman Empire.

Christianity shifted from being illegal to an accepted official religion. This connection between Church and state would have an impact on the Church's history for many centuries to follow.

Would it be good or bad if a president or king led the Church today? Why?

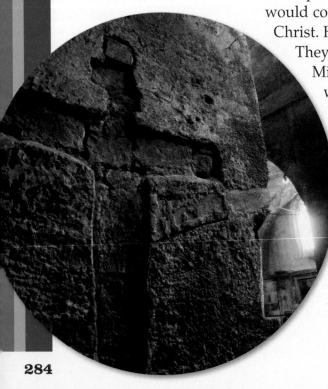

Power Struggles Everybody wanted a piece of the Roman Empire. Europe was in chaos, and the Church was one of the few institutions people could depend on. One leader who shined in the early Middle Ages (A.D. 500 to A.D. 1000) was Pope Gregory the Great, elected in A.D. 590. Gregory fed the poor, rebuilt churches, and opened schools for children. He also worked to prepare better priests. Gregory converted the marauding tribes and helped make peace in Spain, England, and other lands.

The Pope or the Emperor In A.D. 799, Charlemagne (Charles the Great) was a king and warrior who supported Pope Leo III against kings trying to take over Rome. To thank Charlemagne, the pope crowned him emperor of the Holy Roman Empire at Christmas Mass in A.D. 800.

Charlemagne tried to bring power and unity back to the empire. When he won a battle, he insisted that the people he conquered become Christians. He made Latin the language used at Mass in Western Churches, a practice that continued until the 1960s.

This close connection between church and state caused confusion. Sometimes the emperor would obey the pope, and other times he did what he wanted and ignored the Church. The emperor's military and legal power often allowed him to force the Church to support his actions.

The relationship between faith and political power that started with Constantine continued through Charlemagne. The identity of the Church was tied to that of the empire, and lost in the middle were believers.

🔖 **What does this time period tell us about the relationship between religion and political institutions?**

Words of Faith

martyrs

monastery

LOOKING BACK

Benedict was about twenty years old when he fled Rome's turmoil. At first, he lived alone in a cave. Then people came to him, inspired by how he balanced prayer and work. In A.D. 530, he built a **monastery**, a community of men who have taken vows of poverty, chastity, and obedience and have joined in spirituality and service, on a mountain south of Rome.

Benedict's monastery became a model for religious orders around the world. Benedict wrote rules about prayer, work, fasting, and community life. Benedictine religious still follow the Rule of St. Benedict today. During the early Middle Ages, monasteries protected people, art, and writings from invaders. They also sent missionaries to convert invaders and restore Christianity.

ACTIVITY

SHARE YOUR FAITH What thoughts or feelings come to you as you hear about some of the Church's past? Discuss them with another now.

▶ If you could ask a question of someone from the Church's history, who would it be and what would you ask?

THE CHURCH IN TRANSITION

◉ Focus What changes took place in the Church during the Middle Ages and the Reformation?

Most people in the Middle Ages (A.D. 500 to A.D. 1450) lived faithful lives. Many were peasants, unable to read or write, but who worked hard, had little, and found hope and happiness in the Church. It was the center of their lives. Sunday was the highlight of their week. Mass brought beauty and mystery to their lives.

A Challenging Time Pope Gregory VII made a bold move to free the Church of politics. He ruled in A.D. 1077 that the Holy Roman emperor couldn't appoint bishops. Still, the Church depended on the emperor's protection.

Pope Urban II got Christian kings to join forces for the crusades, military efforts on behalf of the Church. The First Crusade, started in A.D. 1095, sought to regain the Holy Land from the Muslims and keep Christians safe on pilgrimages to Jerusalem. The crusades continued for 150 years, and most failed.

As towns grew, cathedral schools and universities were founded. New religious orders emerged. In A.D. 1209, Saint Francis founded the Franciscans, who helped reform the Church through simple living and trust in God. At about the same time, Saint Dominic founded the Dominicans, who were great teachers.

During this same time, some Church members created a court known as the Inquisition to fight heresy. Many Dominican and Franciscan priests were inquisitors. They were seen as educated and pious, good judges of heresy or faithfulness. If heretics refused to confess, they could be burned at the stake, but most were ordered to do penance or make a pilgrimage to prove their repentance.

▼ "The Emperor Charlemagne and His Army Fighting the Saracens," from *The Story of Ogier*, by Antoine Verard (1450–1519)

A Painful Change In the early A.D. 1500s, some people thought they could buy their way into heaven. This led to abuse, often in the form of indulgences. Indulgences are specific works or prayers, offered by the Church, for the remission of temporal punishment due to sins already forgiven. They became like "Get out of Purgatory Free" cards. You still had to be sorry for your sins, but through indulgences, you could avoid temporal punishment and you would not suffer punishment in purgatory. Popes allowed indulgences to be sold and made big profits.

In A.D. 1517, a priest named Martin Luther nailed a poster to the door of the church in Wittenberg, Germany, with his Ninety-five Theses. Luther protested the indulgences to help people avoid repentance and conversion. Eventually, Luther's protest began the Protestant Reformation. He was excommunicated from the Catholic Church. He had wanted reform, not separation. However, thousands of Germans followed him away from the Church. From this group, numerous other Protestant religions came into being.

Then, in England, King Henry VIII, eager for a son to succeed him and fearing his wife could not have one, sought to divorce her. When the pope refused, Henry founded the Anglican Church and made himself its head.

Catholic leaders gathered in Trent, Germany, between A.D. 1545 and 1567. The Council of Trent worked to make Church teachings clearer and discipline stronger. Colleges for training priests were formed and the Church became rededicated to the sacraments. These efforts were part of the Counter-Reformation.

New Lands As Europeans came into contact with Asia and the Americas, explorers and missionaries brought Catholicism to parts of Asia and South, Central, and North America. At times they met resistance, especially when they tried to impose their culture on people they were evangelizing. But their efforts helped make Catholicism the truly universal faith it is today.

CHECK THIS OUT!

Even during times of violence and cruelty as found in the Middle Ages, we can find beacons of hope working with and for the people.

Saint Margaret of Scotland (A.D. 1045–1093), who wanted to be a nun, was shipwrecked in Scotland, where the king fell in love with her; they married, had a family, and she worked for the people, having churches rebuilt across Scotland and helping those who were poor and in need.

Saint Elizabeth of Portugal (A.D. 1271–1336) was a queen who loved the poor. After praying to God for help to feed her starving people, cattle and grain arrived on boats. Every year after, she held banquets for those who had nothing to eat.

ACTIVITY

CONNECT YOUR FAITH Discuss in small groups the challenges missionaries might face today in foreign lands and locally. Name some ways your parish and school help to spread the Good News.

THE CHURCH IN THE MODERN WORLD

Focus How is the Church responding to the needs of our time?

Catholicism in America rode the waves of immigration, first from Europe and now from Latin America, Asia, and other lands. In some large cities, earlier Catholic immigrants from Germany, Poland, Italy, and Ireland might have established four separate ethnic parishes in the same neighborhood. Today, these churches may be places where Anglos, Europeans, Asians, Hispanics, or other ethnic groups worship.

More than a billion people—about one-sixth of the world's population—call themselves Catholic. About 16 percent of Americans are Catholic. These numbers may seem impressive, but they tell a small part of the story.

Mission: Still Possible The Church is still a force for justice in the world. For over a century, she has protected the rights of workers. Like Jesus, she speaks out for the poor and outcasts in our world. She supports basic human rights such as education, health care, and voting. The Church encourages all people to be good stewards of the environment. And she protects the most vulnerable members of society—especially the unborn.

Pope John Paul II was a modern disciple who spread the Gospel around the globe. He lived out the call of the Second Vatican Council to collaborate with other churches and apply our beliefs to the world's needs. In his travels, he promoted peace and solidarity, and encouraged youth to take an active role in the Church. His funeral in 2005 showed the love and respect he earned, as people from every nation, faith, and walk of life gathered to honor him.

Are We Up to the Challenge? "If you want peace, work for justice," was the challenge of Pope Paul VI, who saw connections between poverty and hatred, between oppression and war. Terrorism, genocide, and nuclear weapons are all part of the "Culture of Death" that Pope John Paul II warned us about. He encouraged us to follow a consistent ethic of life that respects and protects all human life, from conception to a natural death.

Our Church also faces challenges from within. The sexual abuse crisis reminds everyone of the need to protect the dignity of all God's children. And forces such as greed and lust continue to distract us from our calling. Still, with the strength and guidance of the Holy Spirit, our Church will continue to grow and help build up God's Kingdom. Jesus reminds us that he is always with us in our challenges "until the end of the age" (*Matthew 28:20*).

✝ **SCRIPTURE**
GO TO THE SOURCE
Read **Matthew 28:16–20**. How does the challenge to "make disciples of *all* nations" make you feel?

ⓐCTIVITY

LIVE YOUR FAITH What is an issue that you, as a Catholic, would like to get involved with? What issue(s) do you want to learn more about?

I'd like to learn about . . .

I'd like to be involved in . . .

IN SUMMARY

CATHOLICS BELIEVE ✝

Faith-filled men and women have made an impact on how the Church responded to the needs of their time.

▶ The Church grew from a persecuted, illegal religion to the religion of the Roman Empire, and people like Augustine, Benedict, and Pope Gregory the Great helped believers keep their faith despite political and social situations.

▶ As the Church faced many internal and external challenges to unity and accurate expressions of faith, everyday people tried to maintain their belief and people like Dominic and Francis tried to help the Church reform.

▶ The Second Vatican Council invites all the members of the Church to give a Christian response to the challenges and opportunities the modern world presents.

CELEBRATION OF THE WORD

Leader: God the Father calls and sends us forth
to be the "Body of Christ,"
with everyone we meet.
Let us listen to the word of the Lord. *(pause)*

A reading from the Gospel according to Matthew.
Read Matthew 28:16–20.

The Gospel of the Lord.

All: Praise to you, Lord Jesus Christ.

Leader: We turn our hearts and minds to God
as we pray:

Reader 1: God, in these times, often filled with fear and doubt,
you call us to be your Church.

All: We will serve the Lord!

Reader 2: God, in these times when it is difficult
for some people to believe in you,
you call us to be your voice.

All: We will serve the Lord!

Reader 3: God,
in these times when hope seems absent,
you call us to share
your vision of life.

All: We will serve the Lord!

Leader: God our Father,
we thank you for sending us Jesus,
to strengthen us for the task that is ours.
Help us to stand together,
to serve you and our brothers
and sisters well.
We ask this in the name of your Son, Jesus.
Amen.

 "For the Life of the World"
David Haas, © 1993, GIA Publications, Inc.

REVIEW

A **Work with Words** Circle the letter of the choice that best completes the sentence.

1. A consistent life _____ respects and protects all human life, from conception to a natural death.
   a. ethic   **b.** virtue   **c.** culture   **d.** theology

2. A _____ is someone who loses his or her life witnessing to Christ.
   a. saint   **b.** martyr   **c.** disciple   **d.** monk

3. The sale of _____ was an abuse that centered on the practice relating to avoiding the temporal punishment for sins in purgatory.
   a. holy water   **b.** indulgences   **c.** salvation   **d.** baptisms

4. A(n) _____ is a religious community of men (or sometimes women) who take the vows of poverty, chastity, and obedience and who are joined in spirituality and service.
   a. sainthood   **b.** priesthood   **c.** monastery   **d.** inquisition

5. The crusades were military efforts on behalf of the Church to regain the _____.
   a. wealth of the Church   **b.** nation of Spain   **c.** Holy Land   **d.** power of the emperor

B **Check Understanding** Indicate whether the following statements are true or false. Then rewrite false statements to make them true.

_____ 6. For over two hundred years, Roman emperors persecuted people who didn't worship their gods, torturing and killing many Christians.

_____ 7. Constantine issued the Edict of Milan in A.D. 313 to free Christians of Roman rule.

_____ 8. Benedict converted the tribes who invaded Europe, and helped make peace in Spain, England, and other lands.

_____ 9. King Henry VIII founded the Anglican Church when the pope refused to grant him a divorce.

_____ 10. The Council of Trent was part of the Reformation, and worked to make Church teachings clearer and discipline stronger.

C **Make Connections: Cause and Effect** Write a one-paragraph response to the question below.

What political or theological issues in the Church affect your experience of faith today? Pick one and write about the effect it has on you.

OUR CATHOLIC FAITH

WHAT NOW?

★ Pay attention to the issues facing the Church today; develop an informed opinion.

★ Read current events in the daily newspaper (not just the fun stuff!).

★ Consider how those events, whether local, national, or global, affect people.

★ Think about ways you might make a difference in the lives of others.

★ Pray for guidance and strength to get involved on an issue that touches you.

ACTIVITY

LIVE YOUR FAITH With your teacher or friends in class, find a story about Pope John Paul II, Oscar Romero, Dorothy Day, Mother Teresa, or some other modern Catholic witness. What issues did they get involved in? Make a list of the gifts they shared (courage, sacrifice, and so forth) that helped them be a force for change.

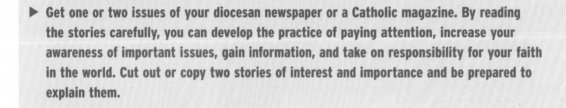

▶ Get one or two issues of your diocesan newspaper or a Catholic magazine. By reading the stories carefully, you can develop the practice of paying attention, increase your awareness of important issues, gain information, and take on responsibility for your faith in the world. Cut out or copy two stories of interest and importance and be prepared to explain them.

 Visit www.harcourtreligion.com for more family and community connections.

 **PRAYER**

God of Justice, help me make a difference.

Blessed Maria Anna Barbara Cope (Mother Marianne)

Throughout the ages, many of the faithful of the Church have devoted themselves to improving the physical and spiritual lives of those around them. One such individual who helped others was Mother Marianne.

Born Maria Anna Barbara Cope in Germany in 1838, she came to the United States with her family when she was one year old. The family settled in Utica, New York, where Marianne's father worked as a laborer. After a brief education, Marianne began working to support her family. However, she knew she was destined for a more fulfilling life through the Church she loved. She joined the Sisters of the Third Order of St. Francis in Syracuse in 1862 and became the supervisor of St. Joseph's Hospital, the only hospital in Syracuse. She made it a hospital policy to care for the sick, regardless of race or religion.

But Marianne was called to another work in 1883. At the time, the island kingdom of Hawaii was suffering an epidemic of leprosy. Victims were exiled to the northern portion of the island of Molokai. Marianne and six of her Franciscans made the long journey to Hawaii.

The sisters cleaned the unsanitary hospital and ministered to the lepers' physical, medical, and spiritual needs. Conditions were improved and the more than two hundred patients started receiving better care. At the time, a Belgian priest, Father Damien de Veuster, was ministering to the lepers in the Molokai colony. Mother Marianne resolved to go there and help him.

By the time they met, Father Damien had already contracted leprosy from his work. After Father Damien's death, Mother Marianne took charge of the colony, attempting to improve living conditions for all.

"Life was to be lived, even in the face of death," Marianne declared. "And when death came it was the gateway to eternal life." Despite criticism, the sisters continued to provide the most humane care possible for the lepers. By the time of her death in 1918, Mother Marianne's record of deeds was on a par with those of Father Damien. Her beatification in 2005 was the first of the pontificate of Pope Benedict XVI.

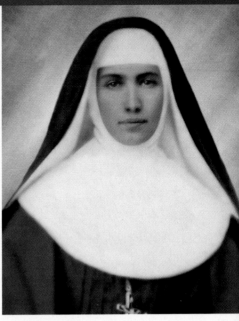

▲ Blessed Maria Anna Barbara Cope, 1838–1918

GLOBAL DATA

Hawaii

- Hawaii was discovered by Polynesian explorers between A.D. 300 and 750.

- Hawaii was renamed the Sandwich Islands in 1778 by British explorer James Cook after the British nobleman the Earl of Sandwich.

- Hawaii was united with all the Hawaiian islands into one kingdom in 1810 by King Kamehameha.

- The first Roman Catholic missionaries arrived in 1826.

- Hawaii was annexed to the United States in 1898.

- Hawaii is home to 230,000 Catholics.

Faith in Action!

DISCOVER Catholic Social Teaching:
Option for the Poor and Vulnerable

IN THIS UNIT you learned about the importance of positive role models and how the witness of the communion of saints should motivate us to serve others.

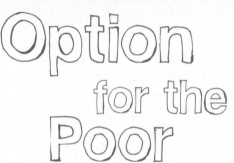

Option for the Poor

▲ **Sister Helen Prejean**

Two contemporary saints who can motivate us to "opt for the poor" are Dorothy Day and Sister Helen Prejean. Dorothy Day clearly modeled Jesus' special love for the poor. Through her Catholic Worker houses of hospitality, she showed us that serving the poor means more than doing things *for* them or giving things *to* them. Service means "doing with" more than "doing for." It means getting to know the poor as people and listening to their stories. It means helping the poor do for themselves, and she was great at giving them responsibility. But Dorothy went beyond the works of mercy and served the poor by challenging the policies and values of our society that allow, or even increase, poverty. Dorothy opted for the poor each time she demonstrated against military spending and the arms race. As our Church says, "the harm it inflicts on the poor is more than can be endured."

Sister Helen Prejean, whose ministry to men on death row was popularized in the movie *Dead Man Walking*, also opted for the poor. Like Dorothy Day, she became friends with the people to whom she ministered, even men on death row. Despite the terrible crimes these men had committed, she saw in them the face of Jesus. And she became the face of Jesus for them. When her death row brother in Christ accepted her offer to be in the observation room at the moment of his execution, she told him to look at her at that final moment and said "I will be the face of Christ for you." Through her social work and her prison ministries, Sister Helen realized the connections between poverty and crime and the high number of poor people on death row and throughout the prison system. She has spoken out for years to change the laws that increase poverty in this country and that continue to punish the poor much more severely than those with wealth. These two women challenge us to go beyond our "comfort zone" and embrace our calling to bring Christ's sacrificial love to those most in need.

❓ **What is it about the witness of Dorothy Day and Sister Helen Prejean that inspires you?**

❓ **How can you be "the face of Christ" for the poor and vulnerable people in your community?**

EMPATHY MEANS TRYING to understand experiences from someone else's point of view. Let's look at how some Florida young people learned empathy.

EMPATHY FOR OTHERS
A "TENT CITY" CHANGES LIVES

On Saturday, November 20, 2004, Sacred Heart Youth Ministry in Pinellas Park, Florida, hosted its sixth annual Thanksgiving homeless tent city. Eighth graders joined high school youth from around the St. Petersburg Diocese to learn what it means to be homeless and how they can help. After the opening Mass at 3:45 P.M., the youth proceeded to the baseball field and began setting up their homemade tents. Youth were allowed to bring three items, but no electronics, cell phones, food, or any other item that a homeless person would not have. Dinner consisted of soup and a few crackers.

After dinner, the youth experienced skits and testimonies from other youth and the police about teen issues like drinking and suicide and issues that affect the poor in their community. Several times later that night, just as the homeless people are made to move from private property by the police, the youth were asked by the local police to move their tent city from one end of the field to the other.

After their morning wake-up (5:45 A.M.) and a breakfast Danish and juice, the youth broke down their tent city. Many agreed to donate their blankets and pillows to the homeless. Next they prepared 200 bag lunches for real homeless people and were driven to Williams Park in St. Petersburg, where they encountered 200 homeless persons waiting for a hot breakfast. The youth spread out through the park and passed out their bag lunches and the blankets they brought with them. Some stood in the soup lines passing out the hot breakfast. Others stood silently, afraid and unsure of what to do. Maureen Boberg, the youth minister who organizes these experiences, found several homeless people willing to share their stories and advice with the youth.

No one is unaffected. "They need us," was a common youth comment. Maureen added, "What started out as a small retreat six years ago has evolved into a passion for the homeless of our community." After this retreat, as with the earlier ones, many of these youth continue to feed the homeless one Sunday a month.

Would you have signed up for this retreat? Which group of youth would you have been with in the park that Sunday morning?

▼ The Thanksgiving tent city, hosted by Sacred Heart Youth Ministry, helps young people experience homelessness and discover what they can do to help.

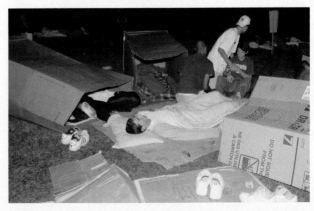

SERVE Your Community

THE WORKS OF JUSTICE ON BEHALF OF THE POOR

Identify with your classmates local and regional groups that are working to change political or economic policies that are harmful to the poor, in addition to the following national groups. You can link to their sites from **www.harcourtreligion.com**:

❶ Institute for Consumer Responsibility—for current consumer boycotts

❷ Bread for the World—for legislation on poverty and hunger in the United States and overseas

❸ NETWORK—for legislation on poverty and related issues

❹ Children's Defense Fund—for legislation on children's needs

❺ The USCCB Office of Social Development and World Peace—for ongoing Catholic justice campaigns

❻ The Catholic Campaign for Human Development—for many justice projects

Work as individuals or teams to research the actions that each group is recommending.

Choose one group's recommendation(s) and create a plan for putting it into practice over the next weeks.

Project Planning Sheet

Who else needs to be contacted about this project?

_____

Groups to present to

_____

How to publicize the project

_____

Other specific tasks

_____

_____

Your specific task(s)

_____

_____

Calendar for completing the project

_____

Why is it hard sometimes to reach out to someone you don't know, especially someone who is economically poor?

_____

_____

_____

What were your thoughts and feelings as you worked with the economically poor?

_____

_____

_____

How do you think the other person(s) felt?

_____

_____

_____

What did you learn about the poverty and the poor in each of these actions?

_____

_____

_____

Why is it important to work to change government or business policies as well as work with individual people who are poor?

_____

_____

What did you learn about Jesus and about your faith in doing the project?

_____

_____

_____

List one thing that might be different about you after doing this project. How will your life be different because of these actions?

_____

_____

REVIEW

A Work with Words Match the words on the left with the correct definitions or descriptions on the right.

_____ 1. communion of saints

_____ 2. sacramentals

_____ 3. icons

_____ 4. blessings

_____ 5. Annunciation

_____ 6. Assumption

_____ 7. Immaculate Conception

_____ 8. devotions

_____ 9. martyr

_____ 10. Constantine

A. Gabriel's visit to Mary to tell her she would be the Mother of God

B. unity of Church members on earth, in purgatory, and in heaven

C. Church's teaching that Mary was kept free from original sin from the first instant of her conception

D. when God took Mary—body and soul—into heaven

E. special sacramentals that include praising God for his great works and gifts and praying for others

F. sacred symbols and objects that help us respond to the grace received in the seven sacraments

G. Emperor who gave freedom of worship to Christians

H. prayers and practices that honor Jesus, Mary, and the saints

I. religious paintings often done by Eastern Christians in a certain style that show Jesus, Mary, other holy people, and religious events

J. someone who loses his or her life witnessing about Christ

B Check Understanding Indicate whether the following statements are true or false. Then rewrite false statements to make them true.

_____ **11.** The emperor Leo III ordered that iconoclasts destroy all crucifixes, statues, and paintings.

_____

_____ **12.** The Mysteries of the Rosary help us focus on events in the lives of Jesus and Mary and apply them to our lives.

_____

_____ **13.** Visitations are special visions or appearances of Mary, Jesus, or the saints.

_____

_____ **14.** Sanctification is the process by which the Church declares someone a saint.

_____

_____ **15.** All faithful members of the Church are called saints because Jesus has called us to be the holy people of God.

_____

_____ **16.** A monastery is a religious community of men (or sometimes women) who take the vows of poverty, chastity, and obedience and are joined in spirituality and service.

_____

_____ **17.** The crusades were military efforts on behalf of the emperor to regain the Holy Land.

_____

_____ **18.** A consistent ethic of life respects and protects all human life, from birth to a natural death.

_____

C Make Connections Write a short answer to these questions.

19. Cause and Effect. Which saint that you have learned about has most influenced your life? How has his or her example affected you?

_____

_____

_____

_____

20. Draw Conclusions. Think about the struggles between the Church and government in the past and today. What is the ideal relationship between Church and government? Use specific examples from the history of the Church to support your answer.

_____

_____

_____

_____

CATHOLIC SOURCE BOOK

THE BOOKS OF THE BIBLE

The Catholic Bible contains seventy-three books—forty-six in the Old Testament and twenty-seven in the New Testament.

The Old Testament

The Pentateuch

Genesis	Exodus	Leviticus	Numbers	Deuteronomy

The Historical Books

Joshua	1 Samuel	2 Kings	Ezra	Judith
Judges	2 Samuel	1 Chronicles	Nehemiah	Esther
Ruth	1 Kings	2 Chronicles	Tobit	1 Maccabees
				2 Maccabees

The Wisdom Books

Job	Proverbs	Song of Songs	Sirach (Ecclesiasticus)
Psalms	Ecclesiastes	Wisdom	

The Prophetic Books

Isaiah	Ezekiel	Amos	Nahum	Haggai
Jeremiah	Daniel	Obadiah	Habakkuk	Zechariah
Lamentations	Hosea	Jonah	Zephaniah	Malachi
Baruch	Joel	Micah		

The New Testament

The Gospels

Matthew	Mark	Luke	John

The Acts of the Apostles

The New Testament Letters

Romans	Ephesians	2 Thessalonians	Philemon	2 Peter
1 Corinthians	Philippians	1 Timothy	Hebrews	1 John
2 Corinthians	Colossians	2 Timothy	James	2 John
Galatians	1 Thessalonians	Titus	1 Peter	3 John
				Jude

Revelation

Creeds

A creed is a summary of the Christian faith. The word *creed* means, "I believe." Two examples of creeds are the Apostles' Creed and the Nicene Creed.

The Nicene Creed

We believe in one God,
  the Father, the Almighty,
  maker of heaven and earth,
  of all that is, seen and unseen.
We believe in one Lord, Jesus Christ,
  the only Son of God,
  eternally begotten of the Father,
  God from God, Light from Light,
  true God from true God,
  begotten, not made, one in Being with
  the Father.
  Through him all things were made.
  For us men and for our salvation
  he came down from heaven:
  by the power of the Holy Spirit
  he was born of the Virgin Mary, and
  became man.
  For our sake he was crucified under
  Pontius Pilate;
  he suffered, died, and was buried.
  On the third day he rose again
  in fulfillment of the Scriptures;
  he ascended into heaven
  and is seated at the right hand
  of the Father.

He will come again in glory
  to judge the living and the dead,
  and his kingdom will have no end.
We believe in the Holy Spirit, the Lord,
  the giver of life,
  who proceeds from the Father and the Son.
  With the Father and the Son he is
  worshiped and glorified.
  He has spoken through the Prophets.
  We believe in one holy catholic and
  apostolic Church.
  We acknowledge one baptism for the
  forgiveness of sins.
  We look for the resurrection of the dead,
  and the life of the world to come.
Amen.

The Apostles' Creed

I believe in God, the Father almighty,
  creator of heaven and earth.
I believe in Jesus Christ, his only Son,
  our Lord.
  He was conceived by the power of the
  Holy Spirit
  and born of the Virgin Mary.
  He suffered under Pontius Pilate,
  was crucified, died, and was buried.
  He descended to the dead.
  On the third day, he rose again.
  He ascended into heaven,
  and is seated at the right hand of the Father.
  He will come again to judge the living and
  the dead.

I believe in the Holy Spirit,
  the holy catholic Church,
  the communion of saints,
  the forgiveness of sins,
  the resurrection of the body,
  and the life everlasting.
Amen.

THE SACRAMENTS

Sacraments of Initiation: Baptism, Confirmation, Eucharist

Sacraments of Healing: Reconciliation, Anointing of the Sick

Sacraments at the Service of Communion: Matrimony, Holy Orders

Order of the Mass

The Mass follows a pattern, with some differences according to the feast or season of the liturgical year. The two great parts of the Mass are the Liturgy of the Word and the Liturgy of the Eucharist.

Introductory Rites

Sign of the Cross and Greeting

Rite of Blessing and Sprinkling Rite or
    Penitential Rite

Glory to God (Gloria)

Opening Prayer

Liturgy of the Word

First Reading

Responsorial Psalm

Second Reading

Gospel Acclamation

Proclamation of the Gospel

Homily

Profession of Faith

General Intercessions

Liturgy of the Eucharist

Preparation of the Altar and the Gifts

Eucharistic Prayer

    Preface

    Thanks and praise for the great
      works of God

Holy, Holy, Holy Lord (Sanctus)

Calling on the Holy Spirit

Consecration of bread and wine

Memorial Acclamation

Offering the Eucharistic sacrifice to God

Prayers for the living and the dead

Doxology and Great Amen

Communion Rite

Lord's Prayer

Sign of Peace

Breaking of the Bread

Invitation to Communion

Communion and Communion Song

Period of Silence or Song of Praise

Prayer After Communion

Concluding Rite

Greeting

Blessing

Dismissal

Celebrating Reconciliation

Rite I—Rite for Reconciliation of Individual Penitents (the person seeking forgiveness meets individually with the priest for the entire sacrament)

Rite II—Rite for Reconciliation of Several Penitents with Individual Confession and Absolution (the person seeking forgiveness gathers with others for prayer, scripture readings, and reflections, but meets with the priest privately for confession and absolution)

Rite III—Rite for Reconciliation of Penitents with General Confession and Absolution, which is not typically celebrated in the United States, and wherever it is used, it can only be in "danger of death" or "serious necessity" [*Code of Canon Law*, 961].

Rite I

1. Welcome

2. Reading from Scripture

3. Confession of sins and acceptance of a penance

4. Act of Contrition

5. Absolution

6. Closing prayer

Rite II

1. Greeting

2. Celebration of the word

3. Homily

4. Examination of conscience

5. General confession of sin

6. The Lord's Prayer

7. Individual confession of sins, acceptance of a penance, and absolution

8. Closing prayer

DEVOTIONS

The Rosary

The Rosary begins at the cross with the Sign of the Cross and then the Apostles' Creed. Then at the first bead, the Lord's Prayer followed by three Hail Mary's—one for each bead. After moving past the third Hail Mary bead, pray a Glory to the Father. At the last bead, announce the first mystery of the Rosary, then pray the Lord's Prayer again.

After passing the medallion move to the right on the Rosary and pray ten Hail Mary's while contemplating the first mystery of the Rosary. After the tenth Hail Mary, pray a Glory to the Father, announce the next mystery of the Rosary, then pray the Lord's Prayer. Pray another ten Hail Mary's until you have announced and contemplated the remaining mysteries of the Rosary.

Mysteries of the Rosary

Joyful Mysteries

Annunciation

Visitation

Nativity

Presentation of Jesus

Finding Jesus in the Temple

Glorious Mysteries

Resurrection of Jesus

Ascension

Descent of the Holy Spirit

Assumption of Mary

Coronation of Mary

Sorrowful Mysteries

Agony in the Garden

Scourging at the Pillar

Crowning with Thorns

Jesus Carries His Cross

Crucifixion

Luminous Mysteries (Mysteries of Light)

The Baptism of Christ in the Jordan

Jesus' Self-manifestation at the Wedding Feast of Cana

The Announcement of the Kingdom Along with the Call to Conversion

The Transfiguration

The Institution of the Eucharist as the Sacramental Expression of the Paschal Mystery

The Great Commandment

"You shall love the Lord your God with all your heart, and with all your soul, and with all your strength, and with all your mind; and your neighbor as yourself."
—*Luke 10:27*

The New Commandment

"I give you a new commandment, that you love one another. Just as I have loved you, you also should love one another."
—*John 13:34*

Beatitudes

The Beatitudes are the promises of blessing made by Jesus to those who faithfully follow his example. They give direction to the human heart for obtaining the happiness that can be found in God alone.

Blessed are the poor in spirit,
for theirs is the kingdom of heaven.

Blessed are those who mourn,
for they will be comforted.

Blessed are the meek,
for they will inherit the earth.

Blessed are those who hunger and thirst for righteousness,
for they will be filled.

Blessed are the merciful,
for they will receive mercy.

Blessed are the pure in heart,
for they will see God.

Blessed are the peacemakers,
for they will be called children of God.

Blessed are those who are persecuted for righteousness' sake,
for theirs is the kingdom of heaven.
—*Matthew 5:3–10*

Works of Mercy

The Works of Mercy are ways to respond to Jesus when we see him in those who are in need. The Corporal Works of Mercy meet people's physical needs, and the Spiritual Works of Mercy bring spiritual hope and healing to others.

Corporal

Feed the hungry.

Give drink to the thirsty.

Clothe the naked.

Shelter the homeless.

Visit the sick.

Visit the imprisoned.

Bury the dead.

Spiritual

Warn the sinner.

Teach the ignorant.

Counsel the doubtful.

Comfort the sorrowful.

Bear wrongs patiently.

Forgive injuries.

Pray for the living and the dead.

WHERE TO FIND IT

Virtues

Theological Virtues

The theological virtues are gifts from God. They are called the theological virtues because they are rooted in God, directed toward him, and reflect his presence in our lives. In Greek *theos* means, "god."

▶ **Faith** means believing in God and all that he has revealed to us and that the Church proposes for our belief.

▶ **Hope** is the desire, bolstered by trust, to do God's will, achieve eternal life and the graces that make this desire come true.

▶ Through **charity** (love), we love God above all else, and our neighbors as ourselves.

Cardinal Virtues

The cardinal virtues are the principal moral virtues that help us lead moral lives by governing our actions, controlling our passions and emotions, and keeping our conduct on the right tract.

▶ prudence (careful judgment)

▶ fortitude (courage)

▶ justice (giving God and people their due)

▶ temperance (moderation, balance)

With the help of God's grace, we develop the moral virtues by means of education, practice, and perseverance.

Glory to the Father (Doxology)

Glory to the Father, and to the Son, and to the Holy Spirit:
as it was in the beginning, is now, and will be forever. Amen.

Gloria Patri

Gloria Patri, et Filio, et Spiritui Sancto:
Sicut erat in principio, et nunc, et semper, et in saecula saeculorum. Amen.

The Lord's Prayer (Scriptural)

Our Father in heaven,
hallowed be your name.
Your kingdom come.
Your will be done,
on earth as it is in heaven.
Give us this day our daily bread.
And forgive us our debts,
as we also have forgiven our debtors.
And do not bring us to the time of trial,
but rescue us from the evil one.

—*Matthew 6:9–13*

Hail Mary

Hail, Mary, full of grace,
the Lord is with you!
Blessed are you among women,
and blessed is the fruit of your womb, Jesus.
Holy Mary, mother of God,
pray for us sinners,
now and at the hour of our death.
Amen.

Prayer to Holy Spirit

Come, Holy Spirit, fill the hearts of your faithful.
And kindle in them the fire of your love.
Send forth your Spirit and they shall be created.
And you will renew the face of the earth.
Lord, by the light of the Holy Spirit
you have taught the hearts of your faithful.
In the same Spirit
help us relish what is right
and always rejoice in your consolation.
We ask this through Christ our Lord.
Amen.

Jesus Prayer

Lord Jesus Christ, Son of the living God, have mercy on me, a sinner.

—(See *Luke 18:38–39*)

Angelus

V.   The angel spoke God's message to Mary,

R.   and she conceived of the Holy Spirit.

Hail, Mary. . . .

V.   "I am the lowly servant of the Lord:

R.   let it be done to me according to your word."

Hail, Mary. . . .

V.   And the Word became flesh,

R.   and lived among us.

Hail, Mary. . . .

V.   Pray for us, holy Mother of God,

R.   that we may become worthy of the promises of Christ.

Let us pray.
  Lord,
  fill our hearts with your grace:
  once, through the message of an angel
  you revealed to us the incarnation of your Son;
  now, through his suffering and death
  lead us to the glory of his resurrection.
  We ask this through Christ our Lord.

R.   Amen.

Act of Faith, Hope, and Love

My God, I believe in you,
  I trust in you,
  I love you above all things,
  with all my heart and mind and strength.
  I love you because you are supremely good and worth loving;
  and because I love you,
  I am sorry with all my heart for offending you.
  Lord, have mercy on me, a sinner.
Amen.

 Visit www.harcourtreligion.com for other prayers in Latin.

WORDS OF FAITH

actual grace The help God gives us in our particular need or to do a particular good act or to avoid evil. (*220*)

angel A spiritual being that praises God and serves him as a messenger to help people understand God's plan for them and creation; angels can think and choose like humans, but they do not have bodies. (*33*)

Apostles The twelve men Jesus chose to be his closest followers and to share in his work and mission in a special way. (*92*)

apostolic succession The term used to describe that the authority to lead and teach the Church can be traced through the centuries from the Apostles to their successors, the bishops. (*135*)

Ascension The taking up of the Risen Christ to heaven. (*96*)

Assumption The Church teaching that, at the end of her life, Mary, body and soul, was "taken up" (assumed) into heaven. The Church celebrates the Feast of the Assumption on August 15. (*273*)

blasphemy The sin of showing contempt or lack of reverence for God and his name. (*180*)

Visit www.harcourtreligion.com for a multimedia faith glossary.

canonization The process by which the Church officially declares someone of heroic virtue a saint. (*277*)

character A permanent, sacramental, spiritual seal that strengthens us to do God's work. A seal is given in the Sacraments of Baptism, Confirmation, or Holy Orders. (*76*)

Church The community of all baptized people who believe in the Blessed Trinity and follow Jesus. (*22*)

clergy Men who are ordained and given sacred authority to serve the Church by teaching, divine worship, and pastoral leadership. (*159*)

common good The Christian principle that all people, either in groups or as individuals, have the opportunities to reach their fulfillment more fully and easily. (*200*)

communion of saints All the faithful Church members on earth, those being purified in purgatory, and the blessed already in heaven. (*260*)

conscience The God-given ability that helps individuals know the difference between right and wrong. (*192*)

conversion A sincere change of mind, heart, and desire to turn away from sin and evil and turn toward God. (*108*)

councils Gatherings of bishops during which they speak about the faith of the Church, its teachings, and important issues. (*23*)

covenant A sacred promise or agreement between humans or between God and humans. (*10*)

D

Decalogue Another name for the Ten Commandments; from the Greek phrases meaning, "ten words." (*12*)

devotions Popular prayers and practices that honor Jesus, Mary, and the saints. (*275*)

diocese A "particular" or "local" Church; a community of the faithful in communion of faith and sacraments united under the leadership of a bishop. A diocese is usually a determined geographic area. (*138*)

domestic Church A term for the Christian family, which is as a holy community where children first learn about God through the love, teaching, and good example of parents and other family members. (*64*)

E

ecumenism An organized effort to bring Christians together in cooperation as they look forward in hope to the restoration of the unity of the Christian Church. (*121*)

evangelical counsels The public vows of poverty, chastity, and obedience that consecrated religious men and women make. (*162*)

F

faith Believing in God and all that he has revealed. Faith is both a gift from God and a free, human choice. (*22*)

filial respect The response children are called to have toward their parents, which includes obedience, respect, gratitude, and assistance. (*188*)

free will The ability to choose and make decisions on a person's own without being forced to choose or act in a certain way. (*8*)

G

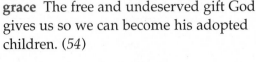

grace The free and undeserved gift God gives us so we can become his adopted children. (*54*)

H

holiness A state of becoming more God-like, living in his presence and with his love. (*32*)

Holy Orders The Sacrament at the Service of Communion in which a man promises to dedicate his life to God and the Church and is ordained as deacon, priest, or bishop. (*232*)

I

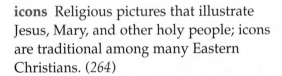

icons Religious pictures that illustrate Jesus, Mary, and other holy people; icons are traditional among many Eastern Christians. (*264*)

idolatry The sin of putting other people or things in God's place, or before God, in our lives. (*178*)

Immaculate Conception The Church's teaching that Mary was preserved free from original sin from the first moment of her conception. The Church celebrates the Feast of the Immaculate Conception on December 8. (*272*)

infallible The quality of being free from error. A teaching is infallible when the pope, as head of the magisterium, speaks officially on a matter of faith or morals that is to be believed by everyone in the Church. (*136*)

J

justification The forgiveness of sins and the return to the goodness for which humans were first created. (*106*)

laity A baptized member of the Church who shares in Jesus' mission and witnesses to him and his message in their homes, work places, schools, and in the broader community. (*159*)

liturgical year The Church's public celebration of the whole Paschal mystery of Christ through seasons and feasts of the Church calendar. (*242*)

liturgy The official public worship of the Church. (*218*)

Liturgy of the Hours The Church's public prayer offered at set times during the day and night to mark each day as holy. (*247*)

magisterium The living teaching authority of the Church first held by Peter and the Apostles and passed down through the generations to the bishops with the pope as their head. (*136*)

marks of the Church The four essential characteristics of the Church and her mission. The Church is one, holy, catholic, and apostolic. (*34*)

martyr A holy person who loses his or her life for witnessing to Christ. The word *martyr* means, "witness." (*284*)

Matrimony The Sacrament at the Service of Communion that celebrates the sacred covenant between a baptized man and women who promise to be forever faithful to each other. (*231*)

missionary mandate The responsibility given by Jesus to the Church to bring his saving message to everyone. (*147*)

monastery A building where a community of religious men join together in spirituality and service. (*285*)

Mystical Body of Christ An image or description for the Church, which stresses the unity of all believers through the Holy Spirit as one holy people, with Christ as their head and themselves as the body. (*78*)

New Commandment Jesus' command, recorded in John 15:12, to "love one another as I have loved you." (*203*)

offices of Christ The three roles of Jesus (priest, prophet, and king) that describe his mission and work among God's people; all those baptized share in these three roles. (*66*)

Pentecost The day fifty days after Jesus' Resurrection on which the Holy Spirit descended upon the first disciples; the Church celebrates the Feast of Pentecost every year. (*53*)

perjury Making a promise under oath which the maker does not intend to keep. (*181*)

precepts of the Church Church laws that name specific actions that all Catholics must carry out to help them grow in love of God and neighbor. (*221*)

righteous To act in accordance with God's will, being free from guilt or sin. (*107*)

sacramentals Sacred symbols and objects that help Catholics respond to the grace received in the sacraments; sacramentals help us pray and remember God's love for us. (*262*)

sacraments Effective signs of God's grace, established by Jesus and given to his Church, by which God shares his life through the work of the Holy Spirit. (*219*)

saint A person who led a holy life giving God glory and who now enjoys eternal life with God in heaven. (*274*)

salvation The loving action of God's forgiveness of sins and the restoration of friendship with the Father brought by Jesus Christ. (*64*)

sanctifying grace God's divine life within us that makes us his friends and adopted children. (*220*)

social sin A term that refers to the sinful social structures that result from personal sin and that lead to social conditions that do not reflect or promote the law of love. (*204*)

soul The spiritual principle in you that reflects God. (*8*)

T

Ten Commandments The ten fundamental moral laws given by God to his people to help them live by the covenant and recorded in the Old Testament. (*12*)

theological virtues Gifts from God that help us believe in him, trust in his plan for us, and love him as he loves us; they are faith, hope, and love. (*25*)

Tradition The living and true teachings of Jesus and his Good News of salvation that are passed down in the Church from generation to generation. (*21*)

Transfiguration The revelation of Jesus' divine glory to Peter, James, and John. (*51*)

 V

virtue A strong habit of doing good that helps people make good moral decisions. (*25*)

giving Holy Spirit, 53
holiness of, 34
images of, 106, 265
prayer to, 110
relationship with, 104–105
relationship with God, 9
salvation, 64
teaching apostles, 136
transfiguration of, 50–51
treatment of people, 92–93
Jesus Prayer, 54, 309
Jewish people, 62, 176
John Paul II, Pope, 104, 167, 201, 210, 288–289
John XXIII, Blessed, 218
John, Gospel of, 20
John, Saint, 36, 94
Josefina (Josephine) Bakhita, Saint, 155
Joseph, husband of Mary, 189
justification, **106**–107, **311**

kings, 158
Kolbe, Maximilian, 276–277

laity, **159**, 160–161, **312**
Last Supper, 116
lay ecclesial ministers, **160**
Lazarus, 95
leaven, **160**
Lent, 108
Leo III, Pope, 264, 285
Litany of Mary, 278
liturgical year, **242**–243, **312**
liturgy, **218**–219, 245
Liturgy of the Hours, 35, 219, 247, **312**
Lord's Prayer, 308
Louis Martin, Venerable, 269
love, 25, 36, 203
Luke, Gospel of, 20
Luther, Martin, 120, 287
Lydia, 97

magisterium, **136**, **312**
Marcella, Saint, 17
Margaret of Hungary, Saint, 193
Margaret of Scotland, Saint, 287
Maria Anna Barbara Cope, Blessed, 293
Maria del Transito de Jesus Sacramentado, Saint, 227
Mariam Thresia Chiramel Mankidiyan, 281
Mark, Gospel of, 20, 22
marks of the Church, 34, **312**
Martha, 95
martyr, **284**, **312**
Mary Magdalene, Saint, 94
Mary of Bethany, 95
Mary, Mother of God, 24, 189, 264, 272–273, 274, 277
Mass, 64–65, 302
Matrimony, Sacrament of, 20, 35, 230–231, 234, **312**
Matthew, Gospel of, 20
May Crowning, 275
Mechthild von Magdeburg, 71
Michael (angel), 33
Michelango, 8, 265
Michael Iswene Tsani, Blessed, 83
Miguel Pro, Blessed, 41
missionary, 150

missionary mandate, **147**, **312**
monastery, **285**, **312**
monks, **163**
monsignor, **138**
Moses, 11, 53
mysteries of the Rosary, 304
Mystical Body of Christ, 78, **312**

natural law, **12**
New Commandment, 203, 305, **312**
Nicene Creed, 21, 137, 301
Ninth Commandment, 234, 235
Noah, 11
nuns, **163**

obedience, vow of, 162
offices of Christ, **66**, **312**
Old Testament, 13
Ordinary Time, 243

parish ministries, 160–161
parishes, 138
Paschal candle, 263
pastor, 138
Paul, Saint, 9, 20, 24, 25, 36, 74, 97, 148, 220
peacemaking, 211–212
Pentecost, 52, **53**, 96, 135, **312**
Pere Jacques Marquette, 209
perjury, **181**, **312**
Perpetua, Saint, 197
Peter Damien, Saint, 143
Peter, Saint, 24, 94, 97, 134, 135
Phoebe, 97
Pieta (sculpture), 265
Pius VII, Pope, 167
polygamy, **234**
pope, 138, 159
    names for, 135
poverty, 294
    vow of, 162
prayer, 35, 55, 108, 220, 246–248, 261, 266, 278, 290
Prayer to the Holy Spirit, 308
precepts of the Church, **221**, **312**
Prejean, Sister Helen, 294
priests, 66, 138, 139, 158, 159, 232–233
Prisca (Priscilla), 97, 101
Profession of Faith, 56
prophets, 66, 158
Protestant Reformation, 120, 287
Protestants, 121
pulpit exchange, 121

racism, 84–85
Raphael (angel), 33
Reconciliation, Sacrament of, 20, 35, 303
relationships, 90–91, 191
religion, **177**
religious orders, 162–163
righteous, **107**, **312**
rights of workers, 168–169
rituals, **218**
Roman Catholic Church, 118–119
Roman Catholics, 121
Rosary, 263, 275, 304
Ruth, 11

Sabbath, 222
sacramental grace, **220**
sacramentals, **262**–263, **313**
sacraments, 20, 35, 77, 219, 302, **313**
sacrilege, 179
saints, 274, 276–277, **313**
salvation, **64**, 149, **313**
Samuel, 10
Samuel Mazzuchelli, Venerable, 125
sanctifying grace, **220**, **313**
sanctuary candle, 263
Sarah, 11, 24
schism, **120**
Scripture, 21
Second Commandment, 180
Second Vatican Council, 23, 204, 218
simony, 179
sins, 106, 108–109, 204
sisters, **163**
Sistine Chapel, 8, 265
Sixth Commandment, 234
slavery, 204
social justice, 127
social sin, **204**, **313**
Solemnity of Mary, 274
solidarity, 203, 210–211
Solomon, king of Israel, 11
soul, **8**, **74**, **313**
Spiritual Works of Mercy, 306
Stations of the Cross, 35, 263
Stephen, Saint, 97
Sunday, 222–223
superstition, 179
Susanna, 11
symbol, **218**

Temple in Jerusalem, 75
Ten Commandments, 11, **12**, 13, 176–177, **313**
theological virtues, **25**, 307, **313**
Therese of Lisieux, Saint, 150–151
Third Commandment, 222
Thomas, Saint, 29
Tobit, Book of, 33
Tradition, 21, 23, 134, **313**
Transfiguration, **51**, **313**
Trinity, 51, 54–55, 245

unity, 114–119, 120–122, 137
Urban II, Pope, 286

vicar, **138**
Victoria Rasoamanarivo, Blessed, 113
vigil lights, 263
virtues, 12, **25**, 204, 307, **313**
vows, 162

war, 210
Woman at the Well, 146–147
Works of Mercy, 306
worship, 21, 35

Zachariah, 33
Zelie Guerin, Venerable, 269